Mosquitoes to Wolves

The Evolution of the Airborne Forward Air Controller

GARY ROBERT LESTER

Air University Press
Maxwell Air Force Base, Alabama

August 1997

Disclaimer

Opinions, conclusions, and recommendations expressed or implied within are solely those of the author(s) and do not necessarily represent the views of Air University, the United States Air Force, the Department of Defense, or any other US government agency. Cleared for public release: distribution unlimited.

Contents

Chapter   *Page*

    DISCLAIMER ii

    ABOUT THE AUTHOR ix

    PREFACE xi

1   EVOLUTION OF CLOSE AIR SUPPORT 1
    World War I 2
    Between the Wars 5
    The American Experience, 1918–42 7
    World War II 9
    Notes 12

2   CLOSE AIR SUPPORT DOCTRINE 15
    Early Navy-Marine Close Air Support 15
    Close Air Support in Korea 16
    Air Force Philosophy in Korea 18
    Navy/Marine Air in Vietnam 22
    Notes 23

3   KOREA: FORWARD AIR CONTROLLERS
    EMERGE 25
    The Fight for Air Superiority 26
    Phase One—Retreat to Pusan 28
    Phase Two—Advance to the Yalu 29
    Phase Three—Second Retreat 29
    Phase Four—Main Line of Resistance
      Stabilized 29
    Phase Five—Air Pressure for Peace 30
    A Substitute for Artillery 30
    Close Air Support in Korea 31
    The Extemporized Air War 32
    The Need for Airborne FACs 33

Chapter		Page
	Command and Control Support	37
	6132d Tactical Air Control Group	38
	6147th Squadron Organized	38
	Immediate Air Requests	40
	Mosquitoes Assigned to Divisions	40
	Mosquito Mission Expands	41
	The 502d Tactical Control Group	41
	Notes	43
4	MOSQUITO OPERATIONS IN KOREA	45
	The Role of the Mosquito	45
	Forward Air Controller Equipment	47
	Visual Reconnaissance	49
	The Tactical Air Control System	50
	Mosquito Mellow	52
	Strike Control Procedures	53
	Problems Encountered	55
	Forward Air Controller Training	60
	Notes	62
5	KOREA: THE STAGNANT WAR	65
	The Argument for Interdiction	65
	CAS along a Stabilized Front	65
	Radar-Controlled Air Strikes	66
	Communications Upgrades	66
	T-6 Upgrades	67
	Operation Thunderbolt	67
	Operation Ripper	69
	Communist Losses in the First Year	70
	Strategy Changes	70
	Pathfinder Operations	72
	The Truce Ceremony	73
	6147th TCG Deactivated	74
	Joint Air-Ground Doctrine	74
	Post Korea	75
	Notes	78

Chapter		Page

6 VIETNAM: THE ADVISORY YEARS 81
    Wars of National Liberation 81
    Developing the Counterinsurgency Force 82
    Farm Gate 82
    Command Structure 89
    Air Operations in 1962 90
    Air Operations in 1963 94
    Air Operations in 1964 98
    The Gulf of Tonkin 101
    New Demands 102
    Notes 104

7 VIETNAM: SLOW FAC OPERATIONS 109
    FACs Come of Age 109
    FAC Aircraft 110
    Personnel Requirements 114
    Seventh Air Force 115
    504th Tactical Air Support Group 116
    Increased Manning Requirements 117
    Qualifications 118
    Rules of Engagement 120
    Locating the Enemy 121
    Visual Reconnaissance Process 122
    In-Country Operations, 1965–72 125
    Employing the FAC Force 129
    Navy Participation 132
    The Battle of Khe Sanh 133
    The Tet Offensive 134
    Cleared in Wet! 135
    Notes 140

8 EXPANDING MISSIONS 145
    Night Operations 145
    Air Operations in Laos 150
    USAF Controllers in Cambodia 160
    Notes 164

Chapter		Page

9 THE FAST FORWARD AIR CONTROLLERS 167
   Out-Country Operations, 1964–65 167
   Commando Sabre 171
   F-4 "Phantom" FACs 181
   Notes 195

10 VIETNAMIZATION AND AMERICAN
   WITHDRAWAL 201
   Vietnamization and Close Air Support 202
   The South Vietnamese Air Force 205
   Cambodia 207
   Lam Son 719 210
   Interdiction in Route Packages I and II 212
   The 1972 Spring Offensive 213
   Linebacker 214
   Notes 221

11 A PERSPECTIVE ON CLOSE AIR SUPPORT 225
   Interservice Cooperation 225
   Airpower in Regional Conflicts 233
   Conclusion 239
   Notes 241

   BIBLIOGRAPHY 243

   INDEX 263

Illustrations

Figure

1 Korean Peninsula 27

2 Vietnam 83

Photographs

Page

T-6 "Mosquito"	35
C-47 "Mosquito Mellow"	39
Farm Gate Aircraft—T-28	85
Farm Gate Aircraft—B-26	85
Farm Gate Aircraft—A-19	86
Farm Gate Aircraft—C-47	86
O-1 "Bird Dog"	97
O-2 "Skymaster"	112
OV-10 "Bronco"	113
F-100 "Misty"	171
F-4D	181
F-4E	188
RF-4C	189
A-10 "Thunderbolt II"	231

THIS PAGE INTENTIONALLY LEFT BLANK

About the Author

Lt Col Gary Robert Lester was born in Bristol, Connecticut, on 3 August 1947. He retired from the US Air Force in 1992 after a 23-year career. He accrued three thousand hours as an F-4 weapons systems officer flying F-4 Phantom II fighters. Colonel Lester served two combat tours in Southeast Asia as a "Fast-FAC." Beginning in 1981, he flew operational test and evaluation missions for advanced weapons and aircraft systems and was an instructor at both of Air Combat Command's test centers. He completed his career as director, Tactics and Test Division, 79th Test and Evaluation Group, Eglin Air Force Base, Florida.

After retirement, Colonel Lester served as associate assistant professor of World Civilization at Okaloosa-Walton Community College and associate assistant professor of American History and Western Civilization for Troy State University, Florida Region.

Lester holds a bachelor's degree in journalism from Wichita State University (1969), a Master of Public Administration degree from Golden Gate University (1985), and a PhD in history from Florida State University (1994). He is also a graduate of Air War College, Air University, Maxwell AFB, Alabama.

Colonel Lester is a member of the Red River Valley Fighter Pilots Association, the Retired Officer Association, the American Historical Association, and the Pensacola Civil War Round Table. He currently resides in Prescott, Arizona, with his wife Penny.

Preface

Comparable to twentieth century cavalry, early forward air controllers (FAC) probed, observed, and reported enemy activity. Flying rickety, underpowered, and unarmed aircraft, they operated on the leading edge of ground combat. The efficient use of airborne FACs never developed in a meaningful way in World War II, with the possible exception of their use in Marine amphibious operations in the Pacific. But the rugged terrain of Korea and the jungle mazes of Vietnam restricted the capabilities of ground controllers to identify targets, thus expanding the need for "eyes in the air." FAC roles changed from those of probing, observing, and reporting, to those of locating targets, marking them for air strikes, and taking an active role in their destruction. This expanded mission resulted in the inevitable evolution of FAC equipment and responsibilities.

Interservice differences regarding the definition of close air support (CAS) caused controversies which clouded ground-support operations in both Korea and Vietnam. The Navy and the Marines saw CAS as the *primary* mission for airpower. The Air Force and the Army saw CAS as the *last priority,* to be employed after air superiority has been gained and maintained, supplies have been interdicted, and the enemy's infrastructure has been damaged.

Even the definition of what constitutes CAS was not resolved by the services. In both Korea and Vietnam, these interservice differences were resolved in favor of the Air Force; a Tactical Air Control System was designed to support the Air Force's concept of CAS, and the FAC became a critical component of that system.

In Korea, the FAC's role began as an observer. It quickly became apparent that the lack of heavy artillery early in the conflict made aircraft bombardment necessary to support friendly ground troops. Getting the observer above the battlefield seemed the best way to identify threats to friendly forces. As the North Koreans swept down the peninsula, targets of opportunity were plentiful behind their rapidly advancing forces—and United Nations airpower was often the only force slowing their advance. *Mosquitoes* were concerned with controlling the "airborne artillery" necessary to protect UN forces in retreat.

Entrenched UN forces at Pusan presented a new problem for the controllers: destroy enemy equipment and supplies before they arrived at the stagnant front. Gen Douglas MacArthur's successful invasion at Inchon and Eighth Army's "breakout" at the Pusan perimeter represented additional challenges to FACs. The rapid offensive advance made identification of friendly and enemy forces more difficult, and FAC responsibilities were extended to a greater range. Lack of a defined "bomb-line" made close control of airpower more important.

Intervention by the Red Chinese in November 1950 turned the conflict into a see-saw slugfest that eventually stagnated along the 38th parallel. The "trench warfare" in Korea between 1951 and 1953 presented other challenges to airpower as the battle lines became fixed and enemy men and equipment were entrenched. Interdiction became airpower's primary mission as CAS became less effective.

Forward air controllers were disbanded during the interwar years (1954–61) as each service competed for defense dollars during the cold war. Strategic weapons and nuclear war on a grand scale occupied Department of Defense thinking for nearly a decade. If the notion of close air support and FACs existed at all, it was a very low priority. The services competed for nuclear submarines, strategic ballistic missile systems, intercontinental bombers, and aircraft carriers. The concept of a conventional confrontation in Europe was approached as being only the beginning of what would become a global nuclear conflict. In this environment, funding for low-technology, light, observer-type aircraft was a low priority indeed.

Preparing for "unconventional" war finally received attention under the Kennedy administration. Soviet "wars of national liberation," announced by Soviet Chairman Nikita Khrushchev in 1960, were recognized as the most probable type of conflict. In 1961, a host of World War II and Korean War aircraft were reactivated in a Vietnamese aid program known as "Farm Gate." These relics were soon replaced by more modern, yet equally unsophisticated, aircraft.

The absence of both a clearly defined enemy and classic front lines made FAC use mandatory for air strikes in South Vietnam. FACs became the eyes of province chiefs, who had the authority to authorize air strikes into their areas. Air controllers became more important then ever in defining the tactical objectives on the battlefield. The FAC motto, "We control violence," took on even more significance. A new command and control network evolved to achieve objectives and protect friendly forces from mistaken air attack.

In the north, however, sophisticated air defenses made light, slow-moving aircraft impractical. "Fast-FACs" therefore took up the mission of interdicting enemy supplies in areas where lack of air superiority restricted the traditional "slow movers." Modern fighter aircraft now took up a FAC role and, although not well suited for this mission, they adapted quite well. By the end of the Vietnam War, advances in technology allowed these FACs to control strikes against targets at night, in bad weather, and with improved precision. Laser-guided weapons systems, new computer navigation equipment, and advanced ground radars combined to provide an effective and lethal capability. If the Mosquitoes were an annoyance in Korea, the Wolves of Vietnam proved to be a deadly addition to the concept of FAC.

THIS PAGE INTENTIONALLY LEFT BLANK

Chapter 1

Evolution of Close Air Support

Close air support (CAS) of ground operations has become a recognized element of modern warfare. As the authoritative Department of Defense (DOD) *Dictionary of Military and Associated Terms* defines it, CAS comprises "air attacks against hostile targets which are in close proximity to friendly forces and which require detailed integration of each air mission with the fire and movement of those forces." This doctrine is also accepted by the North Atlantic Treaty Organization (NATO), Southeast Asia Treaty Organization (SEATO), Central Treaty Organization (CENTO), and the Inter-American Defense Board (IADB). This aspect of warfare is the modern version of one of the oldest air combat missions; it also has become one of the most divisive topics between soldiers and airmen.[1]

The use of airplanes in close support of ground troops appeared early in aviation history, but there were problems. The earliest attempts at influencing the outcome of a ground battle from the air were limited by the fragility of the aircraft and a lack of coherent ideas on its effective use. Taken virtually for granted by troops and aviators today, the employment of airpower in this manner has been controversial from the time bombs were first dropped on ground combatants during the Italo-Turkish War of 1911–12.[2]

The air-to-ground potential of the airplane was tested in several small wars before World War I After an Italian pilot dropped three small bombs on Turkish positions on 1 November 1911, the Italians continued bombing from aircraft and airships.[3] Bombing also occurred during the Balkan Wars of 1912–13. In those wars, however, the bombing was random, incidental, and often at the initiative of the individual aviator.[4] At about the same time, the French Army used aircraft against rebellious tribesmen in Morocco and gained its first experience in cooperation between air units and ground troops.[5]

1

Since the emergence of strategic bombardment during World War I, few airmen have willingly embraced what the British called "army cooperation"; that is, to provide direct support for the infantry. American and British aviators in particular wanted to perform missions that did not involve complicated liaison with ground forces, subordination of air forces to ground requirements, or attrition of air resources in unrewarding missions. They believed their contribution should be through strategic bombardment, air superiority, and interdiction.[6]

The history of CAS during the first four decades of the twentieth century can be divided into three phases. The first—World War I, especially the years 1917 and 1918—was characterized by airpower's rapid development and its increasing combat potential. The second phase (the interwar period to about 1935) was marked by limited doctrinal discussion, restricted development, and a virtual absence of meaningful battlefield application. During the final phase, which continued into the opening campaigns of World War II, there was renewed interest, considerable experimentation, and operational experience in several minor conflicts.[7]

World War I

Trench warfare removed the need for the kind of air reconnaissance that had been crucial in the early months of World War I. The need for accurate trench maps and for corroborating the eyewitness reports of airmen led to a rapid development in aerial photography; the camera became as much a part of the observation airplane as the observer's notebook. Extensive use of aerial reconnaissance led to the camouflaging of important military installations—which led, in turn, to the art of photographic interpretation.[8]

Trench warfare also led to the artillery-spotting airplane. Since indiscriminate artillery barrage did comparatively little harm to a well-sheltered enemy, a way to direct the fire onto specific targets was sought—and the radio-equipped airplane proved ideal. The Germans, quick to realize the specialized nature of this work, formed 14 units exclusively for this task. They wanted each frontline division to have its own artillery-spotting unit. By August 1916, these units comprised 45 of 81 German observation groups.

The airplane also proved useful in determining how far the troops had advanced during an offensive. Communications between forward troops and their rear headquarters were often completely severed when an attack went "over he top"—and even when information did filter back from the fighting area, it was often out-of-date.[9]

In the first part of World War I, military aviation had only one official function: serve as the eyes of the army. During the first weeks, however, aviators from both sides attacked marching columns on their own initiative with whatever weapons they happened to have. By October 1914, officials had begun to sanction and encourage the offensive use of aircraft.[10]

Air-ground communication was difficult at best. Even though aircraft used for artillery spotting often carried wireless transmitters, pilots commonly found it more feasible to drop messages—and ground troops used flares and visual displays (such as arrows laid out on the ground) to signal aircraft.[11]

In 1915, a new tactical reconnaissance aircraft appeared. Called the infantry contact patrol plane, it led to air support along the "cutting edge" of the battle. It was charged with following the progress of the friendly infantry and filling the communications gaps that developed when landlines were cut by bombardment and when backup systems (runners, dogs, pigeons) failed. By 1916, infantry contact patrol systems were serving both Allied and German armies.[12]

Early attempts at air-ground liaison on the battlefield were plagued by a number of difficulties, most of them stemming from the ground troops' fear that use of flares and smoke would advertise their position to enemy artillery. There was less resistance to the use of panels, but compliance was far from perfect; units exhausted from heavy engagement rarely displayed panels.[13]

Since patrol pilots approaching the battlefield could identify enemy as well as friendly positions, they soon began attacking resistance points. Low-level air attacks gained official sanction at the Battle of the Somme, which the British opened in July

1916. The Royal Flying Corps (RFC) assigned 18 contact aircraft for low-altitude "trench flights" with the dual purpose of "close reconnaissance and destructive bombardment."[14]

Low-flying attack units were working in close coordination with the infantry when the great German offensive began in March 1918.[15] By the time of the Armistice, CAS experience had yielded a number of lessons and problems, many of which reappeared 20 years later. A major lesson was that aircraft use had a significant effect on the morale of ground troops. An RFC policy paper drafted in September 1916 noted that hostile aircraft over the front affected morale "all out of proportion to the damage" the aircraft could inflict.[16]

Emphasis on the airplane's psychological impact slowed the development of weapons that were especially suitable to ground attack. Aircraft usually carried small bombs (under 10 pounds) and grenades, and they strafed with machine guns in the .30-caliber/8 millimeter range. The damage these weapons could inflict on field fortifications was negligible. Cannon and rockets appeared in 1918, but there was little effort to exploit their air-to-ground capabilities.[17]

Royal Flying Corps losses were heavy during the German offensive of March 1918 and in the heavy fighting around Amiens five months later. RFC Wing commander Sir John Slessor cited the case of 80 Squadron, which conducted CAS missions almost continuously from March 1918 until the end of the war: "Their average strength was 22 officers, and in the last 10 months of the war no less than 168 officers were struck off the strength from all causes—an average of about 75 percent per month, of whom little less than half were killed."[18] The increased danger to ground-attack aircraft led to a search for models of aircraft that were better suited for such combat.

Air support aircraft in 1918 had two categories of targets: objectives along the enemy's heavily defended front (the "crust") and a range of objectives extending 20 miles behind the crust. By the end of the Great War, a considerable body of opinion held that the chief contribution of aircraft should be against those objectives behind the crust. Additionally, excellent targets often lay beyond effective artillery range—only the airplane could reach them.[19]

While airpower could rapidly be shifted and concentrated, it could not easily be used on a battlefield that was unfamiliar to the pilots or when the battle lines were shifting and fluctuating. Experiments in centralized command encountered opposition from ground forces—the air staff tended to see the benefits of centralized control while the army staff tended to focus on its shortcomings. This fundamental difference remained one of the key problems in CAS.[20] By the end of World War I, much valuable experience had been gained in ground-support operations. Unfortunately, many of these hard-earned lessons were forgotten during the years of comparative peace which followed.[21]

Between the Wars

Technological progress continued during the postwar period. All-metal airframes and more efficient engines were developed. The airplane of 1939 could boast a performance far exceeding that of earlier aircraft; yet many of the world's air forces had difficulty incorporating these innovations.

Air doctrine in the interwar period rested largely on World War I lessons. There was general agreement that the air force now had at least two fundamental missions: win air battles and support ground forces. However, the Royal Air Force (RAF) and the US Army Air Corps (AAC) became convinced that strategic bombardment was their most important mission and they believed it could be decisive in future wars. They viewed air superiority as desirable for intervention in a land battle, but they did not see it as an absolute prerequisite. However, they agreed that the overriding obligation of the air force was to throw its strength into the ground battle at critical times.[22]

The emphasis on indirect (interdiction) rather than close or direct support resulted from two factors: (1) the perception of the battlefield and the targets it offered and (2) the limited offensive capability of airpower in the 1930s. The battlefield offered small targets that were "widely dispersed and usually dug into the ground to protect them against artillery fire."[23] Bombers of the day could attack only broad areas, hoping to hit the specific targets within them. Most authorities concluded that artillery could provide better accuracy, but they agreed that a bomber force was better suited in a surprise offensive because artillery buildups were usually detected by the enemy.

Advocates of separate ground attack aviation argued that only specially trained pilots, flying aircraft designed and armed specifically for low-level attack, could offer effective close support. Opponents argued that such units would suffer prohibitive losses. Whether an air force provided air support through special units or through fighter and bomber aircraft, there was relatively little contact between the Army's ground forces and its Air Corps—and no day-to-day exchange on problems that required cooperation. The mechanics of arranging air support in peacetime often proved cumbersome once a war began.[24]

In the late thirties, proponents of ground attack held that neither air superiority nor fighter escort was a prerequisite for rapid, shallow incursions. Low-level flight, they argued, offered sufficient guarantee that a CAS plane could carry out its mission and return safely.[25] Diving attacks were also under discussion, since tests conducted by the Navy suggested that they could achieve greater bombing accuracy.[26]

Technological innovation had a greater impact on weapons than on aircraft. British wing commander Slessor, for example, maintained that the bomb was "the weapon to use every time."[27] Bombs used in CAS were typically small, fragmentation-type explosives that were effective at a range of 40 to 50 yards from point of detonation. The machine gun and the fragmentation bomb were effective against "soft" targets, such as personnel. They could be used to harass enemy gunners, but they could rarely knock out the guns themselves—and they were of little value against tanks and armored cars.

One important piece of equipment carried by CAS aircraft was the wireless or radio set. Between the wars, the radio telephone was increasingly used in preference to wireless telegraphy. Still, radio communications left much to be desired due to unreliability and limited range. Moreover, the heavy and bulky sets were especially cumbersome to aircraft, where weight was critical. These shortcomings showed up quickly when the US Army Air Corps sought to perfect CAS at the beginning of World War II.[28]

The American Experience, 1918–42

The US Army Air Service, a late arrival to the fighting in France, nevertheless played a significant role at Saint Mihiel in September 1918. In that battle, American and French air forces concentrated 1,500 combat planes to support the ground attack. Col William "Billy" Mitchell, Chief of Air Service for the First Army, directed the air operations. Mitchell listed attack on ground troops as a special mission sometimes assigned to pursuit squadrons. The most attractive targets were reserve troops massing for major military operations. Mitchell believed that bombing and strafing attacks on well-constructed positions had very little effect on either morale or materiel.[29]

The notion of a specialized ground attack branch of aviation found its most emphatic champion in Mitchell. The concept of attack aviation led to a close identity between attack and CAS, the practical result of which was the creation in 1921 of the 3d attack group. The idea still persisted that all aircraft might have to be committed directly to the land battle.[30] Attack aviation was a postwar creation; it had no past, no combat tradition, and no backlog of practical experience.

In the late twenties, the US Marine Corps flew a number of air support missions in Nicaragua. The operation was described during a 1929 lecture at the Army War College.[31] Airplanes served as artillery, intervened in sieges and battles where very little space separated the contending forces, flew escort missions for columns, and broke up enemy attempts at ambush. In subsequent campaigns and exercises, the Marines were to build up a sizable fund of expertise on CAS, particularly as related to amphibious operations.[32] This experience led to adoption of a different philosophy of air support—a difference that would manifest itself early in the Korean War and persist into the Vietnam conflict.

When Brig Gen Henry H. Arnold addressed the US Army War College on air warfare in the fall of 1937, he praised

Japan because "she has not assigned her air force to operate against frontline trenches, as have the Spaniards."[33] Arnold said that high aircraft losses result when aircraft are used "promiscuously and indiscriminately to supplement artillery actions on a large number of petty, heterogeneous missions." "Do not," he said, "detach the air force to small commands where it will be frittered away in petty fighting. Hold it centrally and use it in its proper place; that is, where it can exert its power beyond the influence of your other arms, to influence general action rather than the specific battle."[34]

In 1939, the role of attack aviation was to conduct operations in zones that were beyond the reach of friendly artillery. Cost was a factor in this decision and shifts in doctrinal emphasis continued. Interdiction was a popular concept in the Air Corps at that time, and it had its effect on air support doctrine. Attack aircraft missions should not be roving ones, seeking targets of opportunity. They should instead be carefully prepared beforehand, with the unit commander briefing the crews thoroughly before they took off.[35]

The tactical successes of the Luftwaffe in France, and the close collaboration between Germany's ground forces and its Stukas, led the US Air Corps to contact the Navy in June 1940; the airmen were "extremely anxious" to obtain information on dive bombers.[36] Within a month, General Arnold had created two groups of dive bombers equipped with an Air Corps version of the Navy's A-24 "Dauntless." He also hastened the development of armor protection, self-sealing gas tanks, and a 37 mm cannon. Most important, Arnold took steps to provide effective air support for the armored units that the Army was rapidly organizing.

General Arnold conferred with British military leaders in April 1941. The British had embarked on a crash program of tests and exercises that led to the "Directive on Close Support Bombing" of 6 December 1940.[37] A British organization, called "Close Support Bomber Control" and staffed by both air and ground officers, evaluated and responded to requests for air support. Arnold sent a copy of the British plan to Army Chief of Staff Gen George C. Marshall, recommending "strongly" that the directive be sent to light-bomber commands and armored divisions.[38]

The British scheme proved useful, but less so than a series of tests conducted at Fort Benning, Georgia, between February and June 1941. These tests involved an armored division, two infantry divisions, several pursuit and light-bombardment squadrons, a parachute battalion, and some cavalry units. The tests indicated that aviation support involved "more centralized control" than did artillery support. "Air Support Control" received requests for air support, evaluated them, and ordered intervention when appropriate. Also in 1941, the first extensive army-size exercises ever held in the United States offered an excellent opportunity to experiment with air support. Again, air support control arranged for air support. This time, and for the first time, air reconnaissance seemed to generate more profitable targets than did ground reports.[39]

World War II

The Fort Benning tests resulted in Training Regulation 52 (29 August 1941), which established air-ground cooperation parties (AGCP)—Air Corps advisers assigned to Army ground units for advice on tactical air employment.[40] Field Manual (FM) 31-35 *Aviation in Support of Ground Forces* (March 1942) amplified the role of these parties.[41]

James A. Huston discerned three categories of CAS in World War II. The first category comprised large-scale operations designed to concentrate massive firepower at a decisive breakthrough point in the land battle. In the second category were those special missions extending over a longer period of time for a particular Army; for example, the protection afforded. The third category included unsung and unheralded specific missions that were flown at the request of ground commanders. Ground commanders saw these missions as bread-and-butter aspects of their own operational missions.[42]

As the fighting developed in Southern Tunisia in late 1942, the relationship between air and ground forces became a matter of concern to the Combined Chiefs of Staff and to Gen Dwight D. Eisenhower, commander in chief, Allied Forces

Northwest Africa. There was no centralized control of either the tactical or the strategic air forces, and America's air force was more badly split than the Royal Air Force.[43]

Doctrine called for an air support command attached to an army formation and directed by the ground force commander. There was no concerted effort to gain air superiority over the theater of operations, and the German Air Force (GAF) controlled the air in Tunisia. Friendly losses were so high that the mission of the air forces and the structure of the command and control system had to change. Ironically, Allied airpower had not only failed to achieve air superiority; it had also failed to provide the CAS desired. German fighters, by concentrating against small formations of US and British fighters, made Allied air losses prohibitive. Not until the Allies gained air superiority could they concentrate on providing CAS.[44] Air mission priorities became: (1) gain and maintain air superiority at the front, (2) provide close support for ground troops, and (3) interdict enemy supplies/infrastructure.

A reorganization of airpower was approved in January 1943, at the Casablanca Conference, with British air marshal Sir Arthur Tedder commanding the new organization. Under Tedder was Gen Carl A. Spaatz, commander of the Northwest African Air Force, which consisted of Strategic Air Force, Tactical Air Force, Coastal Air Force, and Troop Carrier Command. All air elements were within a single structure and capable of concentrating on the greatest challenge: gaining control of the air and stopping the German advance.[45]

Naval aviation operating against targets assigned to tactical or strategic forces also came under the theater air commander. During the invasions of Sicily and Italy, the Tactical Air Force commander controlled all airpower used to support the operations.[46] Even carrier forces not directly involved in fleet air defense were under his operational control. This unity of airpower was not only sound in theory; it stood the test of battle and proved to be the most effective method for controlling airpower in a theater of operations.[47]

As the full potential of ground-based air controllers on the front lines became apparent, an experiment called Rover Joe was implemented for the campaign in Italy. A veteran fighter-bomber pilot was placed on high ground near an active part of the Fifth Army's front. He observed the front and selected targets for Allied aircraft, which were assigned directly to him in flights of four every 30 minutes. He described targets and warned pilots about friendly troops and enemy defenses in the area.[48] Gen Mark Clark reported, "Frequently, Rover Joe will put the bombs on targets within 1,000 yards of our troops, and not once have any of our men been hurt."[49] Ninth Air Force employed a similar program in the European Theater.

By the time of the Normandy invasion, numbered tactical air commands had been created to work with each field army; numbered air forces would work with Army groups. Gen Hoyt Vandenberg's Ninth US Air Force worked with Gen Omar Bradley and the Twelfth Army Group. General Vandenberg had three tactical air commands (TAC): IX, XIX, and XXIX. Each worked with the field armies under General Bradley (1st, 3d, and 9th).

The British had a similar relationship between the Twenty-first Army Group and the Second Tactical Air Force. Below the tactical air force level, the British had an air group that was approximately the size of a US tactical air command. Each British and Canadian field army had an air group partner. These similar organizations made it easier for operational control to pass between the US Ninth Air Force and the British Second Tactical Air Force (TAF). When British general Bernard L. Montgomery had priority for a drive on the northern flank, for example, units of the IX TAC were temporarily under the second TAF.

Each tactical air command operated a joint operations center (JOC) to provide command and control. The JOC was run by the combat operations officer, who was an experienced combat fighter pilot. A senior Army officer, a Naval liaison officer (if the tactical situation so required), and various intelligence officers followed the current air and ground situation for the JOC.

A tactical air control center (TACC) executed the JOC's decisions and was responsible for all offensive and defensive air missions within its geographical area to the range of its radars. This organization was also used during the Korean conflict.[50]

The closest thing to an airborne FAC in World War II was the reconnaissance airplane. Modified fighters flew on missions specifically designed to collect intelligence information. Special tactical reconnaissance units (TRU) were organized to perform systematic visual reconnaissance. When a TRU aircraft discovered a target out of artillery range, it called in strike aircraft and led them to the target (functions of a modern-day FAC).[51]

Systems like Rover Joe contributed materially to the success of air-ground operations, and doctrine absorbed these lessons. A revised edition of FM 31-35, issued in August 1946, called for TACPs, each composed of a FAC located near the front to direct air strikes and an ALO collocated with the unit's command post, to advise the commander on the use of airpower. The revised manual dictated that TACPs should be assigned to each combat corps and division, and to subordinate units. Although not entirely consistent on the question of strike control, FM 31-35 did imply that air strikes could be controlled by other aircraft.[52]

Notes

1. Joint Publication 1-02, *Department of Defense Dictionary of Military and Associated Terms* (Washington, D.C.: US Government Printing Office [GPO], 3 January 1972), 61; Woodford Agee Heflin, ed., *The United States Air Force Dictionary* (Maxwell AFB, Ala.: Air University Press, 1956), 119–20.

2. Benjamin Franklin Cooling, ed., *Case Studies in the Development of Close Air Support* (Washington, D.C.: Office of Air Force History [OAFH], 1990), 5.

3. Lee B. Kennett, "Developments to 1939," in Cooling, 14.

4. Henri Mirande and Louis Olivier, *Sur la Bataille: Journal d'un Aviateur Francais a l'Armee Bulgier, au siege d'Adrianople* (Paris, 1913); Kennett, 14.

5. Serge Laine, "l'Aeronautique Militaire Francaise au Maroc, 1911–1939," *Revue Historique des Armees* 5, no. 4 (1978): 107–19; Kennett, 15.

6. Cooling, 1.

7. Kennett, 13.

8. Anthony Robinson, *Aerial Warfare: An Illustrated History* (New York: Galahad Books, 1982), 45.

9. Ibid., 46.

10. Peter C. Smith, *Dive Bomber! An Illustrated History* (Annapolis, Md.: Naval Institute Press, 1982), 9.

11. S. F. Wise, *Canadian Airmen and the First World War, the Official History of the Royal Canadian Air Force*, vol.1 (Toronto: University of Toronto Press in cooperation with the Department of National Defense and the Canadian government Publishing Centre, Supply and Services, Canada, 1980), 343–44.

12. Kennett, 16.

13. Georg Paul Neumann, *Die Deutschen Luftstreitkrafte im Weltkrieg* (Berlin: E. S. Mittler, 1920), 425; Kennett, 17.

14. H. A. Jones, *The War in the Air: Being the Story of the Part Played in the Great War by the Royal Air Force*, vol. 2 (Oxford: Clarendon Press, 1937), 200–10.

15. Kennett, 18.

16. Jones, 473.

17. Jones, vol. 4, 434.

18. Wing Commander J. C. Slessor, *Air Power and Armies* (London: Oxford University Press; reprint, New York: AMS Press, 1936), 100.

19. Kennett, 25.

20. Ibid., 27.

21. Robinson, 48.

22. Kennett, 28.

23. Paul Deichmann, *German Air Force Operations in Support of the Army*, USAF Historical Study no. 92, M-U 27218, Air University Library, Maxwell AFB, Ala.

24. Kennett, 30.

25. Air Corps Tactical School text, 1935–36, "Attack Aviation," sec. 3, US Air Force Historical Research Agency, 2: "The two-seater attack formation, through its defensive fire from the rear cockpits, will be able to continue on its mission unless opposed by greatly superior numbers of hostile pursuit aviation."

26. Smith, 71–72.

27. Slessor, 95.

28. Kennett, 37.

29. Brig Gen William "Billy" Mitchell, "Provisional Manual of Operations," *Maurer Air Service* 2 (23 December 1918): 399.

30. Kennett, 43.

31. "Experiences with the Air Service in Minor Warfare," lecture delivered at the Army War College, 12 January 1929. Text in US Military History Institute, Carlisle Barracks, Pa.

32. Capt Charles W. Boggs Jr., "Marine Aviation: Origins and Growth," *Marine Corps Gazette* 34 (November 1950): 68–75.

33. "The Air Corps," address to the Army War College, 8 October, 37, 10. Text in US Military History Institute, Carlisle Barracks, Pa., 10.

34. Ibid., 4.

35. Army War College text, 1937–1938, "Air Forces and War," 44, US Military History Institute, Carlisle Barracks, Pa.

36. Gen George H. Britt to Chief of Aeronautics Bureau, USN, letter, 8 June 1940, RG 18, Central Decimal Files, 1938–1942, Box 741, National Archives (NA).

37. British War Office, "Directive on Close Support Bombing," WO 106/5162, 6 December 1940.

38. Notation on Brief of Meeting, 17 April 1941, Reel 32, item 1344, George C. Marshall papers, George C. Marshall Research Library, Lexington, Va.

39. Comments for Critique, Second-Third Army Maneuvers, Louisiana, September 1941, File "Maneuvers," Box 224, H. H. Arnold Papers, Library of Congress.

40. Headquarters, Mediterranean Allied Air Forces, "Close Support of the Fifth Army" (Maxwell AFB, Ala.: Air University, 1945).

41. Army Field Manual 31-35, *Aviation in Support of Ground Forces*, GPO, Washington, D.C., 9 April 1942.

42. James A. Huston, "Tactical Use of Airpower in World War II: The Army Experience," *Military Affairs* 14 (Winter 1950): 175–77.

43. Wesley F. Craven and James L. Cate, eds., *The Army Air Forces in World War II*, vol. 2, *Europe: Torch to Pointblank* (Chicago: University of Chicago Press, 1949), 137.

44. William W. Momyer, *Airpower in Three Wars* (Washington, D.C.: Department of the Air Force, January 1978), 40.

45. Arthur William Tedder, *With Prejudice, the War Memoirs of Marshal of the Royal Air Force Lord Tedder* (Boston: Little, Brown & Co., 1966), 393.

46. Craven and Cate, 496.

47. Momyer, 45.

48. "Close Support of the Fifth Army," tab D.

49. Extract from press conference by General Clark, Commanding General, Fifth Army, 2 October 1944; quoted in "Close Support of the Fifth Army."

50. Ibid., 258.

51. "Tactics and Techniques Developed by the United States Tactical Air Commands in the European Theater of Operations," Army Air Forces Evaluation Board in the European Theater of Operations, 1 March 1945, 27.

52. War Department FM 31-35, *Air-Ground Operations* (Washington, D.C.: GPO, 2 August 1946).

Chapter 2

Close Air Support Doctrine

On the eve of the Korean War, a fundamental difference in close air support (CAS) philosophy existed between the Navy/Marines and the Air Force/Army. The Navy system was subordinated to that of the Air Force during the Korean War, but compromises were made on both sides. The philosophical differences were not resolved in Korea, and they arose again in the early days of Vietnam.

Fifth Air Force had made only minor changes to the system since World War II. Except for changes in names, there was no difference between World War II and Korean War organizations. Fifth Air Force provided the same support for Eighth Army in Korea as IX TAC had done for First Army in Europe.[1]

Early Navy-Marine Close Air Support

The seeds of Navy CAS were planted in the 1920s during Marine Corps action in Nicaragua, Haiti, and Santo Domingo; airplanes and infantry functioned as a team for the first time in military history.[2]

Navy-Marine Corps CAS was perfected during World War II. Early in the Pacific campaign, properly controlled air attacks would be a major asset in the successful prosecution of an amphibious advance across the Pacific. Navy and Marine officials believed airplanes could be a valuable "supporting weapon" to help ground troops advance against the Japanese.

Navy-Marine doctrine had its battle test during the Tarawa campaign in November 1943, when frontline units were accompanied by air liaison parties. They assisted ground commanders in selecting suitable targets and in transmitting target information to aircraft pilots. Liaison aircraft were flown by senior aviators who knew the ground plan and were in radio contact with fighter-bombers. The system was improved at Iwo Jima, but the final innovation—attack aircraft being directed by frontline ground units—was not extensively used until the Battle of Okinawa.

By the end of World War II, Navy-Marine CAS was fully developed and battle tested. It had proved itself at Guam, at Iwo Jima, and especially in Okinawa. Navy and Marine Corps aircraft quickly and effectively delivered their bullets and bombs on "close" targets under the direction of frontline troops. This system was available and ready for use at the outbreak of the Korean War.

Largely for economy, but also because existing fighter aircraft were sufficiently versatile to provide either air defense or tactical air support, the Air Force placed the air defense command (ADC) and the tactical air command (TAC) under the continental air command (CAC) in December 1948. The reduced status of tactical air was not popular with the Army, which informed TAC it was no longer satisfied with FM 31-35, *Air-Ground Operations*.[3] In May 1950, Maj Gen Thomas D. White, director of legislation and liaison for the Air Force, was told by Congress that the air support mission might have to be given to the Marine Corps if the Air Force did not pay more attention to it.[4]

Even without the significant technological developments that were impending, the mobilization of additional Army and Air Force units during the autumn of 1950 would probably have forced the Air Force to reestablish a major Tactical Air Command. On 1 August 1950, the Continental Air Command assigned Ninth Air Force (tactical) and available fighter-bombers, troop carriers, light bombers, and tactical reconnaissance units to the TAC. On 15 November 1950, the Air Force specified that TAC would "provide for Air Force cooperation with land, naval, and/or amphibious forces." On 1 December, it made TAC a major command directly responsible to the Chief of Staff, United States Air Force.[5] The vague wording of TAC's mission statement reflected a general uncertainty about the Army-Air Force relationship.

Close Air Support in Korea

The battle at the Pusan perimeter revealed three differences (philosophy, technique, and language) between the Air Force and the Navy. Philosophical differences were at the root of the disparity. The Air Force believed the proper priority for the application of airpower was first on the sources of the enemy's war-making potential and second in the immediate battle area; that is, (1) isolation of the battlefield should take precedence over air strikes on the battlefield and (2) aircraft control must never degenerate to individual ground commanders who had limited perspectives of the battle.

The Navy never fully accepted the validity of the strategic bombing concept—and Navy personnel doubted that "strategic" targets could be neatly separated from "tactical" targets. It was the Navy's view that sufficient force of the proper type should be applied to attain any given objective—and CAS was regarded as indispensable for defeating the enemy's ground forces.[6]

The second major difference was in technique. Navy-Marine CAS required that pilots be trained to recognize terrain and understand the capabilities and limitations of ground arms. With this knowledge and understanding, they could order strikes very close to friendly forces. Marine pilots were especially well trained in this respect; Air Force pilots did not receive the same degree of training.

With regard to the control of airpower, the crux of the difference was that the Marines had 13 tactical air control parties (TACP) in a division: one for each battalion (nine), one with each regiment (three), and one for the division itself. Any of these could request and direct "close" air support. In contrast, the Air Force provided only one TACP per regiment (four for a division). The Marines believed the frontline commander should be able to make his request directly to the supporting agencies. A basic presumption was that unless CAS was immediately available (10 to 15 minutes), its value to the frontline commander was questionable. The Marine controller was on the front lines with the troops. In contrast, Air Force doctrine placed the air controller aloft in a liaison-type aircraft with no close personal contact with the ground commander. The Air Force emphasized central control.[7]

The third difference was in the definition of "close air support." Each service provided CAS, but they viewed its definition differently: "Air action against hostile ground or naval targets which are so close to friendly forces as to require detailed integration of each air mission with the fire and movement of those forces."[8]

To the Navy and Marine Corps, "close" is considered to be 50 to 200 yards immediately in front of friendly troops. The Air Force considered "close" to mean within several thousand yards of the front line . . . the distance to which field artillery could effectively reach.[9] What the Air Force defined as "close" was given another description by the Navy: "deep." The Air Force did not perform what the Marines called "close" air support.[10]

These differences were summarized by Lt Gen Lemuel C. Shepherd, commanding general, Fleet Marine Force Pacific, in 1951: "We believe in providing for a small number of on-station planes; the Air Force does not. We believe in continuous direct communication between the frontline battalion and the controlling air agency; the Air Force does not. We believe that CAS of the frontline troops should take precedence over routine interdiction missions; the Air Force does not."[11]

Air Force Philosophy in Korea

The CAS system used by the Air Force in Korea was derived from the German technique used in World War II, in which USAF planners saw a serious fault: The Luftwaffe was too closely tied to ground forces. USAF and Britain's Royal Air Force (RAF) concluded that tactical airpower should be controlled centrally and applied for the overall objective of gaining control of the air. Only after control of the air had been established should tactical air perform the secondary role of close support.[12]

As for the mechanics of providing CAS, the Air Force system depended on airborne controllers. A light liaison-type plane would circle the frontlines area, spot enemy targets, and direct the bombs and gunfire of other planes.[13]

When the Korean War began, the Air Force system of CAS was not ready. The fundamental reason was that Washington gave far greater importance and priority to strategic air than to tactical air. Another factor was that training for CAS operations was not among Far Eastern Air Force or Eighth Army missions. No effort had been made within Fifth Air Force or Eighth Army to erect a TAC system, train ground liaison officers, stockpile equipment, or conduct air-ground operations training.

Thus, the start of the Korean War saw two different systems of CAS. The Air Force system had largely been developed in the European theater, where the employment of aircraft was coordinated at the Army level by two officers—one air, one ground. Strike planes were assigned to particular missions as approved by the joint operations center (JOC). Upon arrival at the front, they were directed by airborne liaison-type aircraft. CAS targets were those within the immediate battle zone (within 10 miles). However, this system was not immediately ready when the Korean War started.[14]

While there was interservice disagreement on CAS methods, there was disagreement within the Air Force as to CAS's proper priority. General Vandenberg laid out his view on how the air war should be fought: "No successful operations on the surface can be conducted until you get air superiority. And when you go against a hostile air force in order to gain that air superiority, you must first destroy the enemy air force at the place where he is most vulnerable, which is on the ground and in his nest. . . . If you don't do that, your attrition mounts in arithmetical progression. Airpower . . . should go to the heart of the industrial centers to become reasonably efficient. . . . In my opinion, the proper way to use airpower is initially to stop the flow of supplies and ammunition, guns, equipment of all types, at its source. The next most efficient way is to knock it out along the road before it reaches the front line. The least efficient way is after it gets dug in at the front line. Nevertheless, there are requirements constantly where the use of airpower in close support is necessary." For Vandenberg, then, airpower's priorities in Korea were (1) air superiority, (2) interdiction, and (3) CAS.[15]

The Air Force could not adhere to its doctrine, however, because the enemy's war materiel originated in the Soviet Union, which could not be attacked. This war materiel had to be destroyed somewhere south of the Yalu River and, as a rule, "the greater length of road and rail that you can get the enemy from his main source of supply, the more advantageous it is to the Air Force and, therefore, as you decrease it, it becomes less advantageous. . . . As the distance between the Yalu and our troops decreases, the effectiveness of our tactical air forces decreases in direct proportion."[16]

Gen Otto P. Weyland assumed command of the Far East Air Forces (FEAF) on 10 June 1951. He saw airpower's principal task as preventing the Chinese armies from enveloping the retreating United Nations (UN) ground forces. He therefore ordered air interdiction strikes and concentrated CAS, enabling friendly ground troops to withdraw into South Korea.[17]

In the summer of 1950 and the winter of 1950–51, the FEAF provided friendly ground troops with extraordinarily large amounts of CAS. In the intervals between ground battles, however, United Nations interdiction was directed against the "middle miles" of the Korean transportation system that supported the Chinese armies. Constant air attacks against the overextended supply lines drained them of their combat effectiveness. The massive ground attacks mounted by the Chinese in January and April 1951 failed for lack of logistical support.[18]

The Air Force feared that organizational diffusion might lead to a loss in airpower's inherent flexibility. Air Force thinkers therefore questioned the wisdom of dividing airpower into strategic and tactical arms. They also reexamined the mission of tactical air forces. The *Joint Training Directive for Air-Ground Operations*, issued in September 1950, stated that the mission of tactical airpower was related to the strategy and maneuver of ground forces. Late in 1950, however, the Air Force Deputy Chief of Staff for Development suggested that tactical airpower need not be related directly to the maneuver of friendly ground troops. Tactical airpower, he said, might be employed directly against enemy forces in the field without any friendly ground forces being present. "In this new concept, tactical airpower will be entering into direct combat with enemy ground forces—not only supporting our ground forces in their fight against the enemy ground forces. . . . Clearly, it is not acceptable to relegate tactical air to only a supporting role. It is no longer sufficient even to declare that tactical air and ground forces cooperate equally. Rather, tactical air must now be conceived as having a role in the battle against enemy ground forces at times completely on its own."[19]

Unable to secure additional air forces and faced with the prospect of continuing an air war during the ground stalemate in 1951, Weyland could see only two potential employments for airpower: it could either be committed to close support strikes along the front, where the enemy was dug in and relatively invulnerable, or it could be concentrated against interdiction targets in rear areas. Weyland favored the latter and obtained agreement from Gen Matthew Ridgway, commander in chief, UN Command, who was apprehensive that the communists might take advantage of the respite in ground fighting to build up frontline supplies for a renewed ground offensive. Lt Gen James A. Van Fleet agreed to the interdiction campaign, provided that his Eighth Army would receive 96 CAS air sorties each day. Fifth Air Force and Eighth Army then collaborated in planning a comprehensive air interdiction campaign against North Korea's railways. Begun on 18 August 1951, the interdiction campaign took the Reds completely by surprise and was initially very successful.[20]

In August 1952, General Clark held that any comparison between the Army-Air Force and Marine systems of CAS was faulty because the two systems were designed for completely different types of functions and had different allocations of forces.[21] Fifth Air Force, Eighth Army, Seventh Fleet, and First Marine Aircraft Wing representatives met in August 1953 to review the war's air-ground operations. They concluded that "little attempt has been made . . . to reiterate previously published doctrines and techniques which have been found fundamentally sound and workable."[22]

General Weyland knew that the outnumbered UN ground forces in Korea never possessed a proper amount of artillery, but believed that "FEAF and Fifth Air Force had provided adequate CAS."[23] But FEAF's final report contained a warning: "Because FEAF provided UNC ground forces lavish close air support in Korea is no reason to assume this condition will exist in future wars." In a future conflict, it said, the fighter-bomber forces would be hard put to attain air superiority—and air superiority would be more vital to the success of all forces than close support would be.[24]

Navy/Marine Air in Vietnam

The interservice disagreement over CAS lingered through the 1950s and into the 1960s, surfacing again during the Vietnam conflict. Until July of 1966, the Navy maintained a carrier off the coast of southern South Vietnam. Known as Dixie Station, its aircraft were employed in III and IV Corps under the control of the Seventh Air Force commander. They therefore operated under the same tactical control procedures as USAF fighters. In August 1966, the Dixie Station carrier moved north to join the carriers at Yankee Station in the Gulf of Tonkin. Navy and Marine Corps pilots flew predominantly in I Corps, and a large number of the Navy's sorties were flown just above the demilitarized zone (DMZ) where the enemy's entrenched artillery was a problem for US bases and outposts along the southern edge of the demilitarized zone.[25]

When Marine ground units moved into South Vietnam in March 1965, elements of a Marine Air Wing (MAW) moved with them.[26] The Third Marine Amphibious Force (MAF) had reached full strength by early 1966. The First MAW provided support for its divisions. Until February 1968, Marine air was used almost entirely in I Corps to support the First and Third Marine Divisions. The Marines established their own tactical air control system. It scheduled all aircraft into each division area on a planned flow. The system was designed for operations in which a lack of artillery required airpower overhead at all times, but it was a costly way to manage air resources for sustained operations. And when the First and Third Marine Divisions in I Corps settled down to sustained ground combat, with the Army providing heavy artillery augmentation, MAWs employed aviation as though they were still conducting an amphibious operation.[27] This arrangement did not allow airpower to be concentrated on a decisive part of the overall theater campaign.

Until 1968, Seventh Air Force had little influence on how Marine air capability could be used to support other ground force units. Marine sorties not used to support the Marine divisions were made available to Seventh Air Force. But the Marines provided few CAS sorties to the Air Force during this period.

The issue of airpower control led to the assignment of responsibility for controlling fixed-wing aircraft in South Vietnam to the deputy commander for Air Operations, Military Assistance Command-Vietnam (MACV). With the buildup of enemy forces in I Corps in 1968 and the movement of more US Army units into the area, a change in the control of air operations was inevitable. The commander (USMACV) had to be able to turn to a single air commander for advice on when and where to apply the assigned airpower. Thus, the Marine system gave way to the Air Force system of centralized control.

Notes

1. William W. Momyer, *Airpower in Three Wars* (Washington, D.C.: Department of the Air Force, January 1978), 258.

2. Malcolm W. Cagle and Frank A. Manson, *The Sea War in Korea* (Annapolis, Md.: United States Naval Institute, 1957), 48.

3. Tactical Air Command, "Tactical Air Operations," report to USAF Review Board, 21 June 1949, 1-2.

4. Maj Gen Thomas D. White, memorandum to the Secretary of the Air Force, subject: Air Support Mission, 4 May 1950.

5. *History of Tactical Air Command*, 1 July-30 November 1950, vol. I, 1-12; CONARC Reg. no. 26-1, *Organization-Tactical Air Command*, 11 August 1950.

6. Cagle and Manson, 71-72.

7. Ibid., 72.

8. Secretary of Defense, memorandum to chiefs of staff, subject: Close Air Support, 21 April 1948. This same definition remains in Naval Warfare Informative Publication (NWIP) 22-3.

9. Far East Air Force mission summary report, 16 November 1950. Missions as far distant as 20 miles in advance of friendly forces were listed as "close air support."

10. In the period between 26 July and 3 September 1950, almost half of the Navy's CAS sorties were delivered outside the bomb line.

11. Cagle and Manson, 73.

12. Thus, the Army Air Force in the War Department publication FM 100-20, *Command and Employment of Airpower*, July 1943, para.16, stated its opinion of close air support: "In the zone of contact, missions against hostile units are most difficult to control, are most expensive, and are, in general, least effective. Targets are small, well-dispersed, and difficult to

locate. In addition, there is always a considerable chance of striking friendly forces. . . ."

13. Cagle and Manson, 50.

14. Ibid., 51.

15. *Military Situation in the Far East*, report to 82d Cong., 1st sess., 1378–79, 1382, 1385, 1417, 1492.

16. Ibid., 1500–5.

17. Robert Frank Futrell, *Ideas, Concepts, Doctrine: A History of Basic Thinking in the United States Air Force, 1907–1964*, vol. 1 (Maxwell AFB, Ala.: Air University, June 1971), 273.

18. Ibid., 274.

19. "What Can and Should the USAF Do to Increase the Effectiveness of Air-Ground Operations?" Assistant for evaluation, deputy chief of staff for development, USAF, Staff Study, December 1950, 6–7.

20. Futrell, 310–11.

21. Commander in Chief, Far East to CGs, Eighth Army, XVI Corps, FEAF, and ComNavFE, letter, subject: Air-Ground Operations, 11 August 1952.

22. Report of Joint Air-Ground Operations Conference, Fifth Air Force, 8–22 August 1953.

23. Gen Otto P. Weyland, "The Air Campaign in Korea," *Air Force Magazine*, August 1954, 20.

24. FEAF Report, 126.

25. Momyer, 285.

26. William C. Westmoreland, *A Soldier Reports* (Garden City, N. Y.: Doubleday & Co., 1976), 109.

27. Momyer, 286.

Chapter 3

Korea

Forward Air Controllers Emerge

The North Koreans anticipated no resistance from the United States or other nations when they invaded South Korea in June 1950. Further, they felt that any intervention by others could not prevent them from accomplishing their military objectives. They were wrong on both counts: FEAF, the air component of the United States Far East Command (USFEC), was in action over South Korea less than eight hours after the UN voted to intervene.[1]

The United Nations Command (UNC) was organized soon after hostilities began, with a mission to support the Republic of Korea (ROK). In addition to US ground forces, the UNC eventually incorporated ground units from Great Britain, Canada, Turkey, Greece, Luxembourg, Ethiopia, France, Belgium, the Philippines, Australia, Colombia, Thailand, New Zealand, and the Netherlands. Augmenting FEAF units were US Marine Corps and Navy air units as well as British, Australian, South African, Greek, Republic of Korea, and Thai air elements.

The ROK Air Force would be no help; its 16 trainers and liaison aircraft had not a single bomb rack or machine gun mount among them. Fortunately, the North Korean Air Force was also weak; it numbered 62 Il-10 attack aircraft, about 70 Yak piston-engined fighters, and some support planes. Its first combat saw its first defeat; five Yaks struck Kimpo airfield at noon on 27 June 1950. Less than five minutes later, three were burning on the ground. The first USAF kill was credited to Lt William G. Hudson, an F-82G pilot of the 68th Fighter All-Weather Squadron (FAWS). An hour later, four of eight Il-10s were downed by F-80Cs from the 35th Fighter-Bomber Squadron. That evening, President Harry S. Truman told Gen Douglas MacArthur to send the Air Force and the Navy into battle. MacArthur ordered Fifth Air Force (FAF) to hit targets between the battle line and the 38th parallel. In less than one month, the North Korean Air Force (NKAF) was obliterated and the United States had control of the air.[2]

FEAF combat units consisted of 1,172 aircraft located mainly in Japan, with single wings located on Okinawa, Guam, and the Philippine Islands. One medium bomber wing, one light bomber wing, and eight fighter squadrons were committed to the Korean effort. Ten fighter squadrons remained in defense of Japan, Okinawa, and the Philippines.[3]

The Fight for Air Superiority

FEAF began the war with 32 all-weather F-82Gs and 365 F-80Cs. From a stock of North American F-51 Mustang fighters (World War II vintage, formerly designated P-51s) in Air National Guard units, 145 were scraped together for Korean service. FEAF agreed to step backwards; six of its F-80C squadrons would convert to F-51s.

In early air fighting, the NKAF was weak, unskilled, and inexperienced. But the Chinese began firing antiaircraft artillery (AAA) at UN planes patrolling the Yalu area in August 1950 and, on 3 October 1950, Premier Chou En-lai said Chinese troops would defend Korea if UN forces crossed the 38th parallel. MacArthur, however, told Truman it was very unlikely that the Chinese would interfere. Besides, he assured Truman, the Chinese had no air force. (FEAF had submitted intelligence estimates crediting the Chinese with at least three hundred combat aircraft, including jets.)

The Chinese finally yielded to UN air superiority. The UN air forces ruled the daylight skies, throttled the flow of supplies and war materiel, and slaughtered countless numbers of Chinese soldiers. It was, finally, airpower that triumphed.[4]

With air superiority established early, the air effort was committed to support of the hard-pressed ground forces. Close support by air had to make up for a lack in artillery support. Airpower enabled the ground forces to trade space for time and prevented the North Korean People's Army (NKPA) from accomplishing its mission.[5]

Consider the air war as three different, though related, operations: the strategic bombing campaign, a short-lived attack against short-lived targets; the interdiction campaign,

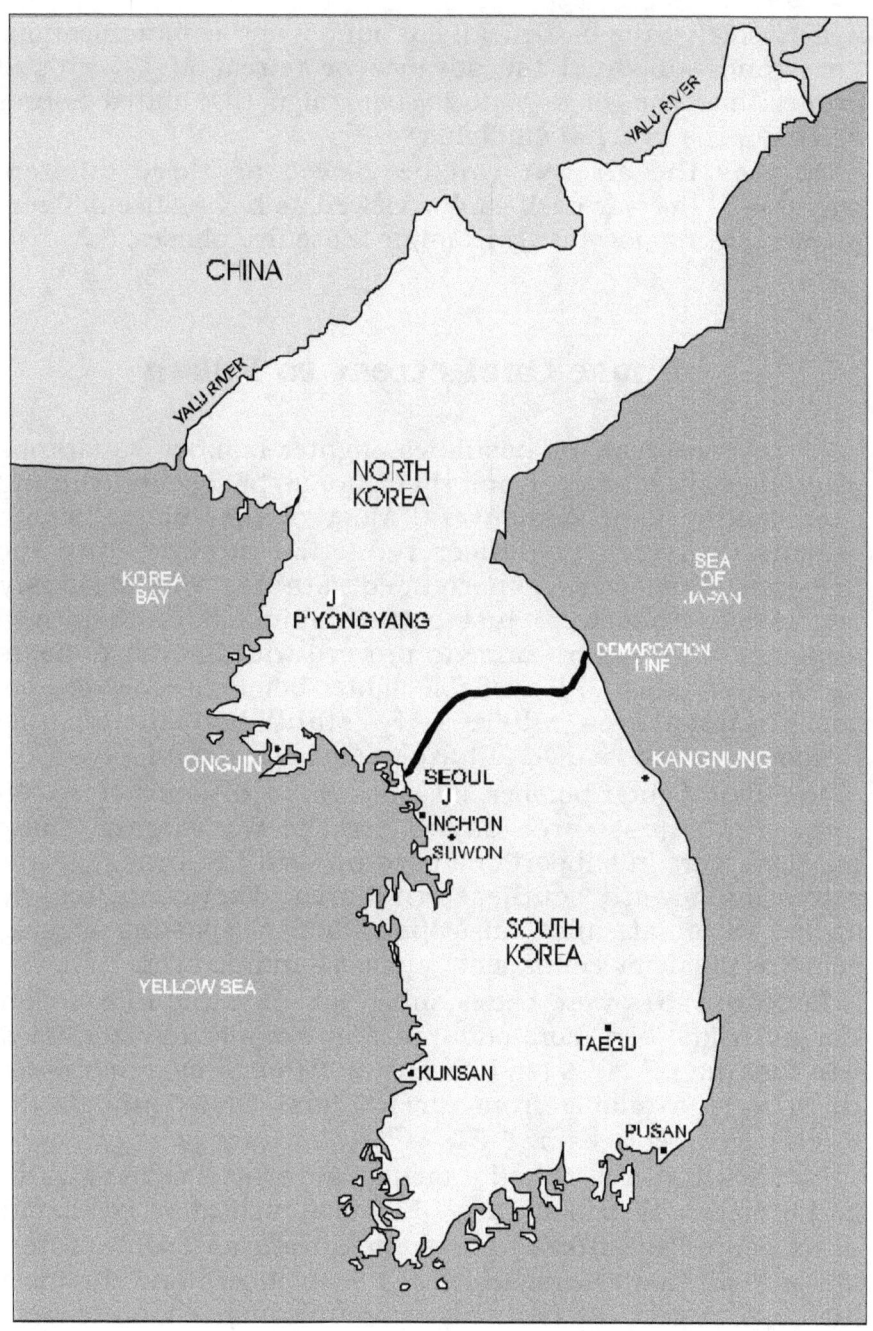

Figure 1. Korean Peninsula

which isolated the battlefield, cut supply and communications lines, and supported the advance or retreat of UN ground armies; and the air superiority campaign that pitted Sabres against MiGs in aerial gunfights.[6]

Just as the air war can be viewed as three different operations, the war itself can be viewed as having five different phases. Let us now briefly examine those five phases.

Phase One—Retreat to Pusan

At the outbreak of hostilities, fighter-bomber squadrons were deployed away from their home bases on training exercises or joint maneuvers. Most of the pilots, having recently survived an officer reduction-in-force from the previous war, were experienced, stable, and seriously aggressive. They were just getting adjusted to their new airplanes when orders came to proceed with aircraft to bases in southern Japan. All available fighter-bombers converged on the Fukuoka area, where FAF established an advance headquarters and a JOC at Itazuke Air Base, Japan

The first fighter-bomber missions were dispatched on 28 June 1950, just three days after the war began. These missions were in support of a hard-pressed UN Army that was retreating toward southeastern Korea. They were mainly armed reconnaissance missions aimed at blasting moving columns of enemy equipment, supplies, and personnel.

Because F-51s were better suited for operating from rough Korean fields, had more endurance at low-altitude, and used less fuel than F-80Cs (and because F-51s and spare parts for them were available from Air National Guard units), the F-80Cs were replaced by F-51s.[7]

By mid-July, a JOC and a tactical air control center (TACC) had been established at Taegu. Eighteen tactical air command posts controlled strikes against the advancing enemy. Later, airborne air controllers helped fighter-bombers find the most lucrative targets. At best, all communication channels were overloaded; the only control many missions had was the information given pilots at briefings.

Phase Two—Advance to the Yalu

As the UN ground forces regrouped and were resupplied at Pusan, the North Korean forces, with their long supply lines under attack by fighter-bombers, grew weaker. The breakout from the Pusan perimeter and the amphibious landing at Inchon in September 1950 set off a fast UN advance to the Yalu. Here, as in the first phase, targets for the fighter-bombers were plentiful: interdiction targets to slow down the enemy's progress, personnel and equipment targets to demoralize and defeat him.

Phase Three—Second Retreat

On 24 November 1950, Eighth Army launched an all-out attack near the Yalu River. Two days later, hordes of Chinese counterattacked furiously on most of the western front. The fighter-bombers devoted almost their entire effort to close support of the hard-pressed UN ground troops. To support the Third Marine and Seventh Infantry Divisions evacuating near the Chosen Reservoir area and along the east coast, fighter-bombers flew 736 combat sorties from 28 November to 20 December 1950.

Most FEAF squadrons were reequipped with F-80Cs, and the jet proved to be a good ground-support airplane. Aircraft control and communications gradually improved during the first six months, even under what would normally constitute adverse conditions. An adequate variety of VHF frequencies reduced the early confusion that was generated by overcrowding the air waves.

Phase Four—Main Line of Resistance Stabilized

Fighter-bomber attacks against the communists' supply lines permitted friendly ground forces to hold along a poorly defined line south of the 38th parallel. Fighter-bomber units flew reconnaissance missions. Pilots became thoroughly familiar with their assigned areas and called in additional aircraft when targets developed; they were able to stop the communists' supply effort during daylight hours. By March

1951, the UN forces were ready again to advance toward the north and the requirement for close-support sorties increased.

Phase Five—Air Pressure for Peace

There were no significant changes in the main line of resistance (MLR) during this period. Ground action by both sides consisted of probing patrols and limited-objective attacks. The communists were never able to launch another major attack, and UN forces never attempted an offensive of their own. The stagnant ground situation did not diminish the fighter-bomber effort. In fact, the highest sustained sortie rates of the war were flown in the closing months, and the F-51s and F-80s were replaced by the fighter-bomber version of the F-86 Sabre during the last six months of the war.

Improvements in control and communications contributed to the increased effectiveness of the fighter-bombers. A stabilized front permitted the installation of a complete tactical control net as targets in the open became so rare and fleeting that fast and dependable communications were essential for aircraft to find them.[8]

A Substitute for Artillery

When Maj Gen William F. Dean's 24th Infantry Division engaged the North Koreans at Taejon early in July 1950, the lightly armed American division needed effective close support to make up for its lack of artillery. On 5 July, Gen Earl Partridge, acting Commander of FEAF, sent a team to set up and run a JOC at Taejon. Two TACPs had retreated from Suwon to Taejon on the night of 30 June and were ready for action when General Dean's troops arrived.

During the critical days after 12 July, when the 24th Division battled to hold Taejon, the entire FEAF—plus B-29s—supported it. In fact, 61.5 percent of FEAF's July sorties were for close battlefield support. "Without question," said General Dean, "the Air Force definitely blunted the initial North Korean thrust to the southward. Without this continuing air effort, it is doubtful that the courageous combat soldiers, spread thinly along the line, could have withstood the onslaught of the vastly numerically superior enemy." Dean's division could not hold against the five enemy divisions attacking it, however, and the North Koreans captured Taejon on 20 July. But the holding battle fought by the 24th Division had given Eighth Army time to get more ground troops to Korea. And FAF flew an average of 239 close-support sorties each day during August, providing a brilliant example of air-ground coordination at its best.[9]

Soon, the only important airfield open to the allies in Korea was K-2 at Taegu. Only Dakotas and Mustangs could be used there, but a Mustang squadron of the Republic of Korea Air Force (ROKAF) flew from an airstrip at Chinhae. Flying from the nearest air bases on Kyushu, Itazuke, and Ashiya, Japan, F-80s could not spend more than 20 minutes over the battlefield—but efficiency was greatly increased when the JOC was set up.

In accordance with the theory that "effects accrue geometrically as the force is increased arithmetically," the Air Force favored interdiction attacks on rear areas as the best way to halt the North Korean offensive. But the demand for close support intensified, and ground controllers directed fire as close as 50 yards ahead of friendly troops while TACPs and T-6 Mosquitoes ranged as far ahead as 10 miles.

Tactical aircraft had operated effectively against the mechanized forces of the Axis powers in Europe, and they were expected to do even better against the primitive Asiatic armies. The contrary was the case, however, since the Korean People's Army was not dependent on mechanical transport.[10] Korean laborers carried an A-frame harness on their backs. Both North Korean and South Korean armies were able to supply troops in rough terrain by use of the A-frame and long columns of laborers.[11]

Close Air Support in Korea

CAS operations provided important fire support for UNC ground troops. Operating under an umbrella of air superiority (established early), UNC air operations deprived the communists of free movement by day, forced them into a massive program of field engineering, denied them supplies for sustained offensives, and demoralized their troops. Three American air organizations mounted tactical offensive air operations: FEAF, principally FAF; First Marine Air Wing; and the US Navy's carrier air groups of the Seventh Fleet's Task Force 77. A limited number of South Korean and UN squadrons also flew sorties under the control of FAF.

The Air Force provided two different types of close control: the ground FAC of the TACP or an airborne tactical air coordinator (A-TAC) flying in either a light observation aircraft or a fighter-bomber.[12] They guided attacking aircraft onto the target and away from friendly troops through combinations of voice communication, marking rockets, artillery smoke shells, and electronic signals. Officers who directed air strikes were pilots with prior experience in flying close-support sorties.[13]

The bomb line (the geographic limit for air strikes not under positive control) tended to coincide with the outer limits of the effective range of corps artillery. Since these limits were normally established by the height of mountains, the ranges were shorter than normal for heavy artillery. Nevertheless, the bomb line normally was five to eight miles from the front lines. The Army did not expect integrated CAS closer than this—and the Air Force did not intend to deliver it except under conditions of clearly marked targets and readily identifiable friendly troop positions, positively observed direction from Air Force ground or air controllers, near absolute safety from friendly artillery fire, and only against targets that could not be attacked with heavy artillery.[14]

Although tactical air operations gave UNC an important advantage over its enemies, the value of CAS remained controversial throughout the Korean War.[15]

The Extemporized Air War

From the invasion of South Korea on 25 June 1950 until the end of the year, air operations over the embattled peninsula had all of the characteristics of a classic American war in its early stages. Coordination between the services was minimal while roles and missions became indistinct and overlapping. Moreover, the lack of preparedness for war ensured confusion, frustration, and inefficiency. Not until

January 1951 did UN air operations show a mature degree of coordination. The first six months of the war also focused attention upon the differences between Air Force and Marine Corps CAS.

Verbal exchanges about CAS obscured some important facts about the Korean air war in 1950. Among them is that air superiority was established early, allowing Air Force planes to fly some 41,500 interdiction and CAS sorties against North Korean forces. Navy and Marine Corps aircraft flew another 13,000 sorties. Lt Gen Walton H. Walker, commander of US Eighth Army, believed that tactical air support allowed the UN to remain on the peninsula and then march toward the Yalu Tactical aviation provided the additional firepower that meant the difference between defeat and victory.[16]

Maj Gen Edward Almond, MacArthur's chief of staff and commander of X Corps, had faith in the efficiency of ground-based FACs. Although he recognized the utility of airborne controllers, he regarded the ground FAC as essential in ensuring that bombs hit enemy troops rather than friendly ones. Almond also believed that the Air Force should dispatch fighter-bombers to engage frontline regiments on a regular schedule. (He did not fully appreciate all the difficulties FEAF faced in providing timely and effective CAS in Korea.)[17]

FAF replaced the F-80Cs of six squadrons with the propeller-driven North American F-51 Mustang, the all-around workhorse of World War II. But the Mustang was a mixed blessing—the modified F-80C or the more capable F-84E had substantial advantages over the Mustang. The jets could provide twice the sorties of the F-51 with only half the maintenance time. In combat, the jets were less vulnerable to ground fire. In 1950, Mustang losses to enemy action were more than twice those of the jets. The jets carried the eight-channel VHF radio while the Mustang had space for only the four-channel radio.[18] Finally, the Mustang's liquid-cooled engine was particularly vulnerable to ground fire.

The Need for Airborne FACs

The rough roads of Korea were very damaging to the ground FACs' old radio-equipped jeeps. Moreover, the TACPs could seldom get far enough forward for maximum effectiveness since the unarmored jeeps could not be exposed to enemy fire. Army units were supposed to request air support missions against specific targets through the JOC. But the 24th Division, in retreat, could not identify enemy strong points along the front lines. American ground troops badly needed close support; yet jet fighters, limited to a short time at lower altitude over the front lines, needed immediate targets.[19]

The technique of having a slower plane spot a target and call in a jet to attack it was born in Korea on 9 July 1950. It was conceived by Lt Col Stanley P. Latiolas, FAF operations officer, when North Korean forces were battering small American and ROK Army units. CAS was needed—in a hurry.[20] On 9 July, Lts James A. Bryant and Frank G. Mitchell brought two L-5G liaison planes to Taejon modified with four-channel VHF radios. Bryant and Mitchell, unable to get their radio equipment to work, borrowed rides in two 24th Division L-17s Although Bryant was attacked by two Yaks over the road between Inchon and Umsong, each airborne controller—"Angelo Fox" and "Angelo George"—managed about 10 flights of F-80s during the day. There was some confusion, since the fighter pilots had not been briefed to expect airborne control, but the results brought the comment that it was "the best day in FAF history."[21]

The next day, 17 communist tanks were destroyed near Chonui by F-80 shooting stars under the air control of Bryant and Mitchell. Lt Col Merrill H. Carlton now took command of this embryo unit, picked up a truckload of equipment, the name "Mosquito," seven new officers, and three enlisted men.[22]

Lt Harold E. Morris brought a T-6 trainer aircraft to Taejon (10 July) and demonstrated that this plane was best able to perform airborne control. One thought was that the T-6 was fast enough to survive enemy air attacks whereas the L-17 was not. (North Korean Yaks had shot down several liaison-type aircraft in the early stages of the war.) Lieutenant Colonel Carlton, who arrived in Taejon on 11 July to direct the airborne control detachment, appealed strongly for more of the unarmed but speedy T-6s, each equipped with eight-channel radio sets.

T-6 "Mosquito"

The airborne controllers demonstrated their value during their first few days of operations. They reconnoitered the front lines, located worthwhile targets, and "talked" fighter-bomber pilots to successful attacks against the enemy. "There was no definite system," said one of the early airborne controllers. "The only thing we had was an aeronautical chart and a radio. . . . We went into the back of the enemy lines and reconnoitered the roads. . . . We saw some tanks, got on each radio channel until we got fighters in the Chochiwon area and any fighter who heard us would give us a call and we would give them the target."[23]

The outfit that did not exist on the books "chartered itself" at Taejon airstrip. By the end of July, the handful of pilots had flown 269 sorties and piled up 670 hours over the front. Commendations and compliments poured in from 24th Infantry Division and the ROK Army. As a result, Colonel Carlton's unit picked up administrative, intelligence, engineering, maintenance, and supply sections, and was given official status.[24]

Immediately after concluding their missions, the airborne controllers went into Taejon City for interrogation by the combat operations section. They furnished current locations of friendly and hostile troops to the combat operations officers. On 13 July, Carlton moved the airborne control function back to Taegu airfield, where he received additional T-6 aircraft and more pilots. Although the organizational status of the airborne controllers remained anomalous, they soon gained a popular name. In a 15 July FAF fragmentary operations order (FRAG), the airborne controllers were given radio call-signs of "Mosquito Able," "Mosquito Baker," and "Mosquito How." The unit was commonly called the "Mosquito" squadron, the controllers and their planes "Mosquitoes."[25]

FAF's jet fighter-bomber wings were based in southern Japan, too far from the targets to spend much time looking for frontline objectives. Flying from Itazuke, for example, the 27th Wing's F-84 Thunderjets were able to spend only 30 minutes at the bomb line.[26]

Seeking to overcome this problem, the 8th and 51st Fighter Groups staged their F-80s through Taegu Airfield. The shooting stars usually flew a first mission from Japanese bases, returned to Taegu for rearming and refueling, and then flew a second mission from Taegu before returning directly to Japan. By using Taegu for a staging base, FAF overcame many of its operational problems—but dependence upon a single base for such heavy operations carried an element of calculated risk.[27]

Two additional factors worked together to alleviate the F-80's range problem. First, the airborne controllers had enemy targets pinpointed for attack when the faster flying F-80s arrived at the scene. Second, most of the F-80 squadrons soon secured "Misawa" external fuel tanks.[28]

Beginning on 26 July, Navy and USAF pilots worked together in support of Eighth Army. Some 60 carrier-based pilots reported to the JOC and were sent to the frontline Mosquitoes, who controlled their attacks. Everyone seemed satisfied, or nearly so. For example, General Walker called for a continuation of the fine work while Vice Adm Arthur D.

Struble, commander of Seventh Fleet, reported that the Mosquito control planes had done an excellent job but appeared to be numerically insufficient to handle both carrier and land-based planes. During the next three days, Task Force 77 (which continued to support Eighth Army) effected a workable solution to the frontline control problem. Navy controllers joined the Mosquitoes and remained on-station with them for up to four hours. Navy attack planes were controlled by either Air Force or Navy controllers, whichever were available. Navy pilots checked out with "Mellow" control and made oral reports on their mission. When the task force withdrew for replenishment, the Navy operations officer told the JOC that the way Navy pilots had been employed was very effective.[29]

Command and Control Support

At the outbreak of Korean hostilities, the USAF possessed only one tactical control group (TCG). It moved quickly from Langley AFB, Virginia, to Korea, but it was not ready to begin operations until early October. FEAF had been committed to a static deployment for the air defense of Japan—a mission that required offensive tactical air operations. Nevertheless, FEAF worked out an interim control organization for Korea with commendable ingenuity. The Eighth United States Army-Korea (EUSAK) made its requests for air support directly to FAF Headquarters, which honored those requests within its means and reported excess requirements to FEAF with an information copy to the new FEAF bomber command. FEAF directed the bomber command to furnish the support FAF could not provide. General Partridge's tactical air force furnished most of the improvised control organization.

The control system was severely hampered by a lack of experienced controllers and a crippling shortage of communications channels. The JOC was relocated near EUSAK headquarters at Taegu on 14 July. Sufficient equipment had arrived by 19 July to establish a full-scale JOC-TACC, except for radar and direction-finding facilities. Advance Headquarters, FAF, opened at Taegu on 20 July, bringing command and control together at one location. The forward element in the control system was the TACP. Six TACPs were flown from Japan to Korea and were on hand when the 24th Division opened at Taejon on 4 July.

FAF would ultimately provide a minimum of four TACPs to each division. A TACP was allotted to each ROK division and to each ROK corps to advise the ground commanders on air capabilities for close support. Under normal circumstances, ground units were supposed to select targets for CAS. But Eighth Army was often unable to identify enemy strong points. FAF, therefore, began using T-6 advanced trainer aircraft to spot targets behind enemy lines. It activated the 6147th tactical control squadron, airborne, to furnish the airborne controllers.[30]

6132d Tactical Air Control Group

On 23 July 1950, the 6132d tactical air control group (TACG) took over control station "Mellow." Its principal duty was to supply the radio communications required by the JOC and the Mosquitoes.[31] The 6132d also absorbed the TACPs in Korea and assumed responsibility for providing additional TACPs to the expanding Eighth Army. Existing doctrine specified no set number or allocation of TACPs, so their operations would depend on the need for CAS. In Korea, General Partridge allocated one TACP to each US infantry regiment and higher unit headquarters, and to each ROK division and corps. As quickly as the Far East Air Materiel Command could fabricate them, the 6132d group provided additional radio-control jeeps along with radio operators and mechanics. Some FACs were obtained from the United States but most came from FAF's tactical groups (which were required to provide combat pilots initially for three weeks' temporary duty as FACs).[32]

6147th Squadron Organized

The airborne controllers proved their worth from the first day they flew over Korea, but the airborne control function continued in an anomalous organizational status until the

"Mosquito" unit was organized on 1 August as the 6147th tactical control squadron-airborne [TCS-A].

Under the command of Lieutenant Colonel Carlton, the 6147th was assigned directly to FAF at Taegu airfield. Eighth Army had begun to attach observers to the "Mosquito" squadron in late July. Riding in the back of T-6s, these Army observers added a ground soldier's view to the aerial control function. And the Mosquitoes continued to serve as the "eyes of the JOC," even though their primary duty was to control air strikes. They remained on station for nearly three hours at a time and messaged observations to the TACC. When the reconnoitered areas were too distant from Taegu to allow direct line-of-sight VHF communications, a plane called "Mosquito Mellow" orbited at an intermediate point and relayed messages to the TACC.[33]

General Partridge placed "considerable stress" on attaching experienced Air Force officers to liaison duty with Eighth Army

C-47 "Mosquito Mellow"

and Task Force 77 units. Their mission was to advise the ground-unit commander on air matters.

Immediate Air Requests

In theory, the procedure for handling requests for immediate air support was as follows: a battalion commander prepared a request and dispatched it through regimental headquarters to the G-3 air officer division. G-3 assigned priorities and, after conferring with the air liaison officer (ALO) and the artillery coordinator, sent the requests to the JOC; the requests were monitored by the G-3 air officer at corps headquarters, who approved or disapproved the air strike.

In the summer of 1950, however, Eighth Army was unable to establish this communications net. "The Army had no equipment available," explained the G-3 air officer at the JOC. "We had no strike-request nets. Everything was in the United States."[34] Regimental commanders soon learned, however, that the TACPs could pass a mission request to a Mosquito, who could relay the request to the TACC. This soon became the accepted communications route for air-support requests.

Mosquitoes Assigned to Divisions

Mosquito controllers were assigned a geographical section at first, but ground commanders soon took a proprietary interest in the Mosquitoes and were reluctant to let the controllers out of sight. The notion that a Mosquito "belonged" to a division became emphatic after 12 August, when the Mosquitoes assumed radio call-signs that coincided with division call-signs. Thus, the Mosquito Cavalry Division called itself "Mosquito Wildwest." Airborne controllers were restricted to limited areas over the front lines, and less thought was given to the enemy's buildup 15 to 30 miles behind the lines. Under these circumstances, Mosquito controllers met situations in which rights of jurisdiction came into play.[35]

Mosquito Mission Expands

As soon as it could obtain the necessary aircraft and controllers, FAF assigned additional Mosquitoes to locate targets in the enemy's buildup areas behind the front. Mosquito controllers working behind enemy lines reported targets through the Mosquito relay aircraft, then controlled armed reconnaissance aircraft as the JOC dispatched them.

In August 1950, Mosquito controllers began using "walkie-talkie" radios to talk directly with tank columns and forward ground patrols. As the ground columns forged ahead, Mosquitoes hovered above them and covered the fronts and flanks of the columns.[36]

Of some importance were a number of spontaneous Mosquito attempts at psychological warfare. On 1 October, for example, Mosquito pilot Lt George W. Nelson spotted about two hundred enemy troops 10 miles northeast of Kunsan Some were in uniform, some in civilian clothes. Nelson dropped a message to them in an improvised container, saying that they should go to the top of a nearby hill and wait until UN troops arrived if they wished to surrender. A second message instructed the men to throw away their arms and wave flags if they accepted these terms (Nelson signed the note "MacArthur"). Soon thereafter, several flags were seen waving on the hill. The Mosquito pilot notified the ground controller, who sent troops forward to take the prisoners in what may have been the first case of enemy troops surrendering to an aircraft.[37]

On another occasion, a Mosquito flushed an enemy T-34 tank with a very low pass and forced it out onto an open road. With the assistance of four F-51s, the Mosquito forced the tank to UN lines, where it was captured. Other Mosquito pilots experimented with various types of noisemakers designed to terrify enemy troops, but these attempts were abandoned due to a lack of research and development facilities.[38]

The 502d Tactical Control Group

Early in the war, General Weyland, who had commanded XIX Tactical Air Command in Europe in World War II, came to

Tokyo to assume the position of vice chief of operations, FEAF. General Weyland brought Col James E. Ferguson to be his deputy. At FAF headquarters, General Partridge received similar assistance from newly arrived Col Gilbert L. Meyers, who became FAF Deputy Commander (operations). Weyland, Ferguson, and Meyers began organizing a doctrinally correct and operationally effective Air Force CAS system.

On 7 October, the 6132d tactical air control group was disbanded. Most of its personnel were used to form the 6132d aircraft control and warning squadron (ACWS) of the 502d TCG. One squadron manned the TACC at Seoul, the others opened tactical air direction centers (TADC) at Kimpo, Taegu, and Taejon. These TADCs provided radar early warning and direction finding, but were given no responsibility for managing the offensive fighter effort. Also in early October, the 20th Signal Company's air-ground liaison arrived from the United States and reported to Eighth Army. This signal company began to furnish the long-needed tactical air request communications net between divisions, corps, and the JOC.[39] These tactical air control units greatly improved air-ground and tactical air operations but there was still work for the Mosquitoes. To get the T-6 controllers closer to the front, the 6147th TCS moved north from Taegu—first to Kimpo on 5 October, and then to Seoul Municipal Airfield (K-16) on 18 October.[40]

With his JOC at full efficiency, Colonel Meyers reinforced the 6147th TCS and gave the 502d TCG control of the ground TACPs. Another change affected Army liaison aircraft, whose normal reconnaissance and artillery-spotting duties had broadened to include requesting and directing air strikes. But having too many spotters caused problems: one midair collision (between an Army L-19 and a fighter-bomber) and many near misses.[41]

In order to provide more controllers and a more logical organization, FAF undertook a general reorganization of the Mosquito and tactical air control functions. The 6147th tactical control group (provisional) was established on 25 April 1951. It included the 6148th and 6149th TCS-A, the 6150th Tactical Control Squadron-Ground (TCS-G), and three support squadrons: maintenance, medical, and air base. The two air control squadrons would provide Mosquito controllers, the ground control squadron would provide enlisted personnel and equipment.[42] FEAF had finally developed and put in place an efficient tactical air control system.

Notes

1. Otto P. Weyland, "The Air Campaign in Korea," in James T. Stewart, *Airpower: The Decisive Force In Korea* (New York: D. Van Nostrand Co. Inc., 1957), 5–6.
2. David A. Anderton, *The History of the US Air Force* (New York: Crescent Books, 1981), 141.
3. Weyland, 6.
4. Anderton, 146.
5. Weyland, 9.
6. Anderton, 143.
7. Col Charles G. Teschner, "The Fighter-Bomber in Korea," in James T. Stewart, *Airpower: The Decisive Force in Korea* (New York: D. Van Nostrand Co. Inc., 1957), 108.
8. Ibid., 109–13.
9. Robert F. Futrell, "The Korean War," in Alfred Goldberg, *A History of the United States Air Force: 1907–1957* (New York: D. Van Nostrand Co. Inc., 1957), 246–47.
10. David Rees, *Korea: The Limited War* (New York: St. Martin's Press, 1964), 50.
11. William M. Cleveland, *Mosquitoes in Korea* (Portsmouth, N. H.: The Mosquito Association, Inc., 1991), 200.
12. For purposes of this analysis, the term *FAC* refers to the Airborne Tactical Air Coordinator. A ground FAC is a member of the tactical air control party at the front lines.
13. War Department Field Manual 31-35, *Air-Ground Operations* (Washington, D.C., 1946); *Evolution of Command and Control Doctrine for Close Air Support* (Washington, D.C.: Headquarters USAF, 1973), 21–25.
14. Robert F. Futrell, *Ideas, Concepts, Doctrine: Basic Thinking in the United States Air Force, 1907–1964* (Maxwell AFB, Ala.: Air University Press, 1971), 182–203; History Branch, Program Division, Combat Development Command, US Army, "History Survey of Army Fire Support," 18 March 1963, section I.
15. Alan R. Millett, "Korea, 1950–1953," in J. Farmer and M. J. Strumwasser, eds., *The Evolution of the Airborne Forward Air Controller: An Analysis of Mosquito Operations in Korea*, RAND report RM 5430PR (Santa Monica, Calif.: RAND, October 1967), 345.
16. Operations Research Office, Headquarters FEC, memorandum, ORO-R-3 (FEC), subject: Close Air Support Operations in Korea: Preliminary Evaluation, 1 February 1951; Headquarters FEAF, *Report on the Korean War*, vol. 1, 1953, 10–12, 62–63.

17. Far East Command, memorandum, subject: Control of Tactical Air Support, 9 June 1950, in "Korean War Miscellaneous," RG 6, MacArthur Memorial Archives, Norfolk, Virginia.
18. Marcelle Size Knaack, comp., *Encyclopedia of US Air Force Aircraft and Missile Systems*, vol. I, *Post-World War II Fighters* (Washington, D.C.: Office of Air Force History, 1978).
19. Futrell, *The United States Air Force in Korea* (New York: Duell, Sloan, and Pearch, 1961), 80.
20. Cleveland, 11.
21. *History of the 6147th Tactical Control Squadron (Airborne)*, (Washington, D.C.: Office of Air Force History, July 1950).
22. Cleveland, 11.
23. Futrell, *The Air Force in Korea*, 83.
24. Cleveland, 11.
25. *History, 6147th*, Barcus Board Report, bk. 2, app., Office of Air Force History, 84.
26. Lt Col William E. Bertram to commander, 27th Fighter-Escort Wing, letter, subject: Tactical Evaluation Board, 15 March 1951.
27. *History of the 49th Fighter-Bomber Group* (Washington, D.C.: Office of Air Force History, 1951).
28. Barcus Board Report, bk. 3, appendix, 220–21.
29. Rees, 50.
30. Cleveland, 33–34.
31. *History of the 6132d Tactical Control Group* (Washington, D.C.: Office of Air Force History 1950).
32. Message AX-9684, Commanding General, Far East Air Force to CINCFE, 29 August 1950.
33. *History, 6132d.*
34. Barcus Board Report, bk. 2, appendix, 84.
35. Futrell, *USAF in Korea*, 108–09.
36. Ibid., 164.
37. Message, AX-1769B, Commanding General, Far East Air Force, to Headquarters, US Air Force, 2 October 1950.
38. Cleveland, 202.
39. Barcus Board Report, bk. 2, appendix, 580.
40. *History, 6132d.*
41. Millett, 368.
42. Lt Gen J. A. Partridge to Lt Gen J. A. Van Fleet, Commanding General, Eighth US Army Korea, letter, subject: Joint Air-Ground Operations Board; *History, 6147th.*

Chapter 4

Mosquito Operations in Korea

The first comprehensive airborne forward air controller program was developed in Korea. Initiated almost immediately upon the outbreak of hostilities, the program grew from a makeshift, very specialized operation to a large, generalized, highly successful program. Within six months, the concept of the airborne FAC had been proven and appropriate techniques had been formulated.[1] The FAC in Korea had a vital mission, but it did not survive in doctrine or organization; it would have to be "reinvented" a decade later in Vietnam.

The FAC concept had been partially accepted by the Air Force prior to the outbreak of hostilities in Korea. Doctrine permitted—but did not dictate—the use of airborne FACs in air-ground operations. No equipment had been allocated, and no FAC squadron had been assembled; the airborne FAC existed only in theory.

Initially, the FAC function was strike control—matching high-performance aircraft with fast-moving targets. To this was soon added the responsibility for performing visual reconnaissance (VR) over the front lines. Later, the FAC was given the additional responsibility of calling in strike aircraft for immediate close air support. The airborne FAC became the focal point of the tactical air control system (TACS), but was still considered temporary. FACs flew in improvised fighter-trainers and grew from squadron to group size, but were still considered transitory. In fact, the stature of the airborne FAC in Air Force doctrine never changed from 1946 to 1966.[2]

The Role of the Mosquito

The first tactical FAC mission pilots were simply instructed to make flights over the front lines, locate targets, and direct friendly fighter attacks.[3] Mosquito commander Lt Col Merrill Carlton was more specific; in July 1950, he told his unofficial organization that their mission was to conduct tactical reconnaissance of frontline dispositions, monitor enemy lines of communication, control air strikes near friendly troops, and control preplanned air strikes as directed by Eighth Army.[4]

The official title given the Mosquitoes was "Tactical Air Coordinator-Airborne" (TAC-A). This was in keeping with the terminology of Field Manual (FM) 31-35 and Air Force doctrine, and is the title still used. In current operations, however, they are almost exclusively called airborne FACs and this nomenclature will be used here.

When the unit was officially formed on 1 August 1950, the role of the Mosquito was expanded: "The mission of the Mosquito primarily consists of providing airborne tactical air control over the front during all daylight hours and at other times, as directed. In accomplishing this mission, the Mosquito directs fighter aircraft to specific targets as outlined by ground controllers or in accordance with visual observations and on the basis of prebriefed information. In addition, the Mosquito performs reconnaissance flights over enemy-held territory and acts as airborne liaison when necessary."[5]

The squadron's commitment was not the extent of its activities, however. As new needs became apparent, the Mosquito was called upon to perform new functions. Perhaps most important was the expansion of his VR role. Among the "special" missions flown by the squadron were identifying guerrilla units, performing penetration reconnaissance deep behind enemy lines, distributing leaflets, performing early evening and dawn reconnaissance designed to limit North Korean night activities, and transporting dignitaries and correspondents.

Throughout the remainder of 1950, the flexibility of the Mosquito was demonstrated. As the significance of the Mosquito's role became more obvious, planners began including airborne FACs in ground operations. For example, a large-scale evacuation of Chinnampo called for three T-6s to rotate coverage,[6] and a paradrop of the 187th Regimental Combat Team was controlled by Mosquitoes.[7] By October 1950, the list of "special" duties included providing continuous cover for convoys, reconnaissance of areas behind advancing UN lines searching for bypassed North Korean People's Army (NKPA) troops, directing loudspeaker-carrying

C-47 "voice" missions, covering the advances of small units, and providing transportation for isolated ground FACs.

In November, a FAC dropped a radio by parachute to an isolated ground controller while another picked up a member of the Korean Military Advisory Group who was stranded at an airstrip under heavy fire.[8] By December, the capabilities of the Mosquito had become well known. Its assignments that month included deep reconnaissance to locate an enemy roadblock, night reconnaissance missions to monitor nocturnal enemy supply activities, and special weather missions.[9]

In five months, the Mosquitoes had gone from official nonexistence to a position of prominence. Ground commanders depended on them—and assumed that the Mosquitoes would fly if any planes flew. While fighters came in spurts, the Mosquito was on station during all daylight hours.[10] The airborne FAC had become associated with good CAS.

Forward Air Controller Equipment

When the airborne FAC was born, the first plane used was the L-5, which was already in use by the Army for artillery spotting. It was considered largely unsatisfactory, however, and Colonel Carlton issued a plea for the T-6 Texan to replace the L-5. The T-6 became the FAC aircraft for the duration of the conflict, but discussion continued over the "dream" FAC aircraft.

While the T-6 was not ideal, it did possess many of the characteristics of a good FAC aircraft. It was relatively simple, easy to maintain, and durable. Modifications of the airframe were easy, and each T-6 in the 6147th Squadron averaged 5.65 hours in the air per day in 1950, adding to the dependability of Mosquito operations. The T-6's low stall speed enabled it to loiter, giving observers a better view of the battle area. It had relatively good maneuverability and its top speed of 210 MPH gave it some ability to respond to emergencies. The T-6's short takeoff roll[11] made it a candidate for basing near the front and for emergency rescues.[12]

One critical feature for any FAC aircraft is the wing. Because observation of the ground is essential, the low wing of the T-6 was considered an obstacle. Mosquito pilots frequently did much of their visual reconnaissance in a continuous bank.¹³ High-winged aircraft afforded excellent downward visibility in level flight, but visibility was restricted in turns.¹⁴

A second critical feature is ruggedness. Since low-level flying made FAC aircraft vulnerable to enemy fire, most observers favored a two-engine design. They felt that the second engine represented an additional margin of safety.¹⁵ This proposition is questionable, however, since there is no evidence that a second engine would have saved a single FAC casualty in 1950.

Navigational aids are also critical features in a FAC plane, and the Mosquito mission suffered from their absence. This problem was worse when the front lines were far from the base and when there was bad weather. In addition, night operations were precluded by the lack of navigational aids. During November 1950, the weather was almost continually poor—and one coast of Korea might be clear while the other was overcast.¹⁶ Smoke and haze presented problems, especially in the north, where mountain peaks eight thousand to nine thousand feet high were often obscured.¹⁷ VHF-Omnirange (VOR) and tactical air navigation (TACAN) were not available in 1950s Korea.

Some observers thought FAC aircraft should be armed. Their argument was based on three factors: (1) the increasing incidence of ground fire, (2) the cumulative frustration of sighting transient targets when no strike aircraft were available, and (3) the occasional success of the marking rocket with white phosphorous warhead as an offensive weapon. Furthermore, once the aircraft was on station, the cost of providing a moderate offensive capability was negligible.

The potential for a limited offensive capability was demonstrated in at least two instances. Lt Chester T. Kochan and his observer, Lt Frank H. Armstrong, made the first claim. They noted tracks leading to a pile of brush at the foot of a hill and flew low to investigate. They saw a partially camouflaged vehicle under the brush, but their radio failed and they were unable to direct fighters to the area. "We sure hated to see the Reds escape, so we tried an experiment," Kochan said. "We wondered what damage a few of our marking rockets would do to the vehicle, so we fired five of them at the vehicle and managed to set it afire. It sure was a pretty blaze."¹⁸ On the second occasion, a frustrated Mosquito pilot, unable to contact fighters, knocked out an enemy machine gun position with his smoke rockets.[19]

On the other hand, many observers argued against ordnance on FAC aircraft. They questioned the necessity of armed FACs, and they wondered how armament might affect the FAC program. In the first place, they argued, FAC planes would not be able to carry and deliver sufficient ordnance to have significant effects. A second argument was that a strike capability would require a more expensive and elaborate FAC aircraft, thereby compromising its simplicity.[20]

On occasion, Mosquitoes made small contributions even without ordnance. In late November 1950, Vic Cole and Lew Neville decided to make a pass on two North Korean soldiers crossing a river in a boat. Cole dove down to an altitude where his prop was kicking up spray and headed right for them. "I went right over the boat and when we looked back it was empty," Cole recounts. "We circled around for a while and they didn't get back in the boat, but hung on the side and slowly made the shore. If they didn't freeze, I'll bet they had a bad cold."[21]

The discussion on arming the FAC included which types of ordnance to use and there was general agreement the aircraft should have machine guns. The operations research office (ORO) suggested two .50-caliber guns with 400 rounds per gun,[22] but considered .30-caliber acceptable.[23] In addition, a light load of either bombs or rockets was recommended. ORO suggested mixing high-velocity airborne rockets (HVAR) with marking rockets when not carrying small bombs.

Visual Reconnaissance

The earliest phase of visual reconnaissance called for a pilot to fly near the front in search of CAS targets. In an attempt to systemize tactics, Mosquitoes were assigned to Army divisions. They were to reconnoiter the area in which their division was fighting and to coordinate strikes with a regimental or divisional TACP. A rotation plan permitted each division to have a Mosquito on station from sunrise to sunset.[24]

While both TACPs and Mosquitoes were responsible for finding targets, they were found almost exclusively from the air.[25] In the first 18 months, 93 percent of all CAS strikes were controlled from the air.[26]

Convinced that a full-scale commitment to a systematic program of deep-penetration visual reconnaissance would be of value, Carlton submitted a proposal to fly 90 sorties a day, 15 at a time during all daylight hours, six operating within the bomb line, six immediately behind enemy lines, two performing "special" VR, and one to oversee the entire operation. The plan was rejected.[27]

Although not authorized to perform "deep-penetration" reconnaissance, the Mosquitoes conducted VR in areas immediately behind enemy lines. All "area reconnaissance" had to be under the operational control of the ground commander—and commanders were reluctant to allow the Mosquito to stray out of sight for fear their units might suddenly need air support.[28] Consequently, the enemy's logistics were relatively unhampered except in the immediate vicinity of the front. The NKPA and communist chinese forces (CCF) moved freely deep behind the front lines.

As the 6147th Squadron's strength increased, it was able to introduce more deep reconnaissance missions. By December 1950, Mosquitoes had begun a fledgling deep-VR program. Mosquitoes assigned to a specific division were given greater freedom to roam further behind the lines and special missions were added to patrol fortuitous points of interdiction.[29] The airborne FACs saw their role develop from a limited target-finding mission within the bomb line to a broad VR program that supported nearly all tactical functions of the Air Force in Korea.

The Tactical Air Control System

The TACS was the mechanism that matched targets with air resources. The Mosquito was an emergency appendage to the TACS and a by-product of the system's deficiencies. The TACS described in the 1946 revision of FM 31-35 incorporated World War II lessons. These lessons were not always applicable to Korea, however, where the allies depended on immediate air support to halt a mercurial enemy advance and avert imminent defeat.

The Air Force section (combat operations) of the JOC had control over tactical air resources. Requests coming to the Army section (air-ground operations) of the JOC were processed and given to the tactical air control center (TACC), where they were matched to specific aircraft.[30] Not until the airborne FAC was given greater responsibilities did a genuinely efficient TACS develop.

The Army was given the task of developing a CAS request network, but it never materialized because of a lack of communication equipment and personnel. The Air Force attempted to establish a signal unit comprised of air liaison officers,[31] but frequent radio breakdowns caused abandonment of the project.[32]

In the absence of a genuine air request network, the Army attempted to forward requests by landline or radio over the divisional command network or the artillery communications network. When units were extended beyond the limits of these systems, however, requests were relayed by Mosquitoes. This procedure worked so well it became the standard technique for submission of immediate CAS requests. The Army's inability to supply an air request network and the fact that a large proportion of the requests originated from Mosquito sightings, placed a heavy responsibility on the airborne FACs to procure close support. The situation was not alleviated until early 1952 when the Army replaced their obsolete radios with a radioteletype system.[33]

Theoretically, strike aircraft were allocated by a daily apportionment of resources called a frag order. This order listed aircraft available for close support, interdiction, reconnaissance, transport, airlift, search and rescue, air defense, and tactical control. For preplanned missions, the frag order specified the targets each aircraft was to hit. For immediate missions, like CAS, the frag order simply stated when the aircraft was to come on duty. These aircraft could be scrambled by the JOC, a procedure that was supposed to give the UN forces the flexibility to meet any contingency.

Practice fell short of theory because communications to Japan were not dependable. Consequently, the air bases in

Japan simply scrambled one mission every 15 minutes.[34] This system left much to be desired, as the enemy sensed that the TACS was in trouble.[35] When ground action was heavy, there was not enough air support to go around; when the front lines were placid, aircraft began to stack up and the TACC released them to perform armed reconnaissance.

The problem was entirely one of communications. The Mosquitoes served as "eyes" for the TACS and remained in radio contact with the TACC while on station. This permitted the center to continuously monitor the entire front and use strike aircraft efficiently.[36]

Mosquito Mellow

The most significant Mosquito contribution came by accident. In the summer of 1950, as the UN gained the offensive and pushed deep into North Korea, direct Mosquito-TACC communication became impossible. By the middle of July, the Mosquito Squadron had determined that some central means of communication should be established between the frontline Mosquitoes and Mellow.[37]

One T-6 named Mosquito Control was designated to serve as a relay. Later renamed Mosquito Mellow, it flew between the front lines and the TACC at 10,000 to 13,000 feet. Initially conceived simply as a communications benefit, Mosquito Mellow was quickly identified as a command and control aid that helped compensate for an overcentralized and inflexible TACS.

The Mosquito Mellow was replaced by the C-47, which was manned by seven controllers. One of the seven, designated "senior controller," had authority to divert fighters from one TACP to another. First adopted as an experiment, the scheme soon proved of great value: "If the Mosquito Mellow senior controller is encouraged to divert fighters but requires worthwhile targets, then the speed of delivering attacks against these targets can be attained to a degree approaching a continuous on-station system of support."[38]

Strike Control Procedures

All the factors that made the FAC aircraft well suited to airborne surveillance—low speed, high maneuverability, and good visibility—worked toward making the high-performance fighter ill-suited for observation. Identifying targets for the fighter pilot was the most important Mosquito function. Controlling a ground strike involves five distinct tasks: traffic control, ordnance selection, target discrimination, target marking, and bomb damage assessment.

Traffic Control

Since the Korean TACS was less than efficient, it was impossible to regulate the arrival of strike aircraft in the target area. If a call went out for substantial air support, dozens of planes might appear over the target simultaneously—all with limited fuel. Aircraft generally arrived in flights of four. The Mosquito instructed two of them to remain at high altitude while the second pair performed the strike, after which the fighters exchanged roles. Finally, they strafed the target before departing.[39]

When the target was especially formidable (e.g., an armored column), it was important to get the aircraft with the greatest effectiveness and the most appropriate ordnance on the target first. The Mosquito customarily stacked strike aircraft in orbits at various altitudes until it was their time to strike.[40]

Ordnance Selection

When a Mosquito FAC notified Mosquito Mellow of the need for strike aircraft, he also requested preferences for ordnance. Since it was not always possible to receive what was ordered, the Mosquito frequently settled for anything available. When aircraft arrived with a variety of ordnance, the FAC decided which ordnance would be used. He generally used the following guidelines: (1) .50-caliber and 20 mm machine guns, plus light rockets, against buildings, trucks, vehicles, oxcarts, troops in the open, bivouac areas, barges, mortar positions, small villages, automatic weapons, and combustible storages or dumps; (2) fragmentation bombs for all troop positions and targets listed above; (3) 500-pound general-purpose bombs and heavy rockets for tanks, bridges, railway tunnels, artillery pieces, and antiaircraft positions; (4) 1,000-pound bombs against major bridges and tunnels; (5) napalm against all targets except railroad tracks. It should be noted that napalm was considered the most effective aerial weapon and the weapon most feared by enemy troops.[41]

Target Discrimination

The Mosquitoes began their operations with no procedures for indicating target location to fighter pilots. This proved to be a difficult problem—one that was solved only through trial and error in combat.

The original procedure was to describe the target over the radio, giving its position in relation to such landmarks as roads, terrain features, and panels.[42] This technique was unsatisfactory for two reasons: (1) the fighter pilot frequently could not find the target and (2) the process further cluttered the already clogged communications channels.[43]

During the first week of airborne FAC operations, one Mosquito's radio went out while he was directing a strike. He nevertheless continued to control the strike by "wagging" his wings in a descriptive manner that identified the target for the fighter. Thereafter, this technique was an effective substitute for a verbal description. Some FACs executed diving passes at the target for the fighter pilot to observe.

In another variation, the lead fighter flew on the Mosquito's wing toward the target. Frequently, the fighter shot his machine guns and the Mosquito described any needed adjustments from the impact pattern. This was an effective technique, but it exposed two aircraft to possible ground fire.

Target Marking

Another class of techniques called for marking the target and its environment. The first marking technique was to drop smoke-emitting or white-phosphorus hand grenades from the T-6, but it was extremely difficult to drop the grenade accurately (only about 30 percent of the grenades continued to smoke after hitting the ground) and the grenades frequently exploded too soon.[44] The Mosquitoes began carrying pistol flares for the same purpose. The difficulties encountered were much the same as with the grenades, however: inaccuracy and short smoke duration.

Another target-marking method involved the use of artillery fire. This technique had been used in World War II for Rover Joe operations.[45] A shellburst that is visible to both the controller and the fighter pilot is used as a reference point from which the exact location of the target may be described. The Mosquito had to be in contact with the ground FAC, who had to be in contact with his unit's artillery officer—and the target had to be within range of artillery, which was frequently not the case.

It was recommended from the beginning that T-6s be equipped with rockets to mark targets, and the rockets began arriving in mid-September 1950. The 2.36-inch marking rockets were mounted by squadron personnel, who also trained pilots in their use.[46]

The airborne rocket proved to be easily visible from the air, which led to an immediate reduction in radio transmission and an increase in bombing accuracy, which resulted in faster target neutralization with less ordnance waste. The marking rocket also proved to be an effective weapon in its own right, and its role in airborne FAC operations grew quickly. In December, the second full month of rocket use, 905 rockets were fired in combat.

Bomb Damage Assessment

Once a strike was executed, the Mosquito performed bomb damage assessment (BDA) to determine whether the target had been neutralized or still represented a danger to friendly troops. The airborne FAC reached his conclusions in conjunction with the ground-based TACP. Whether the fighters that had just executed a strike were of further immediate value for CAS depended on their ordnance and fuel, and on the status of the target just attacked.

Problems Encountered

The value of visual reconnaissance as a source of intelligence was readily apparent, but the Mosquitoes had neither the facilities nor the staff to produce finished intelligence. Nor did they have the equipment to communicate with potential users. The squadron had an intelligence officer, but his main duty was to interpret intelligence for squadron use. The Army commander learned the results of Mosquito reconnaissance through the ground FAC, who received his information from the Mosquito pilot. No procedures were devised for transmitting the Mosquitoes' overall intelligence estimates for the entire divisional front. The Mosquito, who was very helpful in locating specific enemy concentrations,[47] was of less value for more comprehensive information.

The JOC had a high requirement for comprehensive, up-to-date intelligence. But the intelligence did not always arrive in usable form or receive the appropriate attention. And when accurate intelligence did arrive at the JOC, it was considered "only for statistical or historical purposes."[48] In December 1950, the JOC promised Fifth Air Force that intelligence information would receive both tactical and strategic analysis.

Photographic Capability

The absence of a Mosquito photographic capability was serious. Among the potential uses for Mosquito photographs were crew familiarization and training, evaluation of suspicious areas and objects, assessment of enemy tactics, and evaluation of CAS effectiveness.

The Mosquitoes asked for hand-held cameras for the observers. In November, photo-lab and photo-interpreter equipment arrived;[49] the cameras arrived in December. Photo operations began in January 1951, but the results were disappointing. Hand-holding a camera in the cockpit of a vibrating aircraft does not produce sharply defined images.

Relations with Other TACS Elements

The Mosquito's relationship with other TACS components was not defined, and there were duplicating missions and responsibilities. For example, both airborne FACs and ground FACs had strike control responsibility. Army artillery spotters had visual reconnaissance responsibilities, and the Army had responsibility for the strike request system.

With both ground and airborne FACs having the function of directing air strikes, some dissension arose.[50] The Mosquitoes conceded that the ground FAC was helpful in delineating the front line, especially when it was fluid. On the other hand, the ground FAC was not always easy to contact on the radio.[51] Probably the most frequent cause of this inaccessibility was that his radio gear was packed or inoperable.

The FAC radio was a heavy, jeep-mounted device that depended on the jeep for power. Placing the jeep close enough to the front lines for the FAC to observe air strikes meant that it was a target for the enemy. And another problem arose when the front was rapidly changing—boundaries became obscured, with some areas having two FACs and others having none.[52]

The biggest problem in Mosquito relations with ground commanders stemmed from the Mosquitoes' success. The airborne FAC was so effective in locating and destroying targets that he became the ground commander's source of tactical and emotional security; that is, the FAC became associated with effective CAS and lost much of his flexibility. The ground commander developed a proprietary attitude toward "his" Mosquito, frequently refusing permission for the Mosquito to perform deep-penetration reconnaissance because he thought effective CAS depended on the Mosquito being directly overhead.

Control of Navy Fighters

The Air Force was short of fighter-bombers during the all-out defense of the Pusan perimeter. Close support had taken priority over all other air missions, and the Navy was asked to contribute some of their carrier-based aircraft that were normally allocated to interdiction. The Navy initially was reluctant, but an agreement was reached between the Commander of the Navy of the Far East (ComNavFE) and FEAF. Navy planes would provide CAS and be controlled by the TACS and the Mosquitoes.

There were two major difficulties involved with TACS control of Navy fighters: Naval fighter aircraft shared only two channels in common with Mosquito radios[53] and, more serious, carriers launched all their aircraft in a small number of short-duration launches. Consequently, all Navy fighters arrived at the TACC at the same time—with limited fuel supplies. Later, at the insistence of ComNavFE, Navy fighters were allowed to bypass the TACC and go straight to the Mosquitoes.

Crew Effectiveness

Although the Mosquitoes were developed for controlling air strikes, visual reconnaissance served both Air Force and Army. The 6147th TACS began adding Army observers within the first month. The T-6 pilot was an experienced one; the rear seat was occupied by an observer, ordinarily a member of the Army, who gradually became responsible for performing visual reconnaissance, operating the radios, and taking photographs. Many of the observers had been light aircraft pilots or observers in World War II. Their expertise made a significant contribution to the Mosquitoes' effectiveness.[54] Whenever possible, the observer worked in the areas of his parent unit. Thus, each Mosquito crew was fully familiar with ground operations, tactics, and fighter operations.

Initially, Mosquito crews were assigned to units over the entire front to familiarize them with the overall area, but this plan was soon dropped. The Mosquitoes learned that reconnaissance pilots assigned repeatedly to the same area could become extremely sensitive to any changes that might indicate the presence of enemy activity.[55] Crews became bored when they looked at the same area repeatedly, however, so a rotation scheme was devised in which each crew was assigned two areas.

The War at Night

Reconnaissance revealed that the enemy's logistical operations increased at night, when the Mosquito did not fly. Mosquito aircraft lacked basic navigational equipment and effective cockpit heating, and the squadron did not have sufficient men or aircraft for around-the-clock operations.

FAC Survivability

Flying over enemy territory at low speed and low altitude was extremely risky. Twenty T-6s were lost in the first six months of combat in Korea—one every 888.89 hours. (Compare this with the loss every four thousand hours experienced in South Vietnam.[56]) By July 1950, the Mosquitoes were receiving highly accurate 20 mm ground fire.[57] "There was hardly a day when one of the Mosquitoes did not return with a hole in its wing or fuselage or a bullet lodged somewhere near the front or rear cockpits."[58] In October 1951, flak became so heavy that Fifth Air Force began flying flak-suppression missions to support Mosquito safety. In December 1951, serious thought was given to using the F-51 as a FAC aircraft.[59]

Although they received relatively heavy casualties, the Mosquitoes were unwilling to modify their tactics; they assumed the attitude that danger was part of the business. Their typical reconnaissance was performed at 1,200 to 1,500 feet at an airspeed of 120 MPH. By the end of the Korean conflict, however, six thousand feet had been established as the minimum safe altitude for general reconnaissance and control. However, FACs were encouraged to drop as low as they dared for target marking, bomb damage assessment, and closer examination of potential targets, since little could be seen from six thousand feet. Mosquito attrition rates for the first six months of combat are summarized below.

	Aircraft Lost	Fatalities	Sorties/Loss	Hrs/Loss
July	2	0	134/50	335/17
Aug	5	4	206/40	555/42
Sep	3	6	471/33	1,275/58
Oct	4	2	289/25	876/15
Nov	4	4	329/25	943/42
Dec	2	0	608/00	1,612/67
Total	20	16	2,037/173	5,596/241[60]

Every person involved in the design of FAC aircraft emphasized the importance of armor-plating vital areas of the plane, the cockpit, and the engine. The T-6 was preferred for FAC use because of its greater survivability. The L-5, used by the Army for artillery spotting, was neither as fast nor as rugged as the T-6. The ROKAF had some L-5s and had incurred several losses.[61] The Mosquitoes were persuaded to experiment with the L-19 (O-1), the aircraft later used in Vietnam, but it was slower and more delicate than the T-6.

The T-6 was not armed beyond the marking rockets,[62] and the only safety modification made was to paint the wing tips with fluorescent paint to increase the visibility of the FAC to the fighter pilot and reduce the possibility of collision.[63] It is generally conceded that the airborne FAC in Korea survived only in a passive air environment. Had the UN not maintained total air superiority, the T-6's value would have been significantly reduced. It is difficult to imagine an aircraft having the performance characteristics needed by FACs that could defend itself against attack by modern jet aircraft.

Forward Air Controller Training

In response to the expanding need for FACs in Korea, the Air Force's Air-Ground Operations School (AGOS) was activated in September 1950 at Pope AFB, North Carolina. The first class consisted of 17 students. Later that year, however, the Air Force authorized a substantial increase for the school. Thereafter, in both Army and Air Force, a minimum of 120 students per week were trained. The 6147th tactical control group (TCG) received its pilots through normal replacement channels. Observers came from Eighth Army—each division supplied six officers or enlisted men. Many of these observers, who served 90 days on temporary duty, requested extended duty.

After arriving in Korea, a new pilot received a week of intensive ground school training and approximately ten hours of dual and solo local flying before flying a combat mission. He then flew about eight combat missions with a fully qualified observer before receiving a "check" mission to put him on duty status. After 20 missions (at least), the airborne controller went to the front as the ground-based FAC member of the Tactical Air Control Party team. He served approximately 80 days at corps, division, or regimental level and then completed 80 more tactical air controller missions in the T-6.

Formal training for the Mosquitoes was initiated in May 1953, at the Combat Crew Training Center, 3600th Flying Training Group (Fighter) Luke AFB, Arizona. All the instructors were recent combat returnees from the "Mosquito" group. The course was one month in duration, with 55 hours of ground instruction and 22 training flights in the T-6. When the cease-fire agreement was signed on 26 July 1953, the T-6 Airborne Controller course was terminated. The 51-member class that graduated on 15 August 1953 was the last.[64] AGOS was moved to the Highland Pines Inn, Southern Pines, North Carolina, in June 1951 and remained there until January 1957, when a fire destroyed the old inn.[65] Fortunately, preparations were already underway to move the school to Keesler AFB, Mississippi. School and personnel records, however, had to be painstakingly restored.

AGOS reopened at its new home in February 1957, but was moved in 1962 to Hurlburt Field, Florida, where it continues to take advantage of the largest Air Force reservation in the free world—Eglin AFB. The school is subordinate to the air warfare center (AWC), an agency of Air Combat Command. A Navy officer and a Marine officer are permanently attached, and Army faculty members are provided on a permanent basis.[66]

A forward air controller course (FACC) was to provide a reservoir of Air Force pilots trained in the fundamentals of visually directing strikes against surface targets. This course was only for rated officers in USAF, but two other courses were offered for all services. The duration of the FACC was 10 days, five of which were spent in the field for practical training. Emphasis was placed on the capabilities and limitations of the equipment, and on the problems besetting front line commanders.

Notes

1. J. Farmer and M. J. Strumwasser, *The Evolution of the Airborne Forward Air Controller: An Analysis of Mosquito Operations in Korea*, RAND Report RM-5430PR (Santa Monica, Calif.: RAND, October 1967), iii.
2. Ibid., vi.
3. 1Lt Ko S. Samashima, interviewed by US Air Force Historical Research Agency (USAFHRA) staff, 18 November 1950.
4. *History of the 6147th Tactical Control Squadron (Airborne)*, July 1950–July 1951 (Washington, D.C.: Office of Air Force History, 1951), 3.
5. Ibid., August 1950, 2.
6. Ibid., December 1950, 6.
7. Ibid., October 1950, 3.
8. Ibid., November 1950, 3.
9. Ibid., December 1950, 2.
10. From August through December 1950, there were only two days when the 6147th Squadron was unable to fly any sorties, although not all areas could be covered at all times.
11. The takeoff roll of the T-6 is seven hundred feet, as opposed to 1,800 feet for the F-51 and 3,090 feet for the F-80.
12. Standard Aircraft Characteristics: The T-6G Texan, published by authority of the Commanding General, Air Materiel Command, USAF, 12 April 1950; "Standard Aircraft Characteristics: The F-51H Mustang," published by authority of the Commanding General, Air Materiel Command, USAF, 3 July 1950; "Standard Aircraft Characteristics: The F-80A Shooting Star," published by authority of the Commanding General, Air Materiel Command, USAF, 25 January 1950.
13. "Edward R. Murrow and the News," *The Columbia Broadcasting System*, broadcast of 6 February 1951, reproduced in *History of the 6147th Tactical Control Squadron (Airborne)*.
14. Most preferred to perform VR in a continuous bank, observing that the resultant flight path makes the aircraft a more difficult target for ground fire.
15. W. L. Whitson et al., *Preliminary Evaluation of Close Support Operations in Korea* (Baltimore, Md.: Johns Hopkins University, February 1951), 184–85.
16. *History of the 6147th*, November 1950, 29.
17. Supplement to *History of the 6147th*, P. II.
18. William M. Cleveland, *Mosquitoes in Korea* (Portsmouth, N. H.: The Mosquito Association Inc., 1991), 71.
19. Ibid., 257.
20. Farmer and Strumwasser, 76.
21. Cleveland, 79.
22. Whitson, 184.
23. Ibid., 177.
24. *History of the 6147th*, August 1950, 1–2.
25. Whitson, 11.

26. "United States Air Force Operations in the Korean Conflict, 1 November 1950–30 June 1952," USAF Historical Study No. 72, Maxwell AFB, Ala., Air University, 1 July 1955, 195.

27. Ibid., September 1950, 4–5. Although the reasons for rejection were not explicitly stated, it is safe to assume that shortage of men and equipment was the cause.

28. Lt Col Merrill H. Carlton, interviewed by USAFHRA staff, 17 November 1950.

29. *History of the 6147th,* December 1950, 10–11.

30. Farmer and Strumwasser, 32–33.

31. Lt Gen J. A. Partridge points out that a signal unit was sent from the US for the Eighth Army after he briefed Army Chief of Staff Gen J. Lawton Collins on the matter when he was visiting Eighth United States Army in Korea headquarters. There is no indication that such a unit was ever provided for X Corps.

32. "United States Air Force Operations in the Korean Conflict, 25 June–1 November 1950," USAF Historical Study No. 71, Maxwell AFB, Ala., Air University, 1 July 1952, 27.

33. "United States Air Force Operations in the Korean Conflict, 1 November 1950–30 June 1955," USAF Historical Study No. 72, Maxwell AFB, Ala., Air University, 1 July 1952, 86.

34. Whitson, 191.

35. USAF Historical Study, no. 71, Maxwell AFB, Ala., Air University, 28.

36. One squadron of F-51s was stationed in Korea. In addition, Japan-based fighters often landed in Korea if they were low on fuel. These aircraft were refueled and rearmed (giving the operation the nickname "R&R missions"), and immediately flew a second mission before returning directly to Japan.

37. Farmer and Strumwasser, 36.

38. Carlton interview, 2–3.

39. Whitson, 176.

40. Theoretically, the aircraft are prepared to repel hostile air attacks at higher altitudes. However, as General Partridge points out, enemy air was a minimal threat. In fact, no allied aircraft were ever attacked by hostile planes while engaged in close support. Actually, the jets were instructed to orbit at high altitudes to conserve fuel.

41. Farmer and Strumwasser, 42.

42. Robert F. Futrell, *The United States Air Force in Korea* (New York: Duell, Sloan and Pearch, 1961), 181–85. Panels are colored cloths laid on the ground or worn on the backs of advance troops, visible to the pilot, marking the location of the front. Panels were, of course, most important when the front was fluid—precisely the time when they were least faithfully displayed.

43. Carlton interview, 15.

44. "The Standing Operating Procedure of the 6147th Tactical Control Squadron," in *History of the 6147th Tactical Control Squadron (Airborne)* (Washington, D.C.: Office of Air Force History).

45. Samashima interview, 4.
46. *History of the 6147th*, October 1950, 9.
47. Ibid., December 1950, 18–20.
48. *History of the 6147th*, December 1950, 13.
49. Supplement to *History 6147th Tactical Control Squadron*, 11.
50. *History of the 6147th*, November 1950, 33–34.

51. Because the ground FAC is relevant to this study only insofar as he relates to the airborne FAC, no detailed evaluation of his operations is contained here. It should, however, be pointed out that both Army and Air Force personnel voiced nearly unanimous praise of the invaluable contributions made by ground FACs to the success of the air-ground effort.

52. Supplement to *History of the 6147th*, 11.
53. "United States Air Force Operations in the Korean Conflict, 1 November 1950–30 June 1952," 195.

54. Supplement to *History of the 6147th*, 11. Although the Navy had 12 or more VHF channels, including the guard or emergency channel, while Air Force aircraft had four or eight, only two of these channels were common between the services.

55. *History of the 6147th*, 8–11. Beginning 21 August 1950, pilots were rotated back to their parent units elsewhere in the theater after 50 missions, generally flown in less than two months. Notwithstanding this policy, some officers chose not to rotate after their 50th mission, but remained with the Mosquito squadron even during the most intense combat of the war.

56. J. I. Edelman et al., *Airborne Visual Reconnaissance in South Vietnam* RAND Report, RM-5049-ARPA (Santa Monica, Calif.: RAND, September 1966), 31.

57. *History of the 6147th*, July 1950, 14.
58. Ibid., August 1950, 2.
59. "United States Air Force Operations in the Korean Conflict, 1 November 1950–30 June 1952," 195.
60. Farmer and Strumwasser, 65.
61. *History of the 6147th*, July 1950, 5–6.

62. Many FACs said they felt safer in an unarmed plane, reasoning that if enemy ground troops know an aircraft has no offensive capability, they will be less likely to fire at it. This idea was also supported in Vietnam by the experiences of laser "illuminators" who received very little ground fire compared to fighter-bombers who pointed their noses at the ground to deliver the laser-guided weapons. The illuminators maintained level left-hand turns to fire the laser.

63. Supplement to *History of the 6147th*, 195.
64. Cleveland, 56.
65. Ibid., 37.
66. Air-Ground Operations School, "Introduction Pamphlet," 1994.

Chapter 5

Korea
The Stagnant War

Chinese intervention in Korea in November 1950 sent shock waves through the United Nations Command (UNC) and spread quickly to Washington, bringing fundamental changes to American policy. As Eighth Army rose from the ashes of its defeat above the 38th parallel, the Truman administration reverted to its original aim: restoring the Republic of South Korea along its prewar border. Hoping to avoid a higher involvement with both China and the Soviet Union, the administration limited the war. The limitation included air operations.[1]

The Argument for Interdiction

In early 1951, Far East Air Force Bomber Command and Fifth Air Force, reinforced with air strikes from Task Force (TF) 77, began a systematic attack on the communists' supply lines throughout Korea. Between January and June 1951, FEAF aircraft flew 54,410 interdiction sorties and 22,800 close air support sorties. On the day he assumed command of FEAF, Gen Otto P. Weyland wrote Air Force Chief of Staff Hoyt S. Vandenberg that Korea offered an unparalleled opportunity to show how tactical airpower could win a conventional war. The Air Force, he said, should "fully exploit its first real opportunity to prove the efficacy of airpower in more than a supporting role." He thought the Korean experience might provide positive guidance for USAF's force structure and help formulate concepts for the defense of western Europe. That experience, Weyland believed, should come in a massive commitment to interdiction, not to CAS.[2]

CAS along a Stabilized Front

FEAF was to learn that the communist logistics system and field forces could be difficult to destroy. Night, poor weather, and mountainous terrain gave the communists ample opportunity to seek concealment and cover from air attacks. The Chinese proved adept at hiding in caves and tunnels, using natural and man-made camouflage, and digging deep defensive positions. Russian-style mechanized formations and massed artillery positions virtually disappeared from the battlefield in 1951. Major Chinese assaults occurred almost always at night, and they accepted casualties that would have staggered a western army. The communists' tactical adaptations placed new demands on UNC's target acquisition and air direction system.

Radar-Controlled Air Strikes

In the first six months of 1951, FEAF made major reforms in improving the efficiency of CAS. At FEAF Commander Lt Gen George Stratemeyer's insistence, the Air Force increased its commitment to remotely controlled bombardment. The 502d Tactical Control Group (TCG) received ground radar teams, and its B-29s and B-26s were given improved terminal guidance systems. FEAF also improved the accuracy of its level bombing by using bombs that could be guided by the bombardier. But these bombs were in short supply and subject to electronic eccentricities; they had less impact on operations than did proximity-fused bombs. By May 1951, FEAF was employing portable ground radar sets and proximity-fused bombs with increasing effectiveness. Nevertheless, the tactical air control party (TACP) Mosquito system remained intact.

Communications Upgrades

Defects in communications procedures and equipment were at the heart of the CAS problem. The Air Force therefore developed a better jeep, a new radio, and a more powerful generator to run both the radio and a homing beacon. The eight-channel (ARC-3) and four-channel (SCR-522) radios gave the FAC increased capability to talk with aircraft. They also gave Mosquitoes and fighter-bombers their first dependable linkage. Also, TACP ties to air liaison officers

(ALOs) improved in late 1951 when the new radios were installed.³

Tactical air direction nets were increased from four to eight. In addition, the 6147th TCG changed Mosquito Mellow from a T-6 to a specially equipped C-47 that carried a 20-channel VHF radio. To improve TACP assignment and training, FAF sent ground personnel to the 6147th TCG. In addition, the tours of pilot-FACs with ground units increased from three weeks to eight. FAF eventually received enough radars and trained personnel to establish a tactical air direction center (TADC) with each American corps headquarters, and to establish a radar site in each corps area.⁴

T-6 Upgrades

Like the control party's jeep, the T-6 trainer aircraft was not entirely adequate as a Mosquito control vehicle. By the summer of 1951, the Mosquito planes were seldom permitted to penetrate more than two miles into enemy territory—instead, the 45th Tactical Reconnaissance Squadron's (TRS) RF-51s sought targets behind enemy lines. FAF gave some thought to employing F-51s as Mosquito planes, but found it impossible to get additional communications equipment into the Mustangs.⁵ On the other hand, the T-6 was too "hot" to operate from an average ground division's light aviation airstrip. At Eighth Army's suggestion, the 6147th group tested L-19 aircraft as control planes in July 1951 but rejected them as being too vulnerable to enemy ground fire.⁶ The T-6 would continue as the vehicle for the airborne coordinator, but FAF continually worked to adapt it to its mission. Initially, Mosquito controllers "talked" fighter pilots to their targets. By the summer of 1951, however, the T-6s were using 2.25-inch aircraft rockets to designate ground targets.⁷

Operation Thunderbolt

The high degree of cooperation between FAF and Eighth Army meant that air resources could be centered wherever Gen Matthew B. Ridgway, UNC Commander, thought necessary. Thus when American I and IX Corps initiated

"Operation Thunderbolt," FAF's close support centered behind these two corps. To cover the advancing task force, Mosquito controllers moved from Taegu West Airfield (K-37) to the old airstrip at Taejon (K-5). Now, closer to the fighting, the Mosquitoes could remain over the ground troops for up to three hours. They were equipped with infantry radios so they could communicate with ground patrols.

In preparation for the drive northward, the 6147th Squadron put aloft a C-47 airborne relay aircraft with 20 channels of VHF communications. This "Mosquito Mellow" maintained a station 20 miles behind the front lines and passed messages between tactical air control parties, airborne controllers, fighter-bombers, and the "Mellow" station of the TACC.[8] As "Operation Thunderbolt" thrust northward against two divisions of the Chinese Army, the American I and IX corps received effective close support. Air strikes softened points of enemy resistance almost as fast as they developed.

When American ground troops began to move north and northwest of Suwon on 30 January 1951, Mosquito controllers sighted larger concentrations of enemy troops. On 3 February, Capt Edwin "Duffy" LaVigne, flying "Mosquito Cobalt," located a large body of enemy troops opposing the US 25th Division. Within two hours, Captain LaVigne had directed 10 flights of fighter-bombers against enemy positions in the Anyang-Inchon-Yongdungpo area.

Lavigne and his observer, Capt John H. Hargreaves, then proceeded on a reconnaissance for additional targets 25 miles behind enemy lines. The unarmed T-6 fuselage and tail suffered major damage from 20 mm antiaircraft (AAA) fire. Lavigne and Hargreaves dauntlessly made several passes at extremely low altitude to positively identify enemy gun positions for a flight of Navy Corsairs. One of the Corsairs was damaged by AAA fire. Hearing the fighter pilot declare "Mayday," the Mosquito escorted the damaged fighter back to friendly territory. Mosquito Cobalt then returned to the AAA position with a second flight of Corsairs and made several more passes, pointing out additional AAA locations. These missions resulted in neutralizing an enemy stronghold and destroying the guns that had hit the Mosquito.[9]

On 6 February, Capt Dorrence E. Wilkinson, flying "Mosquito Cobalt" in support of the US 24th Division, located a large number of hostile troops in the vicinity of Yangpyong After directing four F-84s, six F-4Us, and six B-26s in attacks against these troops, he estimated that the air strikes caused at least three hundred casualties.

On 12 February, when the Reds attacked South Korean troops (ROK) north of Hoengsong, "Mosquito Liberator" flights were overhead to direct close support for a withdrawal of friendly forces. During the morning, the Mosquito Liberator (piloted by Lt Aubrey C. Edinburgh) found bands of up to 400 enemy soldiers moving by daylight. The Mosquito directed five flights of F-4Us, F-80s, F-84s, and F-51s in napalm and rocket attacks. Later in the day, the relief Mosquito Liberator (piloted by Lt Charles R. Wilkins) found a ROK battalion cut off by enemy roadblocks. This Mosquito controller directed three flights of fighter-bombers in attacks that allowed the friendly battalion to break out of the encirclement.[10]

Operation Ripper

On 7 March, General Ridgway ordered the US IX and X Corps to attack northward in central Korea. Called "Operation Ripper," this attack was designed to create a bulge east of Seoul from which UN forces could envelop the capital city. "Operation Ripper" had one feature of significance to close support management: FAF was able to assign fighter flights to prebriefed TACPs, enabling the fighters to carry maximum ordnance selected for a particular target and range. Until now, squadrons had sacrificed ordnance for extra fuel—which would be needed if the fighter-bombers missed a CAS employment and had to continue north to seek an armed reconnaissance objective.[11]

Quite suddenly, on the night of 14 March, communist forces abandoned Seoul without a fight. On the next day, Eighth Army drove into Hongchon in central Korea. FEAF airmen flew more than 1,000 sorties every day as the Reds broke cover and retreated.[12]

Communist Losses in the First Year

In the first year of fighting, and especially during April and May of 1951, the communist armies in Korea suffered tremendous losses: 163,130 enemy soldiers were in UNC prisoner-of-war camps, and intelligence estimated that the North Koreans and Chinese had sustained 863,949 battle casualties. Altogether, the communists lost almost 1.2 million soldiers through capture, battle loss, and nonbattle causes.[13] FEAF airmen flew 223,000 sorties to drop 97,000 tons of bombs and 7.8 million gallons of napalm, fire 264,000 rockets and 98 million rounds of ammunition, and transport 176,000 tons of cargo and 427,000 passengers and evacuees. FEAF's combat sorties inflicted 120,000 troop casualties and destroyed or damaged 391 aircraft, 893 locomotives, 14,200 railroad cars, 439 tunnels, 1,080 rail and road bridges, 24,500 vehicles, 1,695 tanks, 2,700 guns, and 125,000 buildings. FEAF strategic bombers also neutralized the 18 major strategic targets in North Korea.

In that year, FEAF lost 857 officers and airmen—187 killed, 255 wounded, 412 missing, and three known to be prisoners of war. FEAF also lost 247 aircraft: 188 fighters, 33 bombers, nine transports, and 17 other planes. FEAF's combat record was enviable.[14]

Strategy Changes

The summer of 1951 ushered in a new phase of the war. Both the enemy and the UNC abandoned their identical political objectives of unifying Korea by force, and both gave up their military objectives of capture and control. For both sides, political and military objectives became one—an armistice on favorable terms. UNC air forces were to deny the enemy the capacity to sustain further decisive ground attack, maintain maximum pressure on North Korea, and create a situation conducive to a favorable armistice; the ground forces were to stabilize and maintain a strong defensive line.

It did not take the enemy long to realize that UNC ground force strategy was following the same defensive pattern as his own. He probed with patrols and launched relatively heavy limited attacks to secure defensive posts and salients. The UNC Army also kept up its patrols and counterattacks while friendly air forces roamed the front lines, attacking targets of opportunity. Under attack, the enemy began an extensive effort to construct heavy bunkers, underground supply centers, trenches, tunnels, and well-protected artillery and mortar positions. CAS became less effective as the enemy supplies and equipment were stockpiled, allowing strong attacks supported by heavy artillery fire.

UNC ground forces called for more close aerial support, but CAS had already reached a point of diminishing returns. A greater CAS effort would have cut heavily into the more effective attacks in the rear areas—a concept that was difficult for the Army to understand. Nevertheless, FEAF and FAF made every effort to provide adequate CAS whenever ground forces were actively engaged.

In a static situation, CAS is an expensive substitute for artillery fire. It pays its greatest dividends when the enemy's sustaining capability has been crippled and his supply lines cut by interdiction. Decisive effects can then be obtained as the close support effort is massed in coordination with determined ground action. In the autumn of 1951, it would have been folly to have failed to concentrate the bulk of the air effort against interdiction targets in the enemy's rear areas.

CAS substituted for artillery in some cases; at other times it was used extensively on marginal targets. About 30 percent of all sorties flown during the last two years of the war were flown in close support—a factor that cut heavily into the force which could interdict in rear areas when it should have been the Air Force's aim to reduce enemy firepower before it got to the front rather than try to destroy it after it arrived.[15] Yet, between July 1951 and July 1953, the Air Force flew 155,000 interdiction sorties and approximately 47,000 CAS sorties. The same relative emphasis applied to Navy carrier missions and the First Marine Air Wing.[16]

FAF allocated only 96 CAS sorties per day, an effort that reflected doubts about the relative effectiveness of CAS against a heavily fortified front that bristled with strong concentrations of AAA. Communist flak often drove Mosquito flights above six thousand feet, which made CAS look like an inefficient use of airpower.[17] By 1953, Air Force forward air controllers (FAC) controlled about one sortie per month for each TACP. Communist flak took its toll: aircraft losses per wing normally ran about four per month, pilot losses per squadron about two per month.[18]

By the spring of 1953, CAS operations along the main line of resistance (MLR) had become routine, although incremental improvements continued. Artillery suppression operations developed to a new level of effectiveness and, in April 1953, UNC aircraft flew four thousand CAS sorties with the loss of only one aircraft to ground fire. Both Air Force and Marine Corps air-ground controllers worked on refining radar-guided missions, especially for night operations.[19]

Pathfinder Operations

Recognizing that the Mosquito controllers were extremely vulnerable to hostile ground fire, FAF began experiments with a "pathfinder" fighter-bomber technique in July 1952. A flight of two experienced pilots left the tactical airdrome ten minutes ahead of the main fighter-bomber strike, reconnoitered the assigned target, and subsequently marked the objective by making the first attack. This relieved the Mosquito FAC of target-marking responsibility in high-threat areas. After tests in January 1953, the Eighth Fighter-Bomber Wing recommended that pathfinder aircraft be used on all large-scale close-support strikes.[20]

During the last year of the Korean War, seventeen USAF wings operated in direct support of the fighting: three B-29 wings, seven F-84 and F-86 wings, two B-26 wings, four troop carrier wings, and one reconnaissance wing—a sizable portion of USAF's ready fighting forces.[21]

As renewed fighting broke out on 15 and 16 June 1953, the Mosquitoes broke all previous records on sorties flown during any two-day period in the war. Gen S. F. Anderson, FAF commander, commanded the Mosquito Group's effort in stopping the June 1953 communist offensive. In two days, Mosquito pilots, with fewer than 40 aircraft, directed 332 flights of fighter-bombers against enemy targets for a combined total of 1,632 aircraft.[22]

After three years of hard fighting in Korea, the combatants ended up only a few miles from where they had started on 25 June 1950. But final peace had not come to Korea; only a truce was signed.

The Truce Ceremony

In a special signing hut erected by the communists at Panmunjam, UN representatives and North Koreans began signing the Armistice that would end the fighting at 1001 on 27 July 1953. Eighteen copies, nine for each side, were passed rapidly back and forth across an intervening table while the two chief negotiators signed their names. They finished in 10 minutes and, without speaking, strode out through separate doors. There was none of the thrill and drama of other armistices—this 1953 meeting was a formal and correct tableau by officers who stared through each other when they could not turn their backs. They signed agreements that were reached after history's longest truce talks: 575 bitter meetings spread over two years and 17 days.

1Lt Chester L. Brown of the 6149th TCS flew the last mission flown by a Mosquito. It was Lt Brown's 110th mission as a close support combat pilot. "I am very proud," he said, "to have the honor to be the last one to fly. I have thought for some time the truce would be signed. Now I can go home to my wife and children. I know there must be a lot of happy wives and parents back in the states now that the truce has been signed." The final results, tallied on 28 July 1953, are listed below.

Combat hours flown	11,747,114
Effective sorties	40,554
Tank divisions destroyed	5
Artillery pieces destroyed	563
Vehicles destroyed	5,079
Locomotives destroyed	12
Bridges destroyed	84[23]

6147th TCG Deactivated

By the end of the Korean War (July 1953), Mosquito pilots and observers had flown 40,554 effective missions. The 6147th TCG had received two US presidential unit citations and one Korean presidential unit citation. It had also received coverage by Milt Caniff in his "Terry and the Pirates" comic strip. There was talk of designing a new Mosquito aircraft, but the 6147th TCG was moved to Kimpo airfield, and gradually lost its full combat capability. The unit dropped one of the two Mosquito squadrons and assumed housekeeping responsibility for the airfield.

On 23 June 1956, 6147th TCG became the 6147 Air Base Group (ABG). When the last Mosquito squadron—the 6148th TCS—was then discontinued, the demise of the airborne controllers was aptly worded in the unit's history: "The Mosquitoes fulfilled their job and have a history to be proud of. The success of this organization, born of a wartime necessity, is a tribute to the courage, ability and resourcefulness of the men, both former and present." Thus, the USAF airborne controller became a "peacetime casualty."[24]

Joint Air-Ground Doctrine

At the end of the Korean war, a joint air-ground operations conference representing Army, Navy, Air Force, and Marine Corps met in Seoul and recommended that, in future operations, integration of all services should be secured by an organization and system similar to what finally developed in the last month of the Korean hostilities. The conference also pointed out the need for a joint air-ground doctrine that would encompass all services.[25]

Since it cost far more to deliver aerial bombs than to fire artillery shells, the routine use of airpower as artillery constituted a severe expense to American taxpayers. In times of emergency, however, working in cooperation with friendly artillery, close-support aircraft proved very effective in breaking up the communists' human-wave ground attacks. FAF and Eighth Army worked out techniques whereby friendly artillery could continue to fire upon the enemy during air strikes without endangering close-support aircraft.[26]

While fully appreciating the Mosquitoes' achievements, most observers recognized the risks in using these slow, unarmed, trainer aircraft in future battles. In the future, airborne controllers would fly high-performance aircraft and would operate from fighter-bomber bases. Employing "pathfinder" techniques, these experienced fighter-bomber pilots could lead other jets to close-support targets. In Korea, the Mosquitoes directed most CAS strikes against targets that a FAC on the ground could not observe. Thus, many FACs spent their three-month ground tours without controlling an air strike. As a result, FAF stipulated that FACs would have to control at least one strike per month in order to maintain their proficiency. Despite the fact that FACs on the ground were not effective, Eighth Army required a TACP for each infantry and tank battalion, regiment, and division. On 2 July 1953, Air Force and Army agreed that the Army would provide the equipment and enlisted personnel, and the Air Force would continue to furnish the FAC. Since Air Force and Marine Corps agreed that a FAC had to be a pilot of flight-leader proficiency, the Army requirement of 15 FACs per division would have been extremely expensive in Korea.[27]

The Air Force's declining interest in CAS did not escape the Army. After the failure to draft a joint statement on CAS operations, the Army announced in January 1955 that the principles of the Joint Training Directive had already been repudiated by the Air Force and therefore did not bind the Army. The final irony was that the Army Chief of Staff who found the doctrine so defective was none other than General Ridgway. Perhaps it was especially appropriate that Eighth Army's most famous commanding general would declare void the Korean War's doctrine of CAS. For all practical purposes, the Army and the Air Force agreed not to agree on what part CAS would play in future war.[28]

Post Korea

After Korea, the Air Force was once again without personnel, organization, or equipment for airborne FAC operations. When United States Strike Command (STRICOM) was formed, its manual on Joint Task Force Operations became air-ground operating doctrine; it ignored the Korean experience. Echoing Field Manual (FM) 31-35, it stated, "Tactical Air strikes may be controlled visually by a TACP or electronically by an air support radar team (ASRT)." Later, the manual permitted the use of airborne FACs, which it referred to as tactical air coordinator, when other control means "are not capable of directing operations." In STRICOM doctrine, the airborne FAC was a temporary device to be used a little at a time rather than in a comprehensive program—and he had to be a fighter pilot flying in a two-seat fighter aircraft.[29] These characteristics were repeated in the Tactical Air Command Manual (TACM) on the TACP; Air Force doctrine on the airborne FAC had not changed significantly from 1946 to 1966.

Although the airborne FAC's stature in doctrine did not materially change, its history in the Korean War was strikingly different from its history in Vietnam. In Korea, the program started quickly and sustained itself until peace was restored. In Vietnam, the program started rather slowly and then experienced a steady decline as resources were diverted to other areas and other uses.[30]

The Mosquito program in Korea benefited from a fortuitous set of circumstances. The people who initially staffed the 6147th Squadron showed initiative and a willingness to experiment. Their ability to improvise saved the program from collapse due to improper equipment and a myriad of other technical problems. They found enough adaptable equipment to maintain the program. Without the T-6, for example, the Mosquito probably would never have lasted. The fact that General Partridge and his staff were enthusiastic about the program probably resulted in the diversion of topnotch personnel and equipment to the squadron. The existence of a front line made possible large payoffs from a rather small operation that could be accomplished by relatively few planes and people. Finally, the fact that there was a front line made possible an immediate assessment of CAS effectiveness.

In South Vietnam, circumstances were different. Since there was no front line, an airborne FAC program had to cover more territory—virtually the whole country. The minimal airborne FAC program was much larger in South Vietnam than in

Korea, and the absence of a front line made assessment of combat effectiveness more difficult. Because effectiveness could not be measured and defeat was never imminent, Air Force enthusiasm for the FAC program was never as high in Vietnam as it was in Korea.

In South Vietnam, as in Korea, total air superiority was easily maintained. Given this passive air environment and the FAC's ability to find targets, communicate within the TACS, and increase the accuracy of close support, it seems surprising that a large operation did not immediately come into existence and play an important role. Perhaps an even more important lesson is that the Air Force failed to translate the Mosquito success into organization, personnel, and equipment for future use. Thus, "reinvention" of the solution was necessary each time the problem appeared.

Several factors were involved in the airborne FAC program's failure to survive the interwar years. Air Force interest in strategic forces was one major consideration. There was a general feeling in the military—both Air Force and Army—that nonnuclear limited wars would not occur without immediate escalation. There was also interservice competition to "maximize firepower"— thus, a lack of interest in light aircraft by an Air Force wrestling with the problems of missile forces and space stations.[31]

As the benefits of visual control and reconnaissance were recognized in Vietnam, the ALO/FAC program was expanded to provide airborne controllers for Army units and to provide province-wide coverage. The South Vietnam conflict required an effort that would effectively cover the whole country, and that effort was a major deterrent to an early, effective, airborne FAC system in South Vietnam.

As the Vietnam conflict progressed, however, USAF doctrine began to change. TACM 2-4, *Tactical Air Control Party* (May 1965), recognized the airborne FAC:

> The FAC(A) may control fighter aircraft from any type aerial vehicle, provided it carries communication equipment which will allow direct contact between the FAC(A), the TACP at or adjacent to the requesting unit and the fighter aircraft. It could be a high performance fighter or a helicopter. Target location will primarily dictate what type aircraft

will be selected. A helicopter will do the job well when elevation over friendly territory will provide the FAC visual contact with the selected target. Where the target is deep or on a reverse slope in territory occupied by the enemy, selection of a high performance aircraft will enhance the success of the strike and greatly increase the survivability of the FAC(A).[32]

Thus, between the two conventional wars, there was a time for forgetting and a time for relearning. The relearning began to show up as the beginning of a new doctrine. By the early 1960s, the airborne FAC had begun to reassert his role.[33]

Notes

1. Alan R. Millett, "Korea, 1950–1953," in Benjamin F. Cooling, *Case Studies in the Development of Close Air Support* (Washington, D.C.: Office of Air Force History [OAFH], 1990), 373.

2. Commanding General Far East Air Force (FEAF), memorandum to chief of staff, USAF, subject: "Requirements for Increased Combat Effectiveness," 10 June 1951; Headquarters FEAF, *Report on the Korean War*, I, OAFH, 82–83; Headquarters FEAF, "Weekly Intelligence Roundups," April–May 1951, OAFH; Robert F. Futrell, *The United States Air Force in Korea* (New York: Duell, Sloan, and Pearch, 1961), 313–72.

3. Millett, 375–376.

4. "The Tactical Air Control System," in FEAF, "Report on the Korean War," vol. II, USAF Historical Study No. 154, Maxwell AFB, Ala., Air University, 81–91.

5. *History of the Deputy for Operations*, Fifth Air Force (Washington, D.C.: OAFH, 1951).

6. *History of the 6147th Tactical Control Group*, May–July 1951 (Washington, D.C.: OAFH, 1951).

7. *History of the Office of Operational Engineers*, FAF, May–November 1950 (Washington, D.C.: OAFH, 1951); *History of the 6147th*, May–July 1951.

8. *History of the 6147th*, January 1951.

9. William M. Cleveland, *Mosquitoes in Korea* (Portsmouth, N. H.: Mosquito Association, 1991), 81.

10. *History of the 6147th*, February 1951.

11. *History of the 27th Fighter-Escort Wing*, March 1951 (Washington, D.C.: OAFH).

12. *History of the 6147th*, March 1951; Weekly Activities Report, 27th Fighter-Escort Wing, 12–18 March 1951.

13. Far East Command, Intelligence Summary no. 3214, 28 June 1951, OAFH.

14. Far East Air Forces, public release no. 976, 22 June 1951, OAFH.

15. Otto P. Weyland, "The Air Campaign in Korea" in James T. Stewart, *Airpower: The Decisive Force in Korea* (Princeton, N.J.: D. Van Nostrand Co. Inc., 1957), 20.

16. Millett, 384.

17. Far East Air Force, "Report on the Korean War," vol. I, 96–97.

18. 18th Fighter-Bomber Wing, "History Report," October 1951–July 1953, and 36th Fighter-Bomber Group, "History," July 1951–March 1952, USAF Historical Research Agency (USAFHRA).

19. Millett, 392.

20. History FAF, July–December 1952, 72; 18th Fighter-Bomber Group, "Tactical Doctrine," 25 July 1953, USAFHRA; Capt E. J. Delia, Adjutant, Eighth Fighter-Bomber Wing to Commanding General FAF, letter, subject: Mission Summary, 17 January 1953.

21. Stewart, 286.

22. Cleveland, 146.

23. Ibid., 257–259.

24. Ibid., 57.

25. Report, Col W. J. Yates, chairman, subject: Joint Air-Ground Operations Conference held at Headquarters FAF, Seoul, Korea, August 1953, 22–23.

26. Futrell, 707.

27. Ibid.; message, DA-942830, DEPTAR to CINCEUR and CINCFE, 2 July 1953.

28. Headquarters USAF, *Evolution of Command and Control Doctrine for CAS* (Washington, D.C.: OAFH) 31–33; Robert F. Futrell, *Ideas, Concepts, Doctrine* vol. 2 (Maxwell AFB, Ala.: Air University Press, 1971), 203–7; Gen Otto P. Weyland, USAF, "The Air Campaign in Korea," *Air University Quarterly Review* 6 (Fall 1953): 3–28.

29. "Joint Task Force Operations," (Draft), Headquarters, United States Strike Command, MacDill AFB, Fla.: 15 April 1964, 52.

30. J. I. Edelman et al., *Airborne Visual Reconnaissance in South Vietnam*, RAND Report RM-5049-ARPA (Santa Monica, Calif.: September 1966.)

31. J. Farmer and M. J. Strumwasser, *The Evolution of the Airborne Forward Air Controller: An Analysis of Mosquito Operations in Korea*, RAND Report RM-5430PR (Santa Monica, Calif.: RAND, 1967), 82–83.

32. TACM 2-4, "Tactical Air Control Party," May 1965, OAFH.

33. Col Thomas M. Crawford Jr., *The Airborne Forward Air Controller— Peacetime Casualty*, Maxwell AFB, Ala.: Air War College Professional Study, No. 3894.

THIS PAGE INTENTIONALLY LEFT BLANK

Chapter 6

Vietnam

The Advisory Years

The end of the French war in Indochina (1954) was marked by the Geneva Accord. It provided for an International Control Commission (ICC) to operate under the purview of the United Nations. ICC would be chaired by the USSR and Great Britain, and it would have military members from India, Poland, and Canada. The duties of ICC were to see that the provisions of the Geneva Accord were carried out. France's withdrawal left a considerable vacuum, since the Vietnamese had not been trained for positions of leadership. They were ill-equipped to defend their own government against an increasingly aggressive minority within the country.[1]

Wars of National Liberation

In 1961, Soviet Prime Minister Nikita Khrushchev proclaimed that "Wars of National Liberation" would be the wars of the future. Later that year, President John F. Kennedy met the Soviet leader at Vienna. There followed a vigorous reexamination of US military strategy.[2] Kennedy directed that US forces having special counterinsurgency skills be developed. The intention was for US specialists to provide training and assistance to the South Vietnamese.

This reorientation of US defense priorities prompted considerable debate about how best to cope with unconventional wars. In the Army, most believed it necessary to create forces that were specifically trained and organized for counterinsurgency activities. In the Air Force, many believed that existing tactical forces could adjust without major changes while others argued that the Air Force should build a special force.[3]

Developing the Counterinsurgency Force

A number of technical studies determined that certain propeller-driven aircraft could be put in combat-ready condition quickly. Consequently, the T-28 was modified to deliver bombs.

Another vintage aircraft, the B-26, had been useful in the Korean War and a number of them were still in storage. However, considerable work was needed to restore them to operational condition. Originally designed as an attack aircraft with weapons to be delivered level or in a slight dive, the B-26 was not stressed for dive-bombing in which three or more "Gs" are common. Nevertheless, a decision was made to modify a limited number of these World War II aircraft for counterinsurgency missions.

The final elements of the counterinsurgency force were the tried and proven C-47 and a courier manufactured by Helio Aircraft Corporation. These aircraft were modified for psychological warfare roles: delivering leaflets and broadcasting taped messages through a loudspeaker system. In addition, a flare-dispensing rack was installed in the C-47 to provide illumination at night.[4]

Farm Gate

In the fall of 1961, it looked very much as though the government of South Vietnam was in danger of collapsing from massive Hanoi-based infiltration.[5] Shortly after President Kennedy took office, he sent Vice President Lyndon B. Johnson to Saigon to talk with South Vietnamese President Ngo Dinh Diem. As a result, a mobile control and reporting post (CRP) was dispatched from the 507th Tactical Control Group, Shaw AFB, South Carolina, to Tan Son Nhut Air Base (AB) outside Saigon. USAF's overt participation in Vietnam began when the CRP became operational on 5 October 1961.[6]

The Air Force combat detachment that Kennedy ordered to Vietnam on 11 October 1961 had its roots in a small, secret organization created in the late 1950s when Gen Curtis E. LeMay was Vice Chief of Staff. In March 1961, LeMay responded to the president's instructions to examine how each

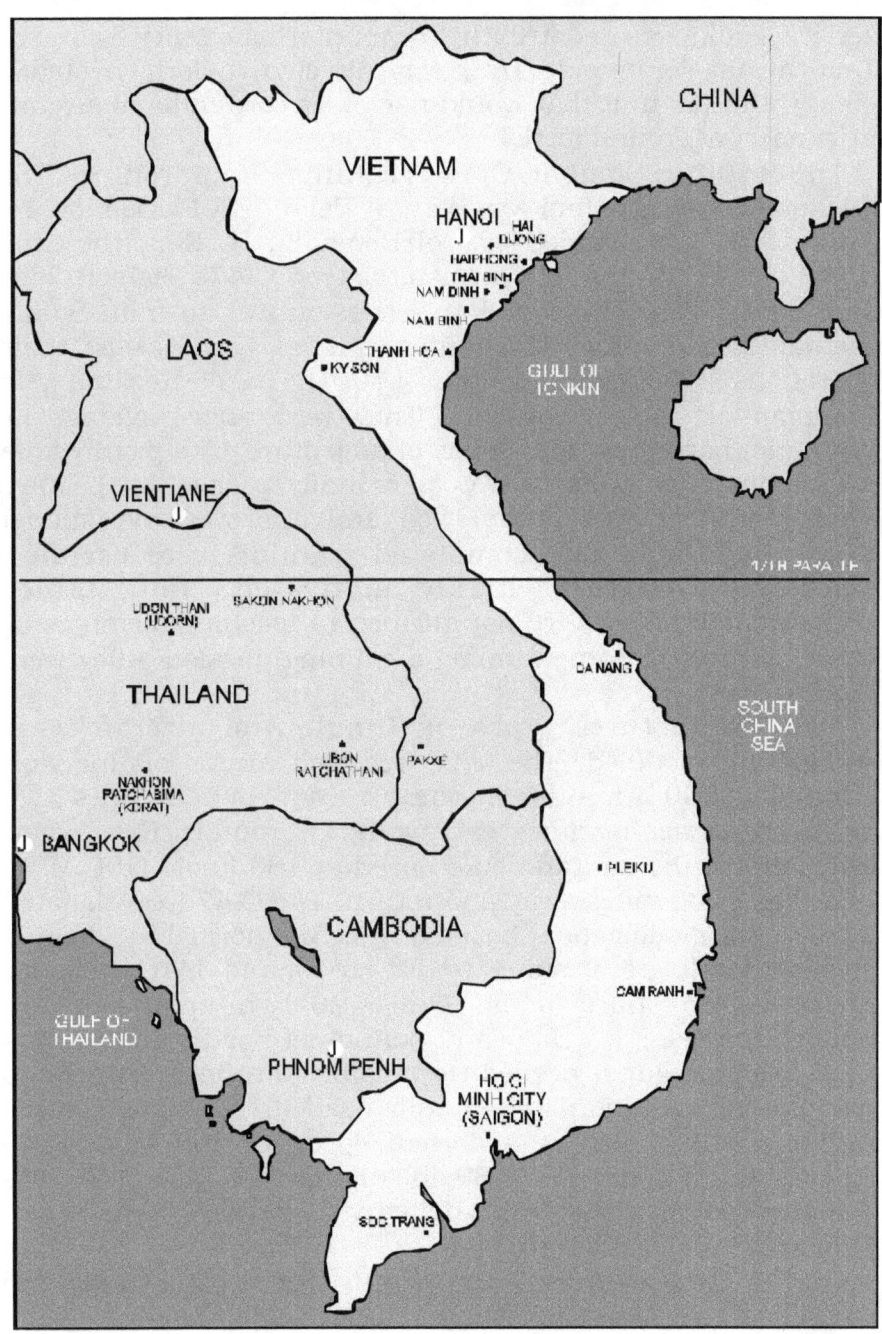

Figure 2. Vietnam

service could best contribute to counterinsurgency warfare. Tactical Air Command (TAC) was directed to form a small, elite, volunteer unit that would use older conventional aircraft in support of ground forces.[7]

The 4400th Combat Crew Training Squadron (CCTS) (nicknamed Jungle Jim) was born at Eglin AFB, Florida, on 14 April 1961. Commanded by Col Benjamin H. King, the unit had 124 officers and 228 airmen, sixteen C-47s, eight B-26s, and eight T-28s. The squadron's mission was to train South Vietnamese air forces in counterinsurgency and assist their operations.[8] Members of the 4400th CCTS (called Air Commandos) were volunteers. They were above average in physique, hardiness, and sense of adventure. The picturesque Air Commando uniform was personally picked by LeMay. Each volunteer was interviewed and approved by Colonel King, and those who completed training were certified emotionally mature, highly motivated, and stable. Unfortunately, they were not attuned to teaching members of other cultures or to performing a training mission—they were combat oriented.

Two of the three types of Jungle Jim aircraft were extensively modified. The T-28 received armor plating and carried 1,500 pounds of bombs and rockets plus two .50-caliber machine guns, each with 350 rounds. Even when fully loaded, the aircraft could speed at 160 knots (190 MPH) to a target 200 miles away and return. The C-47 (redesignated SC-47 after modification) boasted twice the normal fuel load, a stronger landing gear suited to dirt strips, and JATO racks for operating on short fields. The B-26 twin-engine attack bomber, carrying six thousand pounds of bombs and rockets plus machine guns, needed no modification once restored to operational condition. When fully loaded, it had a combat radius of 400 miles at a normal speed of 200 knots (240 MPH)—and it could loiter 30 to 45 minutes. The B-26 was designed for a glide bomb-delivery pattern, not for dive-bombing.[9]

On 24 August 1961, the Joint Chiefs of Staff (JCS) suggested to Defense Secretary Robert S. McNamara that an air interdiction campaign be waged on the trails over which the Vietcong were being supplied.[10] On 5 September,

VIETNAM: THE ADVISORY YEARS

Farm Gate Aircraft—T-28

Farm Gate Aircraft—B-26

Farm Gate Aircraft—A-19

Farm Gate Aircraft—C-47

McNamara informed the three service secretaries he intended to establish an experimental command as a laboratory; later that month, a detachment of the 4400th became operationally ready. If moved to Vietnam, it would acquire counterinsurgency experience and train the Vietnamese.[11] President Kennedy authorized deployment of the Jungle Jim squadron to Vietnam "to serve under the Military Advisory and Assistance Group (MAAG) as a training mission and not for combat at the present time."[12]

But the 4400th was "designed to fight." It had been "singled out" for deployment because its combat capacity and involvement would shore up "South Vietnamese sagging morale."[13] The president now enunciated a new mission statement for Jungle Jim: to train Vietnamese airmen while working with and supporting the special forces that had been sent in five months earlier. One of Jungle Jim's objectives was to forge counterinsurgency tactics—and it was capable of using sod runways to operate austerely in remote areas. It could conduct strike, reconnaissance, and airlift missions; fly close support for ground troops; air-drop small forces (up to company-size); deliver supplies; and perform medical evacuations.[14]

Support arrangements were made, and a tent camp was readied for the detachment's arrival at Bien Hoa Airfield At Eglin, the task force received its formal name: Detachment 2A, 4400th Combat Crew Training Squadron (and its code name, "Farm Gate").[15]

Farm Gate departed Florida on 5 November 1961. Four SC-47s flew to Clark AB, Philippines, and eight T-28s were disassembled in California and ferried to Clark. After reassembly, Colonel King led the T-28s to Tan Son Nhut The detachment became operationally ready on 16 November, though another week passed before the last of the SC-47s and T-28s arrived. Farm Gate also accepted four B-26s that had previously been sent to the Far East. These light bombers reached Bien Hoa near the close of December.[16]

At Bien Hoa, the Farm Gate detachment found a run-down French air base with a flight surface consisting of a single pierced-steel-plank runway, 5,800 by 150 feet. About 700 South Vietnamese soldiers defended the airfield. Farm Gate worked with the two mobile CRPs at Tan Son Nhut and organized a tactical air control system (TACS).[17]

Members of Farm Gate thought they were to conduct combat operations while training South Vietnamese; that was how General LeMay had briefed Colonel King, who was willing to make his unit combat-capable. In early familiarization flights, T-28 crews followed Vietnamese fighter-bombers to targets, observed their attacks, and, when authorized, fired on targets. The men of Farm Gate were highly motivated and eager to fight.[18] On 16 November, however, Farm Gate was tasked with conducting training and pilot upgrade for the Vietnamese. President Kennedy advised that the unit was "training Vietnamese aircrews and supporting Vietnamese operations against the Vietcong."[19]

Morale was lowered from the beginning because of mission uncertainties and the absence of combat. Pilots had expected to carry an air offensive to the Vietcong. Instead, they trained and supplemented the Vietnamese Air Force, seeking to evolve techniques for what McNamara described to the press as "not full-scale warfare but guerrilla warfare." Early Farm Gate operations tended to be improvised and experimental rather than systematic.[20]

Farm Gate also acquired the mission of supporting the Army Special Forces and their Civilian Irregular Defense Group. C-47s operated under an ad hoc system free of MAAG and Vietnamese Army control.[21] While valuable, these missions were not what Farm Gate wanted to do. Gen Emmett O'Donnell, commander of PACAF, permitted Farm Gate to fly combat missions "with at least one South Vietnamese national aboard any aircraft." On 6 December, the Joint Chiefs granted formal authority for Farm Gate aircraft to fly combat if Vietnamese were aboard for training.[22] Together, Vietnamese and Americans were to destroy Vietcong lifelines and support bases. From Bien Hoa, Tan Son Nhut, and combat air bases at Da Nang and Pleiku, air operations provided photo reconnaissance, surveillance, interdiction, and close support of ground operations.[23]

McNamara wanted all flights confined to South Vietnam. Stressing the difference between "riding double" combat training missions and operational missions, he stressed that combat missions be confined to solely "important jobs." In other words, according to McNamara, "Jungle Jim is to be used for training and operational missions in South Vietnam with Vietnamese riding rear seats."[24] Combined crews on combat missions would provide training and allow the Vietnamese to fly these missions alone as soon as possible. The possibility of an independent American combat role came to an end early.[25]

Command Structure

From 1955, the United States was directly involved in organizing and training Vietnamese units. The South Vietnamese Air Force (VNAF), a very small element of their armed forces, had to be built from the bottom up. VNAF's organization, inherited from the French, was considerably different from USAF's arrangement for fighting a theater war. With the introduction of Farm Gate T-28s and B-26s, it became increasingly apparent that a USAF command structure was required to control American flying units. Even though Farm Gate units were restricted to combat training missions, it was inevitable that these missions would involve actual combat.[26] Further, Farm Gate was providing more and more close air support—and air cover for convoys, which were being ambushed with increasing frequency. Since the VNAF could not meet all these requirements, Farm Gate's mission directives provided for its employment in emergency situations.[27]

President Kennedy expanded the training and advisory forces in Vietnam at the same time the Farm Gate project was activated.[28] The airlift force was increased, the Ranch Hand (defoliation unit) detachment was expanded, additional control facilities were dispatched, and more FACs with liaison aircraft were assigned. The MAAG was reorganized and expanded to control the rapidly growing US commitment. On 8 February 1962, Military Assistance Command Vietnam (MACV) was formed with Gen Paul D. Harkins as commander. General Harkins formally separated advisory activities from training and operational activities. In essence, MACV became the headquarters for combat operations.[29]

Early in 1962, General LeMay recognized that the insurgency in South Vietnam demanded a more imaginative employment of airpower. On 23 April, he talked with General Harkins about making airpower more responsive.[30] The command system, LeMay said, was too cumbersome; requests for air cover and for strikes against the enemy's ambush forces were being processed too slowly. He emphasized that airpower, called in quickly enough, could make ambushes very costly. Proper use of the TACS and a more direct method of processing requests would eliminate delays, LeMay argued. He also pointed out that more airmen were needed on the MACV staff to improve the effectiveness of Farm Gate units and to create a better understanding among Vietnamese officers on the use of airpower. To provide significant convoy protection, support for civilian irregular defense groups, and CAS for major ground operations, airpower would have to be centrally and efficiently controlled—which it could be, using the facilities of the already established TACS.[31]

The tactical air control system had proven its worth in World War II and Korea. An air operations center (AOC) afforded centralized planning, direction, and control. Supporting it was a reporting center for radar and other warning services. In addition, each major ground command area contained subordinate air support operations centers and warning posts.

PACAF and Thirteenth Air Force planned such a system for Vietnam in December 1961. An air operations center for overall control at Tan Son Nhut supported the III Corps Tactical Zone headquarters. Subordinate air support operations centers at Da Nang and Pleiku served the I and II Corps headquarters. Secretary McNamara rejected the idea of phasing in this system slowly and directed that it be established at once.[32]

Air Operations in 1962

The system began operating on 13 January 1962. In a move designed to avoid striking innocent targets, President Diem's prior personal approval was required for all air strikes. Gen Bollen H. Anthis, MACV air component commander, briefed Diem and stressed how the system's instant information on enemy and friendly air activities led to a quick response.

Persuaded, Diem permitted the joint operations staff to authorize air strikes without his direct approval.

Forward air controllers were on USAF organizational charts in 1962, but just how to use them was an undetermined issue. There was no clear-cut front line. A FAC on the ground, in a guerrilla/friendly mix-up or obscured in the dense jungle, would have no better view of the situation than an ordinary rifleman. In late 1961, Maj Douglas Evans and Capt Tom Cairney received orders to fly with the VNAF. They became the first American FACs in Southeast Asia.[33]

A number of junior Vietnamese officers were acting as FACs and as air liaison officers (ALO) with ground forces. They were hesitant to control strikes or give advice to ground commanders. Lacking authority and seemingly uninformed, these young officers appeared merely to transmit requests for information to their headquarters over unsecured communications networks. Five additional USAF FACs arrived on 15 February 1962. They were pilots who were highly qualified to direct strike aircraft from observation planes. The initial USAF ALOs got to Vietnam in April 1962.[34]

At first, the USAF controllers were attached to those Vietnamese ground forces judged likely to engage the enemy. Since President Diem wanted rated Vietnamese observers to control strikes, the Americans worked as assistant ALOs They also flew the L-19 for the Vietnamese FACs and served as duty officers in the air operations center.[35] The inexpensive L-19 was the ultimate in maintenance simplicity. Its simple, fixed landing gear of spring steel could handle rough fields as well as rough landings. Normal cruise speed was 90 to 100 MPH and, with flaps, it had a stall speed as low as 55 MPH. With that combination, pilots could work from a 1,000-foot strip or a dirt road.[36]

Crippling the TACS was the limited and failure-prone communications between centers and airfields. PACAF therefore obtained newly developed high-frequency, single-sideband radios for long-distance voice and teletype channels. But when these radios reached Clark on 30 December 1961, problems arose immediately: Operators in the small mobile vans sweltered as temperatures often soared to 130 degrees, atmospheric conditions caused poor transmission, and extensive use cluttered the frequency bands.

In January 1962, USAF planners were convinced they had solved the problem of creating a "clear, realistic, jointly agreed concept for the elimination of Vietcong influence." Their idea called for a quick reaction force of Vietnamese airborne troops, lifted and supported by US or Vietnamese transport and strike aircraft.[37]

Precise targeting was required, and guerrilla warfare blurred distinctions. Insurgents disguised themselves as civilians, found shelter among the populace, and depended on innocent civilians for food and other items. President Diem emphatically insisted that airmen exercise utmost care to avoid angering the people by injuring innocents. In fact, carelessness during an air strike could lead to a prison sentence.[38] Thirteenth Air Force therefore asked Pacific Air Force (PACAF) to lay down rules of engagement for Farm Gate. The request was referred to commander-in-chief Pacific (CINCPAC) for resolution; Adm Harry D. Felt stressed caution.

Because of this cautious approach, more than half of the T-28s flying strike missions in 1962 returned with unused ordnance. One USAF FAC said he saw Vietnamese troops after an engagement "put 60 artillery rounds into a village for no apparent reason and kill women and children." Yet, he knew of no instance when "we indiscriminately went into any area and just for the heck of it bombed and strafed."[39] During the night of 1 March 1962, the Vietcong stormed an outpost about 30 miles north of Saigon in War Zone D. The call for help flashed to the AOC and thence to Farm Gate. An SC-47 flare-ship and two T-28s carrying napalm, rockets, and .50-caliber machine guns scrambled, with radar at Tan Son Nhut vectoring them to the scene. The T-28s pummeled the enemy under the light of blossoming flares, the assault was broken off, and the outpost held. Five enemy bodies were found the following day, along with evidence that more had been wounded.

While lapses in coordination and communications marred some operations, overall results in 1962 infused optimism. On 4 March, a Vietnamese L-19 discovered a company of Vietcong (50 to 70) near the bend of a river 30 miles northeast of Tan Son Nhut. Vietnamese Skyraiders (AD-6) scrambled within 15 minutes, armed solely with 20 mm cannon since the planes were forbidden to carry bombs. Asked to assist, Farm Gate flew a series of strikes at Vietnamese request. Reports the next day claimed 50 to 60 Vietcong dead.[40]

USAF pilots could return fire against "a known source" in self-defense, but they rarely knew a source's exact location. In the daytime, Farm Gate planes could not fire unless under positive control of a Vietnamese FAC, and cooperation with Vietnamese L-19 controllers was frequently difficult. In addition, elaborate reconnaissance and target marking alerted the Vietcong to impending strikes. This impeded action against an already elusive foe.[41]

Air strikes near friendly troops called for cooperation between air missions and ground units. As in Korea, TACPs came to be used. The Air Force supplied a seasoned fighter pilot to serve as the ALO member of the control party. The Army furnished vehicles and mechanics, radio gear and operators. A radio jeep carried the ALO and Army members of the control party. The vehicle's radios linked the FAC and the strike pilots with ground and air units. The control party's work was thwarted whenever the jeep was slowed or stopped by damaged roads, ambushes, jungles, or swamps.[42]

A further frustration was the meager experience of the Vietnamese in coordinating air-ground operations. The shortage of L-19 pilots prevented the assignment of ALOs to ground units. The foremost need was to secure sufficient two-man L-19 crews (pilot and observer) to place strike aircraft on the target. So in lieu of an ALO, the Vietnamese sometimes designated an L-19 crew to serve as a FAC for a ground unit. The pilot and observer reported to the unit, received briefings on the planned action, and became familiar with the terrain. The crew then returned home to conduct other air control and reconnaissance missions. On the day of the operation, the L-19 crew flew back and controlled air strikes for the ground unit.

Unable to operate at night, L-19 crews flew in daytime, usually at three thousand to five thousand feet, far too high for good surveillance and target marking. The air observer marked targets for fighters by radio direction or hand-thrown smoke grenade, commonly by both methods. Criticism and penalty awaited an L-19 crew if ground fire damaged the plane. The observer was subject to severe punishment if he erred in marking a target and friendly casualties resulted.[43]

To communicate with ground troops, L-19s carried Army radios lashed to their back seats. Because the plane could power only its own radios or the Army radio, the crew could not converse with strike aircraft and ground forces at the same time. The ground units wanted man-pack radios that could mesh with existing UHF/VHF airborne sets. No such radios were obtainable in 1962. Complications of this sort paled beside the general insufficiency of the L-19s. They were often simply unavailable. In April, for example, Farm Gate pilots arrived over a target and could see a firefight on the ground but the Vietnamese controller never arrived.[44]

In late 1962, President Diem reorganized the South Vietnamese military. He divided Vietnam into four corps tactical zones, created the new IV Corps in the Mekong Delta, and established the capital military district around Saigon. Combined VNAF-USAF staffs in the direct air support centers (DASC) formed a link in the tactical air control chain. In theory, the DASCs would cover changing areas of responsibility as the battlefield situation progressed. In South Vietnam, however, the DASCs remained fixed in specified regions. A DASC was collocated with the Tactical Operations Center in each of the four Army of the Republic of Vietnam (ARVN) Corps: at Da Nang (I Corps), Pleiku (II Corps), Bien Hoa (III Corps), and Can Tho (IV Corps). The DASCs served as regional extensions of the TACC, receiving and coordinating requests for CAS within their areas of responsibility and working with the TACC to meet tactical air priorities. Corps tactical zone commanders were given greater responsibilities as part of a new National Campaign Plan. They exercised operational control not only over their ground forces but over supporting Vietnamese Air Force elements.

Air Operations in 1963

In 1963, the Air Force regularized the status of its units in Vietnam. CINCPAC Adm Harry Felt spurned the principle that USAF personnel sent to the country had to have prior counterinsurgency training. Farm Gate, he said, was flying conventional missions and airmen could be assigned on a routine basis. This cleared the way for doubling the number of aircrews and maintenance men, and it raised the sortie rate by 25 or 30 percent. Felt also wished to boost the number of liaison aircraft and FACs by two squadrons. This, he said, would be the key to a successful national campaign plan.[45]

In early February, General LeMay pressed for putting US markings on Farm Gate aircraft. He said, "Current classification restrictions on Farm Gate are considered unnecessary. Actual operation is well known through SVN (South Vietnam) and classification has become an administrative burden." Secretary of State Dean Rusk, however, continued to accent the American role as "strictly limited to advisory, logistic, and training functions."[46]

Over the first half of 1963, Vietnamese L-19s (O-1s) escorted truck convoys and trains while strike aircraft covered convoys transporting high-priority cargoes. Vietnamese and USAF planes flew close to 1,000 sorties in these missions. The Vietcong ambushed no surface forces having air cover but were quick to attack transportation that had no aerial escort.[47]

Farm Gate gained fresh aircraft in January 1963: five T-28s, ten B-26s, and two C-47s. By February, Farm Gate had 42 planes and 275 men. By June, MACV had 16,652 people, 4,090 of them Air Force. On 8 July, Farm Gate at Bien Hoa became the 1st Air Commando Squadron (Composite). As 1st Air Commando Squadron, Farm Gate contained two strike sections. The first section consisted of ten B-26s with 23 crews (pilot and navigator) and two RB-26s (reconnaissance version); the second had thirteen T-28s with two crew members per aircraft. There were also two support sections, one with four psychological warfare couriers and the other with six C-47s. The remaining eight B-26s were in detachments at Plaice and Soc Trang.[48]

Air Force and Vietnamese pilots faithfully followed the rule that air strikes had to be handled by a Vietnamese FAC (a precaution against indiscriminate bombing). Crews staging from forward airfields were encouraged to fly low and seek out the enemy. Before they could attack, however, they needed a Vietnamese airborne FAC.[49]

The Air Force's 19th Tactical Air Support Squadron (TASS) was activated at Bien Hoa in July 1963, but the new unit's aircraft and crews trickled in. Four O-1s and 22 crews were on board by July; the remaining 18 planes arrived on the USS *Card* in August. Since Americans were forbidden to direct air strikes, 11 seasoned Vietnamese observers were integrated into the squadron. Operational in September, the unit furnished more and more FACs and ALOs for the National Campaign Plan. Its primary mission was to train Vietnamese pilots in FAC, visual reconnaissance, combat support, and observer procedures. The aim was to replace pilots taken to fill fighter cockpits. The squadron was to remain in Vietnam for one year, then turn its O-1s over to the Vietnamese.[50]

After 25 officers and 69 airmen had completed training (in July and August), they opened the Nha Trang center in September. Trainees took one month of preflight instruction and three months of flight training that included 80 hours of actual flying. Vietnamese liaison pilots in sufficient numbers were ready for combat in early 1964.[51]

In September, Lt Col David S. Mellish, III Corps ALO, received authorization to start an air interdiction program. Vietnamese province chiefs certified certain areas as free of friendly people. The AOC scheduled air strikes, under FACs, into these regions. This interdiction paid off in Tay Ninh and Phuouc Thanh provinces during October, but the Vietcong learned to disperse and take cover as soon as the O-1s dropped smoke grenades to mark targets for the strike planes.[52]

The 19th TASS was fully operational by 15 September. The unit, commanded by Lt Col John J. Wilfong, kept sixteen O-1s at Bien Hoa and six at Can Tho. By year's end they had flown 3,862 sorties: 483 FAC, 1,221 visual reconnaissance, and 1,518 combat support liaison. The "prompt response and can-do attitude" of the crews bred a huge demand for their services. The Americans met with limited success, however, in trying to augment rather than replace Vietnamese liaison operations.[53] A few USAF pilots who flew with Vietnamese FACs realized they had been doing a boring and thankless job

VIETNAM: THE ADVISORY YEARS

O-1 "Bird Dog"

for many years with no end in sight. The average Vietnamese pilot saw the law of averages working against him and was reluctant to fly below two thousand feet. If he mistakenly directed an attack on friendly people, criminal prosecution awaited him. The prevailing American view saw Vietnamese crews as unaggressive and unreliable. By October, this disapproval was being expressed by the overwhelming sentiment that "Americans must run things."[54]

As sorties swelled to meet Vietcong attacks, premission briefings were seldom practical. Responding to numerous requests, Vietnamese FACs frequently flew many miles into unfamiliar areas. They radioed ground units to find the locations of friendly and enemy troops and then marked the targets for strike crews. Air Force officers repeatedly urged the Vietnamese to attach ALOs and FACs to divisions so they could be familiar with local conditions. The VNAF declined, citing the scarcity of qualified officers, the failure of the young ones to work well without close supervision, and the discord between air and ground officers.[55]

By the end of 1963, the government's military offensive was collapsing and the Vietcong were seizing the initiative. Nevertheless, the limited number of USAF and Vietnamese aircraft had scored some tactical gains in the face of severe handicaps.[56] President Kennedy, on 14 November, announced that Rusk and McNamara were going to Honolulu for a meeting to size up the situation and identify how to intensify the struggle and end American involvement. "Now," the president said, "this is our objective—to bring Americans home, permit the South Vietnamese to maintain themselves as a free and independent country, and permit democratic forces within the country to operate." But the assassination of President Kennedy in November 1963 signaled the end of one era and the beginning of another.[57]

Air Operations in 1964

Four days after taking office, President Johnson reaffirmed American objectives in Vietnam. The United States would help the republic win the war against the externally directed and sustained conspiracy, assist the government in developing public support, and keep US military and economic aid at the same level. "This is a Vietnamese war," the president said, "and the country and the war must in the end be run solely by the Vietnamese." He reiterated the October 1963 pledge to withdraw some Americans. Yet, at the same time, he instructed the State Department to prepare a white paper documenting Hanoi's control of the Vietcong and its supply of them through Laos. He further solicited plans for stepped-up clandestine warfare and for cross-border incursions into Laos to check infiltration.[58]

Between January and May 1964, Hanoi sent an estimated 4,700 troops into South Vietnam. Formerly, most of the infiltrators had been ethnic southerners; now there were growing numbers of native northerners, many of them in the North Vietnamese Army. Formerly, the Vietcong had relied on French and American weapons, chiefly from stockpiles captured before 1954 in Indochina and Korea; by 1964, most of their weapons were of Chinese origin, brought by land and sea from North Vietnam.[59]

On 22 January 1964, the JCS proposed a ten-point program of "bolder actions to arrest SVN's military/political decline." The proposal amounted to a virtual takeover of the war from the Saigon government through overt and covert bombing in North Vietnam, large-scale commando raids, mining the sea approaches, ground operations into Laos, and extended reconnaissance over both Laos and Cambodia. The plan also called for committing more US forces to support combat in Vietnam.[60]

The decision to focus on the battle inside South Vietnam underscored the demand to relax the rules of engagement for air operations. On 27 March, MACV authorized strike aircraft to operate to the border if the border could be identified from the air. Elsewhere, they could fly as close as 200 meters when directed by a FAC or five thousand meters without one. However, they were forbidden to fire across or violate the frontier without diplomatic clearance. The State Department sympathized with the JCS stand for hot pursuit into Cambodia under certain conditions, but resisted any easing of those restrictions. State's position governed in 1964.[61]

"The word for the Air Force in Vietnam," MACV Air Commander Gen Bollen H. Anthis wrote in November 1963, "is austerity." War-weary air commando aircraft, a fledgling VNAF, and a slow air request network made it difficult to seize combat opportunities.[62] The USAF 34th Tactical Group was scheduled to phase out of Vietnam. Withdrawal would begin in mid-1964 with the departure of the 19th TASS (which furnished FACs). The 1st Air Commando Squadron, due to receive the first two of 18 rebuilt B-26Ks in June, was scheduled to leave in mid-1965. Farm Gate's B-26s were nearly worn out but 2d Air Division (AD) expected them to survive with careful flying. The new Vietnamese 518th Fighter Squadron got A-1Hs in March 1964. Also that month, the 716th Composite Reconnaissance Squadron received eighteen RT-28s and three RC-47s. During the second quarter of 1964, USAF T-28s were replaced on a one-for-one basis with dual-piloted A-1Hs.[63]

By 1964, Vietnamese and American aircraft comprised only about one-half of the requested support. The reasons lay in air request network troubles and the rising damage to planes from Vietcong ground defenses. On 11 February, after the wing of a B-26 broke off in flight at Eglin AFB, all B-26s in Vietnam were taken out of combat. They were then restricted to only straight and level flight with the lightest ordnance loads.[64] The uncertain combat worthiness of the old B-26s led PACAF to suggest deploying a squadron of the 3d Bombardment Wing's B-57s from Japan to Bien Hoa. Their jet speed spelled a swifter response to air support requests.[65]

At least 1,546 air strike requests were received in the first three months of 1964. Of the 424 not honored, 230 were due to a shortage of planes. But these figures did not present a true picture because ground commanders and FACs disliked filing new requests after having been turned down.

Gen Joseph H. Moore, Second Air Division commander, wanted to enlarge the TACS by adding an air request communications network that would be manned and operated by the Air Force. It would resemble the US Strike Command-Tactical Air Command system that had been worked out during maneuvers in the United States. General Moore hoped to eliminate the long delays encountered in passing air requests up through channels over Vietnamese army communications.[66] The proposed network would enhance USAF advice at lower ground echelons. An Air Force pilot and two radio operators would man TACPs at all levels down to battalion. They would process air support requests, provide advice, and direct CAS strikes. To man this countrywide setup, 2d Air Division drew pilots from the 19th TASS. Moore envisioned a continuing need for Vietnamese controllers, but he saw no reason why Air force controllers and Army and Vietnamese forward air guides could not coordinate their efforts to designate targets for air strikes.[67]

Lt Col John M. Porter, commander of the 1st Air Commando Squadron (ACS), led the original flight of six A-1Es from the Philippines to Bien Hoa on 30 May. The next day, A-1Es flew their maiden strike sorties. Col William E. Bethea, who assumed command of the 34th Tactical Group in June, was impressed by the plane's large and varied ordnance capability, short takeoff roll, extremely long range, and good loitering. But the A-1E's normal cruising speed of 155 knots (185 MPH) prevented a rapid response, and the aircraft could barely defend itself in aerial combat. Nevertheless, 1st ACS soon had twelve A-1Es and the T-28s were retired. On 30 June, the 34th Tactical Group began transition training for Vietnamese pilots.[68]

The natural environment of Vietnam worked against ground TACPs. Their bulky radio gear was hard to transport through the jungle. It was sometimes impossible to direct an air strike safely from the ground. Mountains and heavy vegetation hampered the ground view, and the flat ground of the delta offered no elevation for observation. Numerous tree lines and canal ridges also obstructed the view.

By mid-1964, it was generally agreed that ground TACPs could not replace airborne control even though the plodding Vietnamese O-1s (L-19s) and their often indifferent observers did not provide effective air support. Strong pleas to prevent the demise of the 19th TASS proved futile; the unit remained under orders to transfer its aircraft to the Vietnamese.[69] Also by 1964, FACs had become a prime source of intelligence about the enemy.

The Gulf of Tonkin

On 2 August 1964, the USS *Maddox* reported that North Vietnamese torpedo boats had attacked it while it was on patrol in the Gulf of Tonkin. The attack was apparently in retaliation for US-sponsored South Vietnamese raids along the North Vietnamese coast. Two nights later, the *Maddox* and a second destroyer, the USS *C. Turner Joy* reported additional enemy attacks against them. On 5 August, President Johnson ordered a retaliatory strike against North Vietnamese coastal torpedo bases and an oil storage depot. On 7 August, the president proposed and Congress adopted the Gulf of Tonkin resolution, which authorized him to use all measures—including the commitment of US armed forces—to assist South Vietnam in defending its independence and territory.

President Johnson then approved emergency actions to move additional forces into Southeast Asia. Six F-102 jet interceptors of the 509th Fighter Squadron flew from Clark to Da Nang. Six others from the 16th Fighter Squadron at Naha AB, Okinawa, touched down at Tan Son Nhut. Eight F-100s of the 615th Tactical Fighter Squadron (TFS), on rotational deployment at Clark, went to Da Nang. Thirty-six B-57s of the Eighth and Thirteenth Bomber Squadrons deployed to Bien Hoa. Six RF-101s out of Kadena and Misawa air bases, Japan, augmented reconnaissance planes at Tan Son Nhut. The 405th Tactical Fighter Wing (TFW) sent ten F-100s from Clark to Takhli, Thailand. Eight KB-50s from PACAF's 421st Air Refueling Squadron moved from Yokota to Tan Son Nhut and Takhli. Eight F-105 jet fighters of the 36th TFS flew from Yokota to Clark, then to Korat in Thailand, on 9 August.[70]

Forty-eight C-130 transports from the 314th, 463d, and 516th Troop Carrier Wings arrived at Clark and Kadena between 9 and 21 August. For in-flight refueling, Strategic Air Command (SAC) furnished forty-eight KC-135 jet tankers that operated mainly from Hickam Air Force Base in Hawaii and Andersen Air Force Base on Guam. SAC further formed a task force of eight KC-135s at Clark.[72] On 6 August, General Moore created a 2d Air Division command post at Tan Son Nhut, separate from the combined Vietnamese-USAF air operations center. He began to tie together all USAF units in the area.

On 8 August, at the height of the crisis, PACAF issued orders to inactivate the 19th TASS. Gen William C. Westmoreland expressed surprise, and requested that he be allowed to retain the unit. In lieu of giving the O-1 liaison planes to the Vietnamese, creation of the 116th Liaison Squadron was proposed. Westmoreland requested that U-17A aircraft be purchased to equip that unit. Defense Secretary McNamara approved on 25 September,[72] and the 19th TASS was reactivated at Bien Hoa on 31 October. MACV recommended 30 more planes for it and each of the four Vietnamese liaison units. Until support could be restored, the 34th Tactical Group possessed twenty-four O-1s and only twelve pilots. A detachment of O-1Fs remained at Bien Hoa to train newly graduated Vietnamese pilots.[73]

New Demands

By the end of 1964, the North Vietnamese had begun to escalate the war in South Vietnam.[74] Engagements were now approaching those of battalion-size units. With the appearance of regular North Vietnamese troops in South

Vietnam, aircraft encountered heavier ground fire in all corps areas with a sharp increase in I and II Corps. Whereas most of the ground fire had previously been .30-caliber, .50-caliber now became more frequent. This stronger firepower required most aircraft to change to higher operating altitudes. Aircraft operating below two thousand feet expected to encounter some ground fire. In approaching most airfields, aircrews could expect spasmodic ground fire. This was also true after dark on the approaches to most of the larger airfields; for example, Tan Son Nhut, Bien Hoa, and Da Nang. Aircraft losses increased significantly during this time.[75]

The USAF controller with the 14th Regiment at Tra Vinh was Capt Lloyd E. Lewis. Receiving an O-1 and a Vietnamese observer in September, he began flying day-long surveillance missions in coordination with the Vinh Binh province commander. The result was an appreciable decline in Vietcong activity. Friendly ground forces became more productive, as did interdiction targeting and air strikes.[76]

In September, William B. Graham and Aaron H. Katz of RAND studied the use of USAF ALOs and FACs on constant visual reconnaissance and strike control. They gathered data for a new concept they called the "Single Integrated Attack Team." The idea was presented in Saigon, Hawaii, and Washington D.C. in October, then in a RAND report. The theory favored small and closely coordinated air and ground strike forces as the best counterinsurgency weapon. O-1 crews would carry out continuous and extensive airborne surveillance and strike control. They would work with Special Forces ground teams who would hold Vietcong groups long enough for aircraft to strike them. Unfortunately, the concept was better-suited to an insurgency in its initial stages than to the field warfare the Vietcong were beginning to wage.[77] The continuous surveillance concept could not be properly set in motion during the winter of 1964–65 due to the dearth of aircraft and forward air controllers.

On 9 March 1965, the Joint Chiefs of Staff directed that US aircraft could be used for combat operations in South Vietnam. No strikes were permitted from Thai airfields and American aircraft could not accept missions that the VNAF could carry out. But the planes now boldly displayed US insignia, and a Vietnamese airman was no longer required to be aboard in combat.

Despite a sizable increase in personnel and aircraft between 1955 and 1965, the US advisory mission failed to end Hanoi's support of the insurgency in South Vietnam and Laos. The decision early in 1965 to replace advisors with combat troops recognized two facts that had become clear: infiltration into South Vietnam was growing rather than slowing, and the government of South Vietnam could not cope with the situation. US policy makers saw the confluence of these two factors bringing defeat to the South unless a new approach was taken. Thus, the purely advisory function was abandoned in favor of direct US air and ground participation. The USAF units in place early in 1965 formed the nucleus for the coming buildup.[78]

Notes

1. Maj Gen T. R. Milton, "Air Power: Equalizer in Southeast Asia," *Air University Review* XV (November–December 1963): 3.

2. Townsend Hoopes, *The Limits of Intervention: An Inside Account of How the Johnson Policy of Escalation in Vietnam Was Reversed* (New York: David McKay Co., 1969), 13.

3. William W. Momyer, *Airpower in Three Wars* (Washington, D.C.: Department of the Air Force, January 1978), 9.

4. Ibid., 251.

5. Milton, 4.

6. Momyer, 170.

7. Robert F. Futrell, *The United States Air Force in Southeast Asia: The Advisory Years to 1965* (Washington, D.C.: Office of Air Force History [OAFH], 1981), 79.

8. Lt Col M. M. Doyle, interviewed by TSgt Robert J. O'Neill, 16 February 1963.

9. *History of the 2d Advanced Echelon* (ADVON), November 1961–October 1962 (Washington, D.C.: OAFH), 8; John W. R. Taylor, ed., *Combat Aircraft of the World* (London: Ebury Press, 1969), 491–92.

10. Assistant Director for Joint Matters, Directorate of Operations, USAF (AFXOPJ), *Book of Actions in Southeast Asia* (SEA), item IV-B (Washington, D.C.: OAFH), 961–64.

11. Ibid., Item III-B, 21–22.

12. *Public Papers of the Presidents of the United States: John F. Kennedy,1961* (Washington, D.C.: Government Printing Office, 1962), 84.

13. *History of the Director of Plans, USAF,* 1 July–31 December 1961, vol. 22 (Washington, D.C.: OAFH, 1962), 78.

14. Brig Gen Benjamin H. King, interviewed by USAFHRA staff, 4 September 1962; *History of the Special Air Warfare Center* (SAWC), 27 April–31 December 1962 (Washington, D.C.: OAFH, 1963), 1–10.

15. Director of Plans, USAF, memorandum, subject: briefing on Jungle Jim, 16 October 1961.

16. *History, SAWC,* April–December 1962, 12–13.

17. Message, Detachment 9, 2d ADVON to PACAF, 21 November 1961.

18. *History, 2d ADVON,* 8–9; Victory B. Anthony, *The Air Force in Southeast Asia: Tactics and Techniques of Night Operations, 1961-70* (Washington, D.C.: OAFH, March 1973); Message, CINCPAC to chief, Military Assistance Advisory Group (MAAG) Vietnam (VN), 16 November 1961.

19. Message, CINCPAC to chief, MAAG, VN, 16 November 1961.

20. Message, CINCPAC to Defense Intelligence Agency (DIA), 13 March 1963.

21. Paul S. Ella, Richard P. Joyce, Robert H. Williams, and William Woodworth, "US Army Special Forces and Similar Internal Defense Advisory Operations in Mainland Southeast Asia, 1962–67," Research Analysis Corporation, June 1969, 117.

22. Message, JCS to CINCPAC, 6 December 1961; *History of CINCPAC Command* (Washington, D.C.: OAFH, 1961), 190–91.

23. *History, CINCPAC Command,* 1961, 171.

24. Message, PACAF to chief of staff, United States Air Force (CSAF), 17 December 1961.

25. Message, Thirteenth Air Force to PACAF, 28 December 1961, CSAF to PACAF, 23 March 1963, and JCS to CINCPAC, 26 December 1961.

26. Gen William C. Westmoreland, *A Soldier Reports* (Garden City, N.Y.: Doubleday & Co., 1976), 110–11.

27. Momyer, 67.

28. Lyndon B. Johnson, *The Vantage Point* (New York: Popular Library, 1971), 55–58.

29. Momyer, 68.

30. Corona Harvest Report, "USAF Activities in Southeast Asia, 1954–1964," bk. 1, OAFH, 41.

31. Momyer, 73.

32. Futrell, 105–6.

33. Maj Douglas K. Evans, "Reinventing the FAC: Vietnam, 1962," *Air Force Magazine,* February 1980, 72.

34. Futrell, 106.

35. Ralph A. Rowley, *USAF FAC Operations in Southeast Asia, 1961–1965* (Washington, D.C.: OAFH, January 1972), 15, 18, 24–25; *History, 2d ADVON,* 97.

36. Evans, 74.

37. Director/Plans, US Air Force, memorandum to chief of staff, Air Force, 1 March 1962.

38. Rowley, 19.

39. End of Tour reports, Lt Cols M. M. Doyle and John P. Gilbert, February 1962–August 1963.

40. *History, 2d ADVON*, November 1961–October 1962.

41. Message, 2d ADVON to Thirteenth Air Force, 21 April 1962, and PACAF to CINCPAC, 8 May 1962.

42. Futrell, 143.

43. *History, 2d Air Division*, 1, 110.

44. MACV, Summary of Highlights, 8 February 1962–7 February 1963, 133–34, OAFH.

45. Quoted in message, PACAF to CSAF, 1 January 1963.

46. Message, CSAF to JCS, 8 February 1963, PACAF to CSAF, 20 February 1963, and 2d Air Division (AD) to PACAF, 18 February 1963; *History*, SAWC, January–June 1963, 166.

47. *History, 2d AD*, January–June 1964, VI, Doc 31; Message, 2d AD to Thirteenth Air Force, 15 November 1963.

48. *History, SAWC*, January–June 1963, II, Item 74, and July–December 1963, 119; *History of the Thirteenth Air Force*, January–June 1963 (Washington, D.C.: OAFH, 1963), 72.

49. *History, 2d AD*, January–July 1964, IV, 13–14; 2d AD, Regulation 55-5, 22 January 1963.

50. Futrell, 168.

51. Message, 2d AD to PACAF, 22 March 1963, 29 September 1963, and 5 October 1963, MACV to CINCPAC, 3 October 1963, PACAF to 2d AD, 30 October 1963, CINCPAC to CSAF, 15 March and 11 May 1963.

52. Message, 2d AD to PACAF, 10 January 1964, and III ASOC to 2d AD, 5 February 1964.

53. "Combat Operations, Nineteenth TASS, 31 December 1962," in *History, Thirteenth Air Force*, July–December 1963, III, Doc 80; Message, 2d AD to PACAF, 5 October 1963.

54. End of Tour reports, Lt Col David Mellish, 15 January 1964, and Maj John G. Schmitt Jr., 2 September 1963.

55. End of Tour report, Maj John G. Schmitt, 18 September 1963.

56. Message, MACV to JCS, 13 June 1964, and JCS to CINCPAC, 1 November 1963.

57. *Public Papers of the Presidents, Kennedy*, 1963, 846.

58. *History*, Director of Plans, USAF, July–December 1963, 65.

59. Marguerite Higgins, *Our Vietnam Nightmare* (New York: Harper & Row, 1965), 153–54.

60. *Book of Actions in SEA*, 1961–1964, Item VI-1.

61. Message, MACV to 2d AD, 27 March 1964, JCS to CINCPAC, 12 May 1964, MACV to 2d AD, 29 October 1964 and 20 November 1964.

62. Gen Bollen H. Anthis to Smart, letter, 25 November 1963.

63. Message, PACAF to CSAF, 9 November 1963; *History, PACAF*, January–June 1964, I, pt. 2, January 1964.

64. Message, 2d AD to PACAF, 10 January and 21 February 1964; History, 2d AD, January–June 1964, II, 28.

65. *History*, PACAF, January–June 1964, I, pt 2, January 64; message, 2d AD to Thirteenth Air Force, 23 January 1964.

66. Message, 2d AD to PACAF, 12 April 1964.

67. Message, 2d AD to Thirteenth Air Force, 2 March 1964, to CSAF, 15 April 1964, to PACAF, 20 April 1964, and PACAF to Thirteenth Air Force, 8 May 1964.

68. Message, 2d AD to PACAF, 4 June 1964; *History, PACAF*, January–June 1964, "Weekly Activity Report," 26 June–3 July 1964.

69. *History, PACAF*, January–June 1964, I, pt 2.

70. Futrell, 229.

71. *Book of Actions in SEA*, Item III-P; Message, JCS to CINCPAC, 5 August 1964; *History, TAC*, July–December 1964, IV, Doc 4; *History, 401st Tactical Fighter Wing* (TFW), July–December 1964 (Washington, D.C.: OAFH, 1965), 33–34. The Thai government approved the movement of additional USAF forces into Thailand but was reluctant to have combat sorties flown from the country. The Thais finally agreed to the latter if they were absolutely necessary and if their bases were not publicly revealed.

72. Message, MACV to CINCPAC, 11 August 1964, and CSAF to PACAF, 29 August 1964.

73. *History, PACAF*, July 1964–June 1965, III, October 1964.

74. Working Paper for Corona Harvest Report, "Out-Country Air Operations, Southeast Asia, 1 January 1965–31 March 1968," bk. 1, 16.

75. Momyer, 263.

76. End of Tour report, Lt Clare C. Eaton, undated.

77. William B. Graham and Amron H. Katz, *SIAT: The Single Integrated Attack Team, A Concept for Offensive Military Operations in South Vietnam* (Santa Monica, Calif.: RAND, 1964).

78. Futrell, 240.

THIS PAGE INTENTIONALLY LEFT BLANK

Chapter 7

Vietnam

Slow FAC Operations

With the enemy infiltrating throughout the country, the problem of minimizing civilian casualties was critical. Because there were no front lines, except for the 17th parallel which arbitrarily separated South Vietnam from North Vietnam, the enemy was apt to be anywhere—a distinguishing characteristic of this war in contrast with World War II and Korea. In those wars, once the aircraft passed the bomb line, aircrews could assume that anything moving was a legitimate target. In Vietnam, however, towns and villages were struck only when the enemy used them as supply points or for bivouacking troops. Civilians were not the target, of course, but civilian casualties were a collateral effect of attacks against the military targets.[1] In Vietnam, all villages and towns were in the combat zone. We had no way of telling whether there were enemy forces in the villages unless the villagers were willing to come forward and report them.

FACs Come of Age

To minimize attacks against civilians, forward air controllers became the fundamental means through which all strikes were controlled. With the deployment of the first Farm Gate detachment in 1961, the policy that strike aircraft would be under the control of a FAC became firm.[2] All Farm Gate aircraft were controlled by Vietnamese Air Force (VNAF) forward air controllers (FAC), but the shortage of VNAF pilots and the lack of trained FACs created an unsatisfactory condition.

As Farm Gate aircraft assumed more missions and as the demand for CAS increased, the need for US FACs became apparent. With the requirement to have a FAC control for all air strikes, an expanded force was needed and time was critical. The inability of VNAF to satisfactorily do the job resulted in the deployment of the USAF 19th Tactical Air

Support Squadron (TASS) in June 1963.[3] This unit had twenty-two L-19s and 44 pilots; its role from the outset was not only to control air strikes but to develop information about the enemy through daily visual reconnaissance.[4]

No target was attacked without obtaining permission of the Vietnamese province chief as well as US and Vietnamese military authorities at corps level. Assistance for the strike pilots was provided by the FAC—an Air Force pilot who flew low and slow in a Cessna O-1 Bird Dog to find targets. No target was attacked unless a FAC verified it as legitimate. The FAC guided the fighters into the target area, described the target or marked it with a smoke rocket, observed the strikes, and reported the results.

FACs represented a cross section of the Air Force's fighter pilot population. Most were captains. They were generally young, highly trained, and rated as combat-ready in a current fighter. They had three characteristics in common: (1) they all had an abundance of what Dr. Harold Brown, Secretary of the Air Force, described as "political sophistication"; (2) they were highly competent professional pilots with a thorough background in strike fighter tactics, ordnance, and ordnance-delivery techniques; and (3) they had an intense desire to do their job properly. All were keenly aware of their responsibility to determine which targets were bombed and which were not. Everyone had an intense desire to ensure that innocent people were not harmed.

The FAC corps spent much time in the air. One hundred hours per month was the maximum flying time officially allowed. Many reached this figure every month, and the pressure of combat pushed most over the limit at least once. A FAC flight usually lasted more than three hours, which was the endurance level of his Bird Dog.[5]

FAC Aircraft

It was difficult to find a suitable aircraft for the FAC. After Korea, no special FAC aircraft appeared because it was assumed that the FAC would be ground-based. Therefore, few airframe choices were available when the value of the airborne FAC became evident. The Army provided some L-19s (renamed the O-1) from its inventory in 1963, but the aircraft was not ideal for FAC operations: It did not have all types of radios; it was restricted at night, and in bad weather it was highly vulnerable in a hostile environment; it was underpowered; and it had poor capabilities for marking targets. Yet, despite these drawbacks, everyone seemed enamored of the O-1. Its endurance, easy maintenance, and ability to operate from primitive strips helped make the O-1 easy to operate and fun to fly. The replacement O-2A Super Skymaster brought some improvement, especially in better power performance, but it had about the same strengths and weaknesses as the O-1.[6]

The introduction of the O-2A did not significantly change basic FAC tactics, but it did increase his effectiveness through greater speed, more marking devices, and better night operations.[7]

The search for an aircraft to fill the FAC mission led inevitably to questions regarding the development of a specially designed FAC aircraft. This, in turn, touched on the related issue of arming the FACs. Experience in South Vietnam showed that many small enemy groups discovered by FACs disappeared between the sighting and the arrival of strike aircraft. One Air Force study found that 50 percent of all troops-in-contact incidents ended within 20 minutes and involved fewer than 10 enemy soldiers. Another study revealed that in one four-month period during 1970, 54 percent of fleeting targets detected by FACs at night were not struck because no firepower was available. But the question was raised: "What if the FACs were armed?"

As early as 1965, 2d Air Division rejected suggestions to arm FAC aircraft. Apparently, the deciding factor was the belief—influenced by experiences in World War II—that an armed FAC would be tempted to act like a fighter pilot instead of a FAC. In May 1968, however, USAF Headquarters directed Tactical Air Command (TAC) to test the concept of the armed FAC. These tests were linked to the theory of "phased response," which sought to give some measure of immediate CAS until strike aircraft could arrive.[8] Neither the O-1 nor the O-2A was deemed suitable for these tests, principally because of their vulnerability. TAC agreed to test the OV-10 Bronco. Upon careful consideration, including analysis of both the

O-2 "Skymaster"

tactical air command tests ("Combat Cover") and its own test ("Misty Bronco"), Seventh Air Force began using armed FACs flying OV-10s in June 1969.

One distinct advantage of the OV-10 was its maneuverability and evasive action capability when receiving ground fire. Though the O-1 could make tighter turns, it really only changed direction without making a great deal of progress over the ground. The OV-10 had a much greater climb capability and could maneuver evasively while gaining altitude.[9] It also had these advantages: two engines; better visibility; four rocket launchers; faster response because of higher speed (cruise, 180 knots; dive, 400 knots); and night/all-weather operations. The largest disadvantage was aircrew discomfort due to inadequate cockpit ventilation and the aircraft's greenhouse-like canopy.[10]

Equipped with two 7.62 mm machine guns and four rocket pods, the OV-10 offered limited but highly responsive firepower. During the "Misty Bronco" test period (4 April–13 June 1969), OV-10 pilots handled 78 of 98 requests for CAS by themselves in an average response time of seven minutes.

OV-10 "Bronco"

Some operational problems developed when the OV-10 was burdened with external fuel tanks in efforts to extend its range, but it performed the armed FAC role admirably in the permissive air environment of South Vietnam. Seventy-four percent of OV-10 responses came in five minutes or less.[11] In the words of one Air Force study, "arming the FAC increases overall tactical effectiveness."[12]

The OV-10's in-country operations consisted primarily of visual reconnaissance and CAS for US Army units. Secondary missions included radio relay, convoy escort, air-ground coordination, and artillery adjustment. The 19th TASS, located at Bien Hoa Air Base, received the majority of OV-10s. They were dispersed to the tactical air control parties (TACP) that supported 1st Infantry Division, 25th Infantry Division, 199th Light Infantry Brigade, and 1st Air Cavalry Division. The 20th TASS at Da Nang used its OV-10s to support the

America Division and 1st Brigade of the 5th Infantry Division (mechanized). Forward operating locations were located at Quang Tri, Chu Lai, and Pleiku.

Personnel Requirements

In January 1965, there were only 144 USAF pilot FACs in Southeast Asia. They were joined by 68 VNAF FACs,[13] but this number could not support the rapid buildup of American and free world forces. The FAC shortage caught the attention of Gen Earle G. Wheeler, chairman of the Joint Chiefs of Staff. Soon after his March 1965 visit to Vietnam, the JCS approved 134 additional USAF FAC authorizations and raised the TASS from one to four. In June 1965, the Air Force activated the 20th, 21st, and 22d TASSs. They were manned by September.[14] It also increased the FAC school's output, ordered into production the OV-10 counterinsurgency aircraft, and refined FAC tactics to meet the needs of the jungle-covered terrain of Vietnam.

A problem that emerged with the arrival of US Army troops in 1965 involved ground-based USAF FACs coming into South Vietnam while FACs supporting Army of the Republic of Vietnam (ARVN) units operated chiefly from the air. It took experiences like those faced in Operation Harvest Moon (a combined US Marine Corps [USMC]/ARVN operation in the Song Ly valley between 8 and 15 December 1965) to hasten the evolution to an almost exclusively airborne FAC role. Early in the week-long action, when a four-man USMC ground-air controller unit was unable to contact its air support center, USAF airborne FACs were called in to help direct air support strikes. After that, there were few preplanned ground-controlled air strikes.[15]

With the move to airborne FACs, the ground commander needed a pilot with experience to advise on the best use of air support. Consequently, air liaison officers (ALO) were assigned to advise ground commanders. Also, as a member of the TACP, the ALO acted as ground FAC when circumstances dictated.

The agreement for air-ground coordination signed by the Air Force and the Army in March and April had a direct impact on

FAC resources in Southeast Asia (SEA).[16] It specified that TACPs be assigned to Army units (battalion through field army level).[17] Unfortunately, the Air Force had not maintained a FAC force sufficient to fulfill this agreement. To do so would require a doubling of FAC levies.[18] By 31 December 1965, the Air Force had 224 FACs assigned to SEA and additional temporary duty FACs manning another 49 TACPs.

TAC furnished and trained the bulk of the FACs, and it supplied most of the fighter pilots for the Vietnam War. But with the increase in fighting, a pilot shortage emerged. An obvious solution was to train more pilots. However, it took almost three years to train a fighter-qualified pilot, give him one year of experience, and put him through FAC training. Relaxing the fighter-pilot qualification for FACs seemed the ready answer, but it was a step TAC was reluctant to take.[19]

To stretch its meager FAC resources, TAC deployed barely enough to permit one to each US Army battalion—a violation of the Air Force's agreement with the Army to furnish two.[20] The Army insisted that ATC furnish 90 FACs for the 45 battalions programmed to be in-country[21] by 30 April. In May 1966, Pacific Air Force (PACAF) reported to Headquarters USAF that five hundred FACs would be needed to fill all quotas under the Army/Air Force agreement.[22]

Setting a quota for FACs was one thing; filling it was quite another. A shade over half of the FACs authorized were in place by October 1966, with the Air Force hard-pressed to satisfy the remaining minimum needs. Despite the joint agreement, scarcity forced the pooling of FACs at brigade level. They then deployed to battalions when they were needed. Pooling had its advocates. An air liaison officer with the 3d Brigade, 9th Infantry Division, deemed pooling better than parceling out FACs piecemeal. He saw it as easing the shortage and giving the FAC force more flexibility.[23]

Seventh Air Force

As more US units moved into Vietnam, 2d Air Division expanded to become Seventh Air Force on 1 April 1966.[24] Three months later, Gen William W. Momyer replaced Lt Gen Joseph H. Moore as the unit's commander. At that time, and until the Tet offensive of 1968, all air operations within South Vietnam were flown by units based in South Vietnam or on carriers in the Gulf of Tonkin. Although Momyer had operational control of all USAF units in Thailand, he didn't employ them in South Vietnam until January 1968. Thai leaders were concerned about the international political implications of allowing US aircraft based in Thailand to provide CAS to ARVN divisions in South Vietnam. Seventh Air Force had authority to use Thailand-based units if the situation in South Vietnam became critical. Beginning with the Tet offensive, Seventh Air Force commanders used Thailand-based units as needed.

The command and control system facilitated the employment of airpower wherever it was needed. Seventh Air Force's aircraft in South Vietnam and Thailand were based throughout the theater; no target was ever more than a few minutes away from strike aircraft.[25] Additionally, KC-135 tankers made it feasible to use fighters from one end of the country to the other.

By early 1967, hundreds of thousands of troops were in-country. Seventh Air Force was well established by this time to support these US, ARVN, Korean, and Australian ground forces in all of the four corps areas. Centralized control of airpower was the only feasible means by which each of these ground forces could get air support when needed.[26]

504th Tactical Air Support Group

The 504th tactical air support group (TASG) was the parent organization for all FACs assigned to Southeast Asia. It received approximately 80 new FACs per month to replace those that rotated. A large, sprawling, and complex organization, the group was responsible for ground communication equipment, flying safety, standardization, personnel manning, and logistical support. By October 1968, the TASG had 2,971 personnel; 668 were FACs.

The 504th TASG had operational units at 70 locations. The group was involved in-country with seven direct air support centers (DASC). Assigned ALO/FACs worked with two field force headquarters, 10 Divisions, 34 Brigades, and 119

Battalions. In supporting the ARVN, ALO/FACs worked with four Corps Headquarters, 10 Divisions, 43 Provinces, and 63 Special Forces camps. Personnel of the 504th TASG also operated out-country.

The five TASSs within the 504th were located as follows: 19th TASS at Bien Hoa; 20th TASS at Da Nang; 21st TASS at Nha Trang; 22d TASS at Binh Thuy; and 23d TASS at Nakhon Phanom, Thailand. Essentially, the mission of these squadrons was to provide the TACPs with personnel and logistical support. The 504th TASG accounted for a third of the total combat time flown in Southeast Asia in 1967 and 1968. Their 325 aircraft (O-1, O-2, and OV-10) averaged 26,000 hours per month. In 1968, the Group averaged 29,000 flying hours per month.

Increased Manning Requirements

In October 1968, a survey team was sent from PACAF to Southeast Asia to determine FAC manning requirements. It examined both in- and out-country commitments, and determined that 835 FAC-qualified pilots were needed through February 1969. The team then decided that the requirement could be cut to 736 through better use of the 612 FACs on hand (as of November 1968).[27] Even so, there was still a shortage of 124 assigned FACs.

A bright spot in the survey team's report concerned the use of navigators as FACs. The 23d TASS received its first navigators in early 1967 and trained them in the OV-10. Navigators became most useful in base defense and in the strike control and reconnaissance (SCAR) of the out-country war. They performed visual reconnaissance, target-spotting, and navigation while the pilot flew the plane and controlled air strikes. Navigators in the FAC force enjoyed over 100 percent manning (45 functioning, 40 authorized). The PACAF team suggested that navigator assignments be upped to 69 so that FAC requirements could be pared to manageable levels.[28]

Two events abetted efforts to ease the FAC shortage—the November 1968 bombing halt and, later, the scaling down of American participation in the war. The 504th TASG[29] hoped for a fully manned FAC force by March 1969.[30] For one thing, the bombing halt applied solely to North Vietnam (only a small part of the total FAC force operated there). Moreover, the halt canceled few sorties. Air activity expanded in South Vietnam and Laos, creating a corresponding need for additional FACs. But the demand tapered off as some US ground troops prepared to leave SEA. In June 1969, the 504th TASG attained 84 percent manning with 660 of the 791 FACs authorized. This was well ahead of the 70 percent manning average over the past four years.[31] In August 1969, commander in chief, Pacific Air Force (CINCPACAF) forecast a need for 831 FACs through June 1970.[32] It decreased this to 761 in December as US troop withdrawal was accelerated. The 504th TASG then experienced 100 percent manning for the first time.[33]

Qualifications

The one year of fighter pilot experience required for FACs hindered FAC manning. Nevertheless, some advocates deemed the required experience desirable. The fighter-pilot FAC knew strike aircraft capabilities intimately, and he knew the effects of different types of ordnance on any given target. Hence, he was well-equipped for advising the Army ground commander. Others insisted that a FAC could do just as good a job without fighter experience. They suggested dropping or relaxing the fighter-pilot requirement in order to produce more FACs. Debate flourished from 1965 to 1970.

The supporters of fighter experience were adamant in their position. On 20 January 1967, Maj Gen Thomas G. Corbin, special air warfare center (SAWC) commander, informed Gen Gabriel P. Disosway, TAC commander, that assignment of inexperienced pilots to FAC duty could be detrimental and dangerous to the air war. He said it could lead to errors in judgment, needless casualties, and a loss in overall effectiveness.[34] Maj Lawrence L. Reed, a FAC with over 1,100 combat hours, thought nonfighter pilots required more training and more time to match the skill of experienced fighter pilots. Also, a nonfighter pilot could not speak with "complete authority based on personal experience" to those he advised.[35] The deputy director, direct air support centers

(DASC) Alpha, declared in December 1967, that a FAC without fighter experience could not be completely confident in counseling ground commanders. He warned that poor advice would erode the FAC's status and weaken the Air Force position on CAS.[36]

There were those who strongly believed "performance of nonfighter trained personnel . . . reportedly met the demands of the SEA operation and has been comparative to those with fighter qualifications."[37] In 1968, Maj Kenneth A. Kirkpatrick, chief of Air Operations for 504th TASG, said that fighter experience gave a FAC deeper insight into weapons effects and some techniques of aircraft control. Nevertheless, it was the pilot's personal qualifications that really counted; a FAC without fighter experience could become a competent and well-qualified controller in three months.

Other FACs sounded a like theme: a controller could spend years as a fighter pilot and be no more skilled in controlling aircraft than a nonfighter pilot. Fighter experience was helpful for the first month or two, after which it was no great advantage—more time spent in FAC aircraft would probably have been more beneficial. Fighter experience was a luxury requirement levied to give the Army more confidence in USAF CAS.[38] Additionally, evidence at Headquarters USAF disclosed no great performance difference between FACs with fighter backgrounds and those without.[39] Gen Albert P. Clark, TAC vice commander, believed that leadership qualities were, in the long run, more important than background. Competence, he said, could be acquired through time and experience.[40]

As early as October 1965, the Air Force recognized that something had to be done to shore up the FAC force. The major commands (PACAF, TAC, and USAFE) were tasked to consider relaxing the requirement for tactical fighter experience. The three commands hesitated to remove it entirely. PACAF did agree to use previously qualified fighter pilots as FACs until currently qualified ones arrived. On 12 October, after considering the commands' misgivings, Headquarters USAF waived the one year of operational experience requirement and approved assignment of combat crew training course graduates directly to FAC duty. The Air Staff assured TAC that FAC positions would be filled with experienced fighter pilots to the "maximum extent possible."[41] The waiver lifted the burden at first, but the swell of US ground forces in SEA during 1966 forced a search for more FACs.

During March 1966, a worldwide tactical fighter symposium developed workable criteria for assigning FACs to units according to their experience and training. The conferees believed that the waiver of the fighter experience qualification hinged on the type of duty performed. If, for example, the FAC acted as an air liaison officer, fighter experience would help him in advising ground commanders. The Army and Air Force wanted fighter-qualified FACs for American units because their main job was controlling strike aircraft near friendly ground troops. In contrast, USAF FACs with ARVN units spent much time on visual reconnaissance and liaison, little on controlling air strikes. Few VNAF air controllers had fighter backgrounds. The symposium suggested that the Air Force assign some nonfighter pilots to FAC duty with ARVN, VNAF, and in the out-country war. FACs performing SCAR and interdiction in the out-country war operated in areas of few friendly troops and civilians. Consequently, FACs without fighter experience could be used.[42]

Rules of Engagement

Before 1965, the rules of engagement (ROE) allowed VNAF observers/FACs to control air strikes while limiting the USAF FACs to advice only. These rules were later relaxed to keep pace with the expanding US troop commitment, but they still required the FAC/strike team to avoid injuring non-combatants.[43]

In 1966, a major revision in ROE specified that all targets selected for attack had to be approved by either the Vietnamese province chief or a higher authority. The single exception was in MACV-designated areas declared free of friendly forces and civilians. Control of USAF air strikes in support of US Army forces was confined to Air Force FACs except when no USAF FAC was available; a VNAF FAC could be used then. If no FACs were available, a ground commander or US pilot supporting the operation could designate targets.

Such tight restrictions on air strikes against known or suspected enemy targets in populous areas reflected the deep desire of US officials to protect noncombatant civilians and their property.

Similarly, the controller and the ground commander meshed their efforts to prevent accidental attacks on friendly forces. The FAC needed to know intimately the action occurring below and to secure the ground commander's permission before clearing strike aircraft onto the target. Ground troops marked their own positions as often as necessary for each flight of strike aircraft. The ground commander checked the FAC's target-marking. If he found it to be inaccurate, the target was marked again.

The ROE stipulated that a VNAF observer/FAC accompany the Air Force controller whenever USAF aircraft supported ARVN troops. The VNAF FAC could break off an air strike anytime the situation warranted. As a further safeguard, the FAC was required to keep either the target or the target-marker constantly in view. He was also to know at all times where the friendly troops were.

Locating the Enemy

The FAC's effectiveness lay in his ability to direct air strikes and inhibit enemy movement. But first, he had to find the enemy. To do this, the FAC needed to know the enemy's habits, how he traveled and subsisted, and how he employed tactics. Much of this information came from aerial reconnaissance, which accounted for up to 60 percent of a controller's flying time.

Gen William M. Westmoreland sensed a need for organized visual reconnaissance geared to the expanding war. On 2 June 1965, he directed that a program for repeated reconnaissance of all corps areas be established. Subsequently, each corps area was divided into sectors[44] that an O-1 could cover in two hours. Each corps commander worked with his air liaison officer to obtain daily reconnaissance of topographical features and problem areas. One O-1 operated in every sector, more than one in sectors requiring close coverage. Scanning the same sector day after day enabled the O-1 crew to detect anything different or unusual. The visual reconnaissance program operated jointly because no single service could muster sufficient O-1s to do the whole job. At the program's start, O-1s numbered 376: 152 Army, 110 Air Force, and 114 VNAF. However, Army O-1s were less available and not so widely dispersed as those of the Air Force because the Army used O-1s for battlefield reconnaissance and artillery adjustment. And since VNAF O-1s covered mainly the Saigon area, the brunt of visual reconnaissance responsibility fell to USAF FACs.[45]

The widely dispersed FACs were in excellent position to gather countrywide reconnaissance information. Notwithstanding, the shortage of O-1s and controllers ruled out complete coverage of South Vietnam. Some areas received little or no coverage while others received too much.[46] By 1968, however, the shortage of aircraft and controllers had been mostly overcome and single management of air support established. From then on, single-management visual reconnaissance coverage of South Vietnam was more balanced.[47]

Visual Reconnaissance Process

The best way to get an idea of the difficulties encountered in visual reconnaissance (VR), especially over a crowded rural area, was to go along on a mission. You might ask, "How can you possibly tell the Vietcong from the friendlies?" J. S. Butz Jr. had the best answer: "We can't. Look for yourself. It's just about like flying over Manhattan Island at one thousand feet and trying to pick out all the Italians."

A FAC gathered information in three ways. One was by discovering that people were shooting at him. (The FAC left open the two back windows of his O-1. At one thousand feet, he could hear shots fired from the ground; these were presumed to be unfriendly.) Another method was to spot evidence that the Vietcong were in the vicinity or had been there recently. A third method was to actually catch the Vietcong at work.[48]

South Vietnam challenged the FAC with topography ranging from unbroken jungle to plains, mountains, and cleared farmland. Once the jungle vegetation bloomed, the double-and triple-canopied foliage prevented the FAC from seeing the ground at all from fifteen hundred feet. He either had to dip lower, endangering himself and the aircraft, or concentrate on the open areas—and the Vietcong shunned open areas, preferring the jungle or the marshes of the delta.[49]

If the FAC gleaned the basics of reconnaissance in FAC school, he arrived at expertise through field experience. It took him at least a month to master VR techniques and learn his assigned sector thoroughly. Even then, he had to have a significant number of missions behind him before he could spot an object with the naked eye from fifteen hundred feet— unless the object moved.[50] To counter Vietcong infiltration, the controller needed to know when the villagers ate and slept, their work schedules and habits, how they traveled, and how many were in a given location. He, likewise, required information on the latest locations of friendly and enemy troops. Since he could not trust the maps completely, he memorized landmarks such as roads, trails, streams, villages, and structures.[51]

FAC operations varied widely in the four corps areas and in the various Army units. Some of the differences were dictated by the terrain or peculiar conditions of the locality. Others were due simply to the preference of the Army commanders. Many different flight techniques were used. In the pancake-flat delta, in the southern part of the country, most FACs stayed at twelve hundred feet or higher. They reasoned that if they got very low, they would offer too much target to the Vietcong.

In the rubber plantations and jungle terrain north of Saigon, the FACs often flew right on the treetops. Here, a man on the ground has only one chance to hit a FAC—and he must fire straight up. The chances of scoring a hit were slim.

In the mountainous country of the north, FACs usually traveled in pairs, one at three hundred feet and the other well over one thousand feet. FACs flying in the deep valleys could not be tracked by radar, and their radios often were ineffective. When a FAC was flying in one of those valleys, his only link with friendly forces—and his only chance for rescue—lay with the FACs flying above.[52]

Seventh Air Force set up priorities to satisfy needs. Top priority went to VR requests from ground commanders; these consumed a great deal of controller time. FACs spent any remaining time controlling air strikes or flying area reconnaissance. They covered vital coastal regions at least twice a day and other critical areas at least once. Noncritical areas got attention about every three days. Because the enemy liked to move at night, most reconnaissance took place at dawn or at dusk, when the FAC had a better chance of catching the enemy breaking/making camp or preparing a meal.

Once airborne, the FAC kept radio contact with both the TACP and ground units in the surveillance area. The controller usually started reconnaissance at the point of reported enemy activity and fanned out from there. He flew irregular patterns to keep the enemy from predicting his route. A complete sector search commonly consumed more than two hours. Maj John F. Campbell, 22d TASS, said a thorough search of his sector took from six to eight hours, with several O-1s being used.[53]

Flying below fifteen hundred feet improved sector coverage, but there were drawbacks—overall view was reduced and the chances of being shot down increased. Hence, FACs flew below fifteen hundred feet only when ground fire was unlikely or there was an emergency. To support troops in contact with the enemy, for example, they would fly at treetop level.[54]

The value of VR obviously depended on the controller's experience and the area surveyed. Targets were difficult to locate in the thick jungles of South Vietnam's central highlands, so the FAC's chief value was in harassment. The enemy, never knowing whether he had been seen, was forced to stay hidden—and hiding sapped his effectiveness. (In contrast, the controller could easily monitor enemy movements in the open areas of southern South Vietnam.)

Visual reconnaissance reports were filed quickly when the FACs landed. If the information was needed immediately, the controller radioed it in for a quick response. Oral reports excelled written ones; the FAC could broaden his account and clear up cloudy details.

Laboratory and field research invented new ways to locate the enemy, but none were completely successful. They included side-looking airborne radar (SLAR), infrared radar/optics, lasers, "people sniffers,"[55] and photography. Some FACs took along their own cameras as an aid. Despite film-processing delays, Seventh Air Force established a small, experimental, hand-camera program in April 1967.

From 1968 onward, an intensive VR effort forced the enemy to stop nearly all daytime movement. Even then, he seldom escaped the surveillance of Army patrols and special forces units. As enemy activity accelerated, the Air Force extended reconnaissance into the hours of darkness. The O-1 was of little value at night, except for harassment. On the other hand, combining the O-2A, OV-10, and FAC-carrying flareships produced excellent results. The total visual reconnaissance effort accounted for over 60 percent of all targets generated in South Vietnam.[56]

In-Country Operations, 1965–72

As airpower in Vietnam escalated dramatically in 1965, the Tactical Air Control System progressed to a highly workable operation. The introduction of jet aircraft, combined with the large influx of US forces, created a growing need for close air support. In-country strike sorties increased from 2,392 in January to 7,382 in June and to 13,274 in December 1965. By 1966, in-country strikes were averaging fifteen thousand sorties per month.

Quick reaction and responsiveness were the primary concerns of the USAF in 1966. Diverting aircraft already airborne to targets of higher priority was accomplished through a separate immediate air request network. The FAC played a key part in this procedure. The Air Force/Army Agreement of March–April 1965, with the provision that the Air Force provide vehicles, communications, and FACs, did much to facilitate the rapid reaction needed in CAS requests.

During the late 1960s, the Air Force FAC held one of the most hazardous jobs in Vietnam. He lived with the ground forces in far from ideal conditions, and he was required to represent the Air Force in a variety of situations. Professional competence, flexibility, and clear thinking were necessary talents. He was required to fly an aircraft that was marginal under combat conditions, downright dangerous in bad weather or at night.[57]

Because there was no forward edge of the battle area (FEBA), a very firm system of target identification and strike control was essential. The airborne FAC evolved as the most effective way to achieve this. Ground FACs were seriously restricted by the triple canopy of foliage prevalent in much of Vietnam. In late 1966, FACs became engaged in practically every type of ground operation. They operated in the central highlands, delta lowlands, below the demilitarized zone (DMZ), in the monsoon rainy season, and in special actions.

In addition to mounting attacks against the Americans, Vietcong troops had made impressive gains in the jungles of the II Corps area by 1965. On 19 February, General Westmoreland—invoking authority given him three weeks earlier to use jet aircraft under emergency conditions—sent 24 Air Force B-57s against the Vietcong Ninth Division's base camp deep in the jungles of Phuoc Long province along the Cambodian border. Two days later, an Army special forces team and a civilian irregular defense group (CIDG) company were caught in a communist ambush at the Mang Yang pass on Route 19. US helicopters moved in, supported by F-100 and B-57 strikes, and successfully evacuated 220 men who might otherwise have been lost.[58]

The events of February 1965 marked a turning point in the war. Washington officials no longer talked about withdrawing American military advisors; they now recommended deployment of additional US forces to Southeast Asia. A campaign of air strikes against North Vietnam was being readied, and major restrictions on air strikes in South Vietnam were lifted. On 6 March, Westmoreland received authorization to use US aircraft whenever the VNAF could not timely respond. In addition, the requirement that USAF planes carry Vietnamese crewmembers was dropped.

Vietnamese markings were removed from US aircraft in March 1965. Major US forces were brought in, and USAF airborne FACs were permitted to mark targets and direct strikes. Nevertheless, all air strikes still had to have at least the tacit approval of the Vietnamese government (through the Joint General Staff and the Tactical Operations Center in Saigon).

Three categories of FAC missions developed. One mission was to support forces from other countries (US, Korean, Australian, and Thai). A second was to either work with specific Vietnamese contacts (ARVN units and local officials) or to cover a certain geographical area. The third mission was to support out-of-country operations.[59]

As American ground forces increased, so did US airpower. In February 1965, Strategic Air Command (SAC) deployed two B-52 squadrons to Andersen Air Force Base, Guam, for possible use over South Vietnam. In April, the Air Force activated four O-1 squadrons in South Vietnam. The first US Marine F-4Bs arrived at Da Nang on 12 April and immediately began flying CAS missions. A number of Air Force tactical fighter and bomber squadrons also deployed to Vietnam on temporary duty (later made permanent). In October 1965, the first of five F-100 squadrons moved to Bien Hoa and Da Nang. They were followed in November by F-4C Phantoms of the 12th Tactical Fighter Wing (TFW) at Cam Ranh Bay and by experimental AC-47 gunships from Tan Son Nhut. By year's end, the Air Force had more than five hundred aircraft and 21,000 men at eight major bases in South Vietnam. The deployment of USAF, Navy, and Marine units to Southeast Asia in 1965 represented the greatest gathering of American airpower in one locality since the Korean War. More than 142,000 USAF combat sorties were flown and more than 56,000 tons of munitions were dropped on enemy targets. The joint USAF-VNAF effort accounted for an estimated fifteen thousand enemy dead and thousands of other casualties in 1965.

During 1966, American troop strength reached 385,000. The allies also were bolstered by the arrival of a second Korean infantry division and additional Australian and New Zealand forces. Air equipment arriving in South Vietnam included an F-5 squadron, two F-4 squadrons, and additional AC-47 gunships.

The only significant enemy success in 1966 occurred in March in the Ashau valley when a Special Forces camp was overrun. Located astride a section of the Ho Chi Minh trail two miles from the Laotian border and 60 miles southwest of Da Nang, the camp was defended by 219 Vietnamese irregulars and 149 Chinese Nung mercenaries assisted by 17 American Special Forces advisors. Before dawn on 9 March, an estimated two thousand North Vietnamese regulars opened an attack on the outpost. Due to poor weather, only 29 sorties were flown on the first day.

On 10 March, the North Vietnamese Army (NVA) launched repeated assaults against the camp under cover of a thick overcast which hid the tops of the surrounding hills and mountains. Almost miraculously, an A-1E pilot made his way into the valley through an opening in the cloud cover. Other aircraft followed him down and flew 210 strikes, temporarily slowing the enemy attack. According to one American survivor of the battle, tactical air crews tried to hold off the enemy by flying under such dangerous conditions that they "had no business being there." General Westmoreland later called the air support "one of the most courageous displays of airmanship in the history of aviation." The camp commander, Capt Tennis Carter, US Army, estimated that the A-1E pilots of the 1st Commando Squadron killed 500 enemy troops outside the camp walls.

During the day's action, Maj Bernard C. Fisher became the Air Force's first Medal of Honor recipient in Southeast Asia when he made a daring rescue of a downed fellow pilot, Maj D. Wayne Myers. Myers' badly damaged A-1E had crash-landed on the camp's chewed-up airstrip. Major Fisher made a quick decision to try to rescue Myers. Covered by his two wingmen, Fisher landed his A-1 on the debris-strewn runway, taxied its full length, spotted Myers at the edge of the strip, picked him up, and took off through a rain of enemy fire.

Of the 17 Americans involved in the confrontation, five were killed and the others wounded. Only 172 of the camp's 368 Vietnamese and Nung defenders survived the evacuation. The North Vietnamese suffered an estimated eight hundred deaths, most from air strikes.

The increasing effectiveness of airpower in 1966 was in large measure the result of improved tactics and weapons. Airborne FACs developed an effective system of VR. Assigned to specific geographic areas, they were able to identify changes in the landscape below that might indicate the enemy presence. Night reconnaissance was enhanced by several research and development programs and by refinement of existing instrumentation. The starlight scope, for example, amplified starlight and moonlight, enabling its operator to see movement on the ground. Infrared viewers were also used for night aerial reconnaissance. Munitions introduced included cluster bomb units (CBU), each of which contained several hundred bomblets, and a delayed-action bomb that could penetrate heavy tree cover. Another tactic of importance was the employment of AC-47 gunships for night hamlet defense. Their ability to remain aloft for many hours—and to respond quickly to calls for CAS—proved indispensable to hundreds of besieged posts, villages, and hamlets.

Communist military experts from China, Cuba, and North Korea visited South Vietnam in the spring of 1967 and concluded that time was no longer on Hanoi's side. North Vietnamese forces had not won a single major battle in almost two years. US firepower, especially tactical air, had decimated their main force's strength. Desertion was rampant and the Vietcong infrastructure was being destroyed. Against this background, Gen Vo Nguyen Giap and other North Vietnamese officials flew to Moscow. Subsequently, the Soviets sent more planes, high-altitude missiles, artillery, and infantry weapons. They also provided factories, means of transportation, petroleum products, iron and steel, nonferrous metal equipment, food, and fertilizer. The number of Soviet vessels reaching North Vietnamese ports rose from one hundred twenty two in 1966 to one hundred eighty five in 1967.[60]

Employing the FAC Force

Between 1965 and 1968, 65 to 70 percent of Seventh Air Force strength was employed on preplanned missions. The Army conducted search and destroy operations for which air support was planned in detail. Additionally, fighters were scheduled into areas at frequent intervals to handle targets of opportunity. These preplanned strikes provided air support for all aspects of the operation and ensured that airpower was available to handle those parts of the action in which artillery was insufficient.

The air effort not committed to preplanned missions was used for "immediate" or troops-in-contact (TIC) situations. All ground operations were designed to find the North Vietnamese and force an engagement in which allied superior firepower could be employed. After contact with the enemy had been established, allied ground forces would pull back a sufficient distance to allow artillery and airpower to be used without restraint. The Army would then attack with reaction forces, fighters would be diverted from preplanned missions, and aircraft being held on ground alert would be scrambled.

On a given day in South Vietnam, Seventh Air Force flew about three hundred preplanned sorties, the Marines in I Corps another two hundred, and the VNAF one hundred. The number of aircraft on ground alert varied according to the number of ground contacts expected throughout the country. On average, 40 aircraft were held on alert—and scrambled three or four times a day. In a typical day, day in and day out, 750 to 800 sorties were flown in support of ground forces. Because the tactical air control system spanned the country, all combat aircraft were under positive control.

When ground alert aircraft were launched, backup forces were brought to alert status to replace them. In a matter of minutes, a major air effort could be applied to any area. For missions already airborne and diverted, it took 15 to 20 minutes to get fighters into an area and in contact with the FAC. The time it took to put munitions on a target was determined by the speed with which the FAC could get clearance from the ground force commander. If the FAC had received prior clearance, it required only a matter of minutes to mark the target. To save time, the FAC briefed the fighter pilots while they were still some distance from the target. All that remained was for the fighters to visually acquire the target.[61]

Ground alert aircraft normally took 35 to 40 minutes to get bombs on the target.[62] (It took 40 minutes in the Korean War and about 45 minutes in World War II). When a faster reaction was needed, it was provided by either diverted aircraft or airborne alert aircraft.[63]

Despite complex procedures that involved many communication links, layers of coordination, and delivery of ordnance close to friendly forces, response times to requests for immediate assistance evolved to produce a general formula: 20/40. This guideline meant that "immediates" would be answered within 20 minutes (by airborne aircraft being diverted from lower-priority missions) or 40 minutes (by scrambling aircraft on the ground). By 1968, ground commanders had incorporated the 20/40 formula in their planning. As a follow-up to this process of classifying response times, a joint Army-Air Force study group in 1972 set the criteria that at least 50 percent of the requests for immediate air support should be answered within 15 minutes, 75 percent within 20 minutes, and 100 percent within 40 minutes.

A proficient FAC had to be "a politician, administrative officer, radio operator, and effective weapons controller."[64] The best FACs had four attributes in common: (1) knowledge of standard procedures; (2) an understanding of the capabilities and limitations of strike aircraft; (3) special techniques, such as briefing methods or marking targets; and (4) familiarity with the various types of ordnance.

Gunships: An Alternative To Quick Response

In seeking an alternative FAC aircraft, the Air Force turned to an unlikely source. Transport aircraft were modified as gunships for an unprecedented role of quick-reacting close air support. With longer and relatively less expensive loiter times, the gunships filled a gap in tactical air capabilities—especially at night.[65]

The AC-47, the first of the "new" gunships, arrived with the 4th Air Commando Squadron in late 1965. It carried its own flares and three mini-guns. Each could fire six thousand rounds per minute. The aircraft lived up to its call-sign (Spooky), and the performance of the mini-guns prompted its fire-breathing nickname, taken from a popular song, "Puff, the Magic Dragon." The mission of the AC-47s was almost exclusively for CAS at night. Within the first year of operation,

"Spooky" defended five hundred outposts. In one 90-day period (July-September 1966), AC-47s claimed to have spoiled 166 enemy night attacks.

Success with the AC-47 led to the development of the Gunboat (later Gunship II) program, which involved arming C-119s and C-130s. In using these larger, faster transports, the Air Force sought to overcome some of the weaknesses of the AC-47 (slow reaction time, poor cockpit visibility, and aircraft vulnerability).[66]

With their tremendous rate of firepower, the gunships proved effective in the CAS role, although their relatively slow airspeed and poor maneuverability rendered them unsuitable for some phases of close air support. When used at night or in bad weather to defend isolated outposts, the gunships played a key role. One Air Force study calculated a 24-minute average response time for gunships as compared with a 40-minute average for jet aircraft.[67]

Navy Participation

Although most of the Navy's tactical strike aircraft flew interdiction missions in North Vietnam, the Navy did participate in some CAS in the south. In fact Westmoreland, who had been impressed with the capabilities of carrier-based aircraft for close air support, requested that the Navy establish a carrier-based "Dixie" station similar to the "Yankee" station in the northern Gulf of Tonkin. By June 1965, the Dixie station (100 miles southeast of Cam Rahn Bay) and the Yankee station required five carriers each. After 1965, however, the number of Navy CAS sorties, most of which were either in the delta (IV Corps) or integrated with Marine ground operations in I Corps, steadily decreased. In December 1966, the Navy flew only three CAS missions (compared to 5,120 by the Air Force; 312 by the VNAF; and 265 by the Marine Corps). In December 1967, the totals were one by the Navy; 8,526 by the Air Force; 775 by the Marines; 326 by the VNAF; and 142 by the Royal Australian Air Force.[68]

The Battle of Khe Sanh

By 1968, more than 486,000 Americans—56,000 of them USAF personnel—were in South Vietnam. During this climactic year, the Air Force flew 840,117 combat sorties in support of allied ground forces. The OV-10A made its appearance, as did low-light television equipment and laser-guided bombs.

As the year 1967 closed, another unilateral cease-fire was declared by the United States; the North Vietnamese and Vietcong used the occasion to strengthen their positions. This time, however, the communists had several clear objectives designed to draw international attention to their ability to thwart American military power. The first move was to squeeze the US military base at Khe Sanh, a remote outpost off the Ho Chi Minh trail in the northwest corner of South Vietnam. The communists intended to repeat their decisive defeat of the French at Dien Bien Phu by concentrating their forces at Khe Sanh and strangling the base. Unlike the 1954 battle, however, the communists had to face an effective air resupply system and the combined firepower of land-based US Air Force units and carrier-based US Navy squadrons. The Johnson administration, determined that Khe Sanh would not fall, provided heavy support for the beleaguered troops and resumed raids on North Vietnam.[69]

Cargo carriers were in the minority around Khe Sanh. On a typical day, three hundred and fifty tactical fighters would hit enemy positions while sixty B-52s from Guam carried out carpet bombing missions. About 30 FACs would be working the strikes, marking targets and calling in specific aircraft. A dozen RF-4Cs would race low across the battlefield, cameras rolling. At night, AC-47 gunships used their batteries of mini-guns to shatter the enemy. They also served as night FACs and battlefield illuminators.

All incoming tactical aircraft reported to the airborne battle command and control center (a C-130 in orbit above the area) and were assigned to a specific FAC. The FAC brought in each individual strike; often, aircraft were stacked in holding patterns up to thirty-five thousand feet, waiting to drop their ordnance.[70]

During the 78-day siege, which began on 22 January 1968, six thousand Marines and South Vietnamese Rangers stood against an enemy force three times that number. By the time the siege was broken, tactical aircraft had flown almost twenty-five thousand sorties and expended more than ninety-five thousand tons of ordnance under the direction of nearly 1,600 FAC sorties. The Air Force contributed about 75 percent of that total in a joint effort with Marine and Navy aircraft. The after-action estimate of fifteen thousand enemy killed led one State Department official to describe Khe Sanh as "the first major ground action won entirely, or almost entirely, by airpower."[71] The Khe Sanh siege illustrates the effectiveness of close air support.[72]

Maj Gerald T. Dwyer flew his O-1 in support of the defense of Khe Sanh. Flying as Nail 55, he was on a combat mission over the extreme western end of the Ashau valley on 21 May 1968. Suddenly, a 37 mm projectile struck his aircraft and blew off one of the wings. As the aircraft began to tumble, Major Dwyer released the aircraft's entry door and dove out the open hole. He pulled the ripcord and was rewarded by the shock of an opening parachute. While in his descent, Dwyer received small arms fire from enemy troops on the ground. He landed without injury and discarded his parachute to begin evasion. Within minutes, he was being pursued by five heavily armed enemy soldiers. He made contact with search and rescue forces on his survival radio, but antiaircraft (AAA) fire was too intense for a helicopter pickup. Major Dwyer continued to evade through the jungle until he was instructed to ignite a smoke-flare in preparation for helicopter pickup. His pursuers attacked him with rifle fire, pistol fire, and hand grenades. He killed three of the attackers with his .38-caliber revolver and the remaining two were dispatched by an air strike. Dwyer was then rescued by helicopter. It was the second time in two months that he had been shot down.[73]

The Tet Offensive

As if to test America's commitment, the North Vietnamese launched their strongest offensive on the morning of 31 January 1968. During the cease-fire for Tet (the Buddhist new year) celebrations, Vietcong and North Vietnamese troops sneaked into Saigon and other key points for a series of well-orchestrated attacks on American and South Vietnamese installations.[74]

In simultaneous attacks throughout South Vietnam, they struck at 36 of 44 provincial capitals and hamlets. The initial fury of the attack enabled the attackers to seize temporary control of 10 provincial capitals. They succeeded in penetrating Saigon, Quang Tri City, Da Nang, Nha Trang, and Kontum City. However, except for Hue, which took several weeks of fighting to clear, the enemy troops were ousted in two or three days. Most of the 23 airfields that were attacked were soon back in full operation.

Outside the cities, USAF crews launched heavy attacks against communist forces. FACs remained aloft around the clock, directing strikes at enemy storage areas and troop areas, and providing CAS for allied units in contact with Vietcong and NVA forces.[75]

Cleared in Wet!

There was nothing a fighter-pilot-turned-FAC would rather do than catch a large Vietcong force in the open. But this rarely happened. Many a FAC served his year's tour in Vietnam without ever participating in a major battle. An average FAC might see clearly identifiable Vietcong troops only three or four times in a year. A typical FAC mission went like this.

"Peacock, this is Sabre 21. Are we cleared to FAC freq? Over."

"Roger, Sabre 21. Contact Cider 45 on 301.5. Your rendezvous—340, 25 miles off channel 107."

"Sabre 21 Flight—let's go 301.5."

"Sabre 22."

"Hello, Cider 45. This is Sabre 21."

"Sabre 21, this is Cider 45. Read you loud and clear. How me?"

"Cider, you're five square. Want our line-up?"

"Rog . . . ready to copy."

"Sabre 21 is a flight of two F-100s, mission number 2311. We're carrying eight 117 slicks, point oh-two-five, and 1,600 rounds of mike-mike."

"Rog, Sabre. I copy. Ready for target info?"

"Rog."

"OK, your target is a known VC location. We got some mortar fire out of here last night. Also, there is at least one .50 cal in the vicinity. I'm not being shot at now, but the FAC up here this morning took a hit. So you can expect auto weapons fire. Copy?"

"Rog. Sabre 21 copies."

"OK, the friendlies aren't too close to this target. There is a fire-support base about 700 meters southwest of the target. When you get below the clouds, you'll be able to see it on a bald hilltop. Target elevation is 2,700 feet. We've got a pretty stiff wind from the east, about 15 knots on the surface and at 2,000, and 20 knots at 5,000 and 7,000. Copy?"

"Rog. Do you have a preferred run-in heading?"

"Rog, Sabre . . . I don't want you to overfly friendlies. Make your runs from southeast to northwest, breaking right after your drop. That way, bomb smoke won't obscure the target on your run-in heading. Over."

"Rog, Cider 45 . . . I understand—friendlies 700 meters to our left as we attack from southeast to northwest . . . break right. I'm down below the clouds at the rendezvous point. Don't have you in sight. I think I have the fire-support base in sight. Over."

"Rog, Sabre . . . I'm about one k north of that and I see you. I'm at your three o'clock low. I'm rocking my wings. Over."

"This is Sabre 21. Have you in sight. We're ready to go to work."

"Stand by, Sabre. I'm getting final clearance from the Army on FM."

"Standing by."

"OK, Sabre. We're ready now. If you have me in sight, the target is just off my right wing. Call me when you want a mark."

"Rog, Cider. I'm turning base now—go ahead. Sabre Flight, set 'em up hot—arm, nose, and tail."

"Sabre 21, my smoke rocket is away. I'll hold to the south. I have you in sight. Do you see my smoke?"

"Rog. I have your mark. Am I cleared in wet?"

"You are cleared in wet. Hit ten meters to the right of my mark."

"Understand cleared in wet. I have you in sight. You want me to hit ten meters northeast of your mark. Two away. Sabre 21 is off right."

"Good hit, lead. Two, do you have lead's bomb?"

"Rog. I see it."

"OK, move yours up the hill 20 meters."

"Rog. Understand 20 meters at 12 o'clock."

"That's right. I have you in sight, on base. You are cleared in wet."

"Rog, Cider. I understand cleared in wet. I have you in sight to my left . . . Two away—off right."

"OK. Good hit . . . outstanding. Now, Sabre Flight, hold high and dry while I take a look."

"This is Sabre 21 . . . high and dry."

"Sabre 22, high and dry."

"Cider 45, this is Dusty 41. We're over rendezvous."

"Dusty 41, this is Cider 45. Stand by—I'm working another set of fighters. How much loiter time do you have?"

"Cider, this is Dusty. We're fat; we can wait quite a while."

"Good . . . I should be able to work you in shortly."

"Cider, this is Sabre . . . they're shooting at you. I see flashes right below you."

"Rog, Sabre. I hear 'em and I see it now. If you're ready, I'll plunk a mark in there and you guys can shake 'em up a little."

"Rog . . . mark."

"Marks away. Hit my smoke, Sabre!"

"Rog. Sabre 21 is out of position. If you're right, 22, go on in."

"Sabre 22, turning in. I have the smoke . . . I have the FAC."

"Rog, 22. I have you in sight. Cleared in wet."

"Cleared in wet. I can see the flashes just right of your mark."

"Rog. Go get 'em boy."

"One away . . . off right."

"OK, good; excellent! Lead, if you have two's bomb in sight, put yours right in the same place."

"OK . . . lead's turning final. Have you in sight."

"Outstanding hit, lead. That should get some results. Go high and dry and watch me. I'll go over the area again and see if I can draw more fire."

"Roger . . . have you in sight."

"Sabre, this is Cider. You really creamed them. Through the hole you blew in the trees, I can see the remains of a gun position, a beat-up quad .50, and one body. Let's put your last two bombs between this position and the original target. About half way. Want another mark?"

"This is Sabre 21. Yes, if you have enough rockets left to mark for the next flight."

"OK, Sabre. I'll save my rockets and drop a smoke can. Have you got me?"

"Rog . . . turning base. I see the smoke just starting to appear."

"OK, Sabre lead, put your last bomb 20 meters at 12 o'clock to the smoke . . . and two, put yours 20 at six. I have you, lead; you're clear in wet."

"Rog, cleared wet—20 at 12, that is, to the northwest . . . one away—off right."

"Right where I wanted it. Hey, lead, you got a big secondary with that one!"

"Cider, this is 22 turning in. Am I cleared?"

"Right, 22. Forget my last instruction. Put your bomb right in lead's smoke. Let's see if we can get another secondary."

"Rog. Am I cleared wet? Cider 45, this is Sabre 22, am I cleared wet?. . . Sabre 22 going through dry."

"Sabre 22 . . . Cider 45 here. Sorry about that, but the Army had me tied up on the other radio. Save your last bomb a minute. Go high and dry. They say they have spotted something. I'm going to drop another smoke can where I think they want your last bomb. I'll get confirmation from them before I clear you to drop. Do you copy?"

"Rog. I'll stand by. I'm high and dry."

"Sabre, my mark's away. Do you have it?"

"Rog."

"OK, stand by one . . . OK, that's near where they want it. Hit ten short—that's ten meters southeast. Copy?"

"Rog . . . 10 at six o'clock."

"Rog. I have you on base. You're cleared in wet."

"Understand, cleared wet. One away and off to the right."

"Beautiful, 22—you guys are really sharp today. That's all your hard stuff, isn't it?"

"Cider 45, this is Sabre 21 . . . right, we're clean of bombs. You want our 20 mike-mike?"

"No, Sabre. I've got Dusty standing by to come in. Check with Peacock on your way home. Somebody will be needing your guns. I'm going in to get your BDA now."

"Rog. You're covered, Cider."

"Sabre 21, Cider 45."

"Go ahead, Cider. Ready to copy."

"OK, Sabre. Your target coordinates were Yankee Alpha 360 080. Your rendezvous time was 10, you were on target from 15 to 33. You put 100 percent of your bombs on target. Really outstanding bombing—all within 10 meters. Target coverage was 60 percent due to its large area. On the first bomb, I can see nothing but smoke and foliage. However, with the other bombs, I'll give you one gun position destroyed, one automatic weapon destroyed, and one KBA confirmed. I'll add two more KBA estimated. And, oh yes, one large secondary explosion and secondary fire with black smoke. Copy?"

"Rog."

"You guys really did a job. The Army commander down here has been into my ear on the other radio. I think you did a lot more damage than I can see and give you credit for. The Army's going into the area today. I'll pass on any extra BDA they come up with."

"Thanks a lot, Cider 45. We'll appreciate that. It was a pleasure working with you. If you're clear of the target area, we'll leave your freq."

"Sabre 21. Let's go channel 5."

"Sabre 22."

"Dusty 41, this is Cider 45. I'm ready to copy your line-up."

And so it went for FACs providing close air support.[76]

Notes

1. William W. Momyer, *Airpower in Three Wars* (Washington, D.C.: Office of Air Force History [OAFH], January 1978), 266.
2. Corona Harvest, "USAF Activities," 2–19, 2–20.
3. Ibid., vol. 2, bk. 2, 6–34.
4. Momyer, 267.
5. J. S. Butz Jr., "Forward Air Controllers in Vietnam—They Call the Shots," *Air Force and Space Digest*, May 1966, 60–62.
6. *USAF FAC Operations in Southeast Asia, 6–7, 51–52* (Washington, D.C.: OAFH, January 1972), 6–7, 51–52; *The Air Force in Southeast Asia: Tactics and Techniques of Close Air Support, 1961–1973* (Washington, D.C.: OAFH, February 1976), 102–7.
7. Maj Richard M. Atchison, "The Slow Mover FAC Over the Ho Chi Minh Trail: 1965–1972," Headquarters PACAF, Working Paper, CHECO Project, 3 February 1975, 11.
8. *The Air Force in Southeast Asia: Tactics and Techniques of CAS*, 120–31. The concept of phased response was first suggested in Nov 1966 by the joint Army-Air Force Tactical Air Support Analysis Team. This study also reported that 24 percent of troops-in-contact incidents lasted longer than 20 minutes but still involved small enemy contingents. Strike aircraft arrived in time to attack these targets but often wasted firepower in the "overkill" of small enemy groups. Only 23 percent of troops-in-contract incidents were rated as "large." This study indicated that many FACs were jerry-rigging grenade launchers and machine guns to their wing struts. Capt Donald R. Hawley created the "Hawley Cocktail" by placing live grenades in peanut butter jars and throwing them out his aircraft window.
9. Maj James B. Overton, Seventh Air Force, interviewed by Maj John T. Sutphen, Introductory Evaluation Team (Combat Bronco), 19th TASS, 504th TASG, undated.
10. Ibid., *FAC Operations in Close Air Support Role in South Vietnam*, Headquarters PACAF, Project CHECO report, 31 January 1969, 22–23.
11. "Summary of Misty Bronco Operations, April–June, 1969," 30–31, OAFH.
12. Walter Andrews, "OV-10s 5-Minute Response," *Armed Forces Journal*, 6 September 1969, 15.
13. *History of the Second Air Division* (2d AD), July–December 1964, III (Washington, D.C.: OAFH), 27–28.
14. *History of Military Assistance Command-Vietnam*, 1965 (Washington, D.C.: OAFH), 46–48; Headquarters USAF draft report, "Effective SEAsia Tactics (TACS)," 1969, 3–1. Including the 19th TASS, the squadrons were at these locations in South Vietnam: Bien Hoa (19th), Da Nang (20th), Pleiku (21st), and Binh Thuy (22d). In September 1966, the 21st TASS moved from Pleiku to Nha Trang.
15. Overton interview, 31–32; Kenneth Sams, *Operation Harvest Moon* (Headquarters PACAF, Project CHECO, 3 March 1966); TAC/TAWC report

"Forward Air Control Operations in Southeast Asia," 1 January 1965–31 March 1968, and 10 November 1969, III, 5e.

16. Team Report, "Requirements for ALO/FAC/SCAR/Navigators and Aircraft in SEA," PACAF, 22 November 1968, 3 (hereinafter referred to as SEA FAC.

17. Under the agreement, the TACP at battalion level consisted of one ALO, one FAC, vehicles, and communications personnel and equipment. The TACP at brigade, division, and, if required, corps and field army level, comprised one or more ALOs, vehicles, and communications personnel and equipment. (Hereinafter, the term *FAC* will denote a "FAC," "ALO," or "strike control and reconnaissance (SCAR)" pilot. The semantic problem of "FAC" versus "SCAR" is well documented in Maj A. W. Thompson, "Strike Control and Reconnaissance (SCAR) in SEA," Headquarters PACAF, Project CHECO, 22 January 1969).

18. "Effective SEAsia Tactics," 1–65.

19. *History, TAC,* January–December 1965, I, 329–30.

20. "Effective SEAsia Tactics," 3–1.

21. "In-country" is that part of the Southeast Asian conflict within South Vietnam; "out-country" that part outside of South Vietnam, i.e., Laos and North Vietnam.

22. *History, PACAF,* January–December 1966, 397–98.

23. Overton interview, 32–33; SEA FAC Requirements, 3.

24. George S. Eckhardt, *Command and Control, 1950–69* (Washington, D.C.: Department of the Army, 1974), 64.

25. William W. Momyer, *The Vietnamese Air Force, 1951–1975: An Analysis of Its Role in Combat,* USAF Southeast Asia Monograph Series, vol 3, monograph 4 (Washington, D.C.: US Government Printing Office [GPO], 1977), 33.

26. Ibid., 274.

27. SEA FAC Requirements, 15; talking paper, Deputy Director Director/Strike Forces, Director/Operations, subject: FAC and Strike Control and Reconnaissance (SCAR) Working Group, 18 August 1969.

28. SEA FAC Requirements, 5; Thompson, SCAR in SEA (Headquarters PACAF, Project CHECO, 22 January 1969), 75–76.

29. Activated in December 1966, the 504th TASG provided administrative, maintenance, and supply support for the FAC program.

30. *History, 504th TASG,* July–September 1968, I, 7–8.

31. Officer Manning Analysis for June 1969–December 1970, , AFMPC; Message , 504th TASG to Seventh Air Force, 301414Z June 1969, subject: ALO/FAC and Aircraft Status Report as of 27 June 1969; *History, 504th TASG,* April–June 1969, 11.

32. Message , CINCPACAF to Seventh Air Force, 131943Z, August 1969, subject: FAC/ALO Requirements.

33. *History, 504th TASG,* July–September 1969, I, 12, October–December 1969, I, 10.

34. Maj Gen Thomas G. Corbin, SAWC commander, to Gen Gabriel P. Disosway, TAC commander, letter, subject: Quality of FAC Trainees, 20 January 1967.

35. Maj Charles O. Lescher Jr., "Forward Air Controller Selection Criteria and Vietnam Tour Length," thesis (Maxwell AFB, Ala.: Air Command and Staff College), June 1968, 35.

36. Thompson, 18.

37. Quoted in *History, TAC*, January–December 1965, I, 332.

38. Thompson, 18–21. It was mentioned at an ALO/FAC training conference that one reason for the fighter-experience requirement was to keep the Army out of the airborne FAC program since the requirement did not make that much difference after a FAC gained experience. PACAF ALO/FAC Training Conference Report, 3 September 1968), atch. 2, 2–3.

39. William G. Greene, operations analyst, to Maj George Partridge, Air-Ground Control Branch Director of Operations, letter, subject: Comments on Working Copy of the Draft Report by the FAC and SCAR Working Group, 4 August 1969.

40. *Visual Reconnaissance (VR) in SEA, 1 January 1962–31 March 1968* (Washington, D.C.: OAFH), 76–77.

41. *History, TAC*, January–December 1965, I, 332–33.

42. William G. Greene to Maj George Partridge, letter, subject: Comments on working copy of draft report by the FAC and SCAR Working Group, 4 August 1969.

43. Maj John Schlight, "Rules of Engagement: Continuing Report, 1 January 1966–1 November 1969," Headquarters PACAF, Project CHECO, 31 August 1969, 37–40.

44. Thompson, 60–62. From 214 sectors at the program's start, the number rose to 225. Sector size ranged from as big as a province (open terrain) to only a few square miles (densely populated or jungle areas).

45. Working paper 66/11, "Seventh Air Force, An Evaluation of the Visual Reconnaissance Program in South Vietnam," 20 September 1966, 5–12, OAFH; J. I. Edelman et al., *Airborne Visual Reconnaissance in South Vietnam* RAND Report RM-5049-ARPA (Santa Monica, Calif.: RAND, 1966), 2–4; Thompson, 65–66.

46. Only 65 percent of VR sectors were covered daily. J. I. Edelman et al., *Airborne Visual Reconnaissance in South Vietnam* , RAND Report RM-5049-ARPA (Santa Monica, Calif.: RAND, 1966), 2–4.

47. Lt Edward P. Brynn, "Reconnaissance in SEAsia, July 1966–June 1969," Headquarters PACAF, Project CHECO, 15 July 1969, 27–28.

48. Butz, 62–63.

49. Maj Louis Seig, "Impact of Geography on Air Operations in SEA," Headquarters PACAF, Project CHECO, 11 June 1970, xi, 11–14, 29–30.

50. A former FAC said a man could stand motionless under a tree in full view of the aircraft and go unseen.

VIETNAM: SLOW FAC OPERATIONS

51. Working Paper 66/11, Seventh Air Force, 20 September 1966, 5–12; Lt Col George I. Wilkins, "The FAC Factor in South Vietnam," thesis (Maxwell AFB, Ala.: Air War College), November 1970.

52. Butz, 66.

53. 504th TASG Manual 55-3 "Forward Air Control Tactics," 1 March 1970, 2-1, 2-2.

54. Maj John F. Campbell, 22d TASS ALO/FAC, interviewed by Ralph Rowley, 4 January 1972. Major Campbell was an ALO/FAC with ARVN in Kien Phong Province, IV Corps, during 1969.

55. The "people sniffer" (airborne personnel detector [APD]) detected human waste by processing air samples chemically.

56. "VR in SEA," 1 January 1962–31 March 1968, 9.

57. Overton, November 1968, 5–7.

58. Ralph A. Rowley, "The In-Country Air War, 1965–1972," in Carl Berger, ed., *The United States Air Force in Southeast Asia, 1961–73* (Washington, D.C.: OAFH, 1977), 33.

59. John J. Sbergo, "Southeast Asia," in Benjamin Cooling, ed., *Case Studies in the Development of Close Air Support* (Washington, D.C.: OAFH, 1990), 435–36.

60. Rowley, 44.

61. Momyer, 278.

62. *Command and Control*, bk. 2, p. 2 (Washington, D.C.: OAFH), 4–20.

63. Momyer, 278.

64. United States Air Force, *Evolution of Command and Control Doctrine for Close Air Support* (Washington, D.C.: OAFH, March 1973), 53.

65. Sbergo, 436.

66. Jack S. Ballard, *The Development and Employment of Fixed-Wing Gunships* (Washington, D.C.: OAFH, 1982), 23, 55. This study quoted from the Seventh Air Force operations order on the primary purpose of the AC-47: "To respond with flares and firepower in support of hamlets under night attack, supplement strike aircraft in the defense of friendly forces, and provide long endurance escort for convoys".

67. O. D. Cunningham Jr., "Close Air Support Aircraft," Special Study, M-41780-68 (Maxwell AFB, Ala.: Air Command and Staff College), 1–2.

68. Keith R. Tidman, *The Operations Evaluation Group* (Annapolis, Md.: Naval Institute Press, 1984), 272. These figures were for actual "close air support" sorties. The Department of Defense kept records for "attack" sorties, which were defined as including "strike, armed recce, flak suppression, interdiction, close air support, and direct air support sorties."

69. Anthony Robinson, *Aerial Warfare: An Illustrated History* (New York: Galahad Books, 1982), 286.

70. David A. Anderton, *The History of the US Air Force* (New York: Crescent Books, 1981), 188–89.

71. Air Force Policy letter for commanders, Supp., 9 September 1973, OAFH, 23.

72. Ronald Brown, USAF course outline, Maxwell AFB, Ala., Air War College, 40.

73. Atchison, 12.

74. Robinson, 286.

75. Rowley, 52–56.

76. F. D. Henderson, "Cleared in Wet!", *Air Force Magazine*, August 1968, 38–40. For those not familiar with the terms, the following explanations are offered. "Peacock" is the call sign of a Combat Reporting Center (CRC) in South Vietnam, which controls all tactical aircraft in its area. Peacock's instructions pertain to a tactical air navigation (TACAN) fix, on a compass heading of 340 degrees from the CRC at a distance of 25 miles. "Sabre 21" is the call sign of the flight leader, or "lead" with Sabre 22, his wing man, being second, or "two," in the flight. (A four-plane flight would be made up of lead, two, three, and four.) "Cider 45" is the call sign of the FAC, who must mark all ground targets and approve each specific bomb or strafing gun. A "wet" run is one in which weapons may be fired. If no clearance is obtained from the FAC, the pilot must make his run "dry." The term *117 slicks, point oh-two-five* refers to the M-117 general-purpose 750-pound bomb with low-drag fins, fuzed to detonate .025 seconds after impact. "Mike-mike" is phonetic for mm, or millimeter. The F-100 Supersabres on this mission carry four 20 mm cannon, each loaded (in this instance) with 400 rounds. To avoid excessive radio interference, Army units normally employ FM equipment while Air Force aircraft use VHF and UHF radio. The FAC plane is equipped with all three types.

Chapter 8

Expanding Missions

During the peak years of the Vietnam War (1965–70), the controller's responsibilities steadily expanded. Night operations, for example, triggered a search for new ways to find, mark, and strike targets. It eventually spawned the starlight scope, lasers, new flare techniques, and a tighter FAC-gunship relationship. Mounting enemy aggressiveness sparked an upturn of both in-country and out-country interdiction.

Night Operations

The step-up in enemy night activity in 1965 stimulated development of new tactics and equipment. Night air operations were difficult under the best conditions but decidedly worse in bad weather and over jungle/mountainous terrain. Darkness held other drawbacks; for example, vertigo and spatial disorientation of crew members, difficult and dangerous rendezvous between FAC aircraft and fighters, and difficulty in marking targets accurately enough to separate friendly from enemy troops.

Marking

The enemy took advantage of the FAC's difficulty in identifying friendly positions at night, but ingenuity came to the rescue. During an Ia Drang valley operation in 1965, one FAC suggested that the ground commander fill empty 105 mm howitzer casings with sand-soaked JP-4 (jet fuel). Then, when the enemy attacked, these improvised torches would be put at the four corners of the perimeter and lit. The ground commander said, "Gee, then they'll know where we are." The controller replied, "When they hit you they [already] know where you are. Give us a chance to find out where you are, too." The torches were an excellent reference, enabling fighters to drop ordnance as close as 50 yards from the perimeter. A like method had 50-gallon drums cut in half and filled with jellied gasoline mixed with sand. Trip-flares were attached so the enemy would trigger them and light up the drum torches. The ensuing fires enabled fighters to drop napalm and FACs to give strike corrections. Also, US Army troops adopted the Vietnamese trick of pointing flaming arrows toward enemy positions.

Frequently, a ground commander lacked the means and/or time to mark his perimeter with torches. Under such circumstances, air support was available only under a full moon and a cloudless sky. Starting in 1965, however, flareships overcame this drawback. Dropping flares commonly deterred the enemy from attacking or caused him to break off an ongoing attack.

Marking targets under flarelight was difficult, however. The 2.75-inch white phosphorous (WP [willie-pete]) marker rocket—a mainstay for daytime FAC operations—worked poorly at night, especially against moving targets. The rocket's smoke lasted only two or three minutes and easily drifted away from the target. The controller could not divert his attention for even an instant, or he would miss the rocket's short impact flash and have to mark again. The ideal marker would have been a long-burning, high-intensity flare, fired as a rocket and capable of illuminating a target even in bad weather—but no such marker existed.[1]

For night target-marking, the Air Force introduced ground marker logs. Although an excellent reference for directing air strikes, the markers at times could not be seen in mountainous or heavily forested areas. Moreover, the enemy created confusion by setting ground fires of his own. The FAC countered with brighter, longer-burning, red/green logs.[2]

The M-151 WP rocket came into service in 1968. Although superior to the 2.75-inch rocket, the M-151 had a short burn-time and was hard to see from the air.[3] Air Force testing for an improved marker rocket continued through 1970, but with marginal success.

Starlight Scope

Flarelight alerted the enemy, curbed his movement, and canceled surprise. To sidestep these shortcomings, the Air

Force experimented with various infrared sensing devices, low-light-level television (LLLTV), and other light-intensifying instruments. The US Army had developed several items for night detection. Of these, the Air Force selected the starlight scope for testing in 1965. Using the starlight scope at night, the FAC could see objects invisible to the naked eye; for example, people moving, canals, tree lines, buildings, roads, trucks, and sampans. However, this capability vanished when clouds obscured the moon and stars.[4]

Initial testing of the starlight scope utilized the O-1 Bird Dog. The O-1's small rear cockpit, however, cramped the scope operator and restricted coverage. Since the operator held the scope in his hands, aircraft vibration caused additional problems. Further, distortion caused by the cockpit window affected the scope picture.[5] Despite these snags, however, controllers found the starlight scope helpful for night visual reconnaissance.

The O-2A Super Skymaster began flying combat missions in 1967. Evaluation of the aircraft, which extended until the spring of 1968, included finding the right starlight scope. The Air Force's new Eyeglass, an early front-runner, gave a superb view under bright moonlight/starlight. From up to four thousand feet altitude, the scope detected truck and boat traffic; from up to one thousand feet, it picked out people.[6]

Equipped with a smaller version of the Eyeglass scope, the OV-10 Bronco was no match for the Super Skymaster at night. From 29 October to 15 December 1969, the 23d TASS at Nakhon Phanom tested a modified starlight scope fitted with a binocular viewer and mounted in the Bronco's camera port. Although the test turned out well, the required high-cost modifications prompted the Air Force to put Pave Spot in the OV-10s instead.[7]

Interdiction in South Vietnam

In 1965, the Air Force launched interdiction operations against the complex of lacing roads, rivers, trails, and passes known as the Ho Chi Minh trail. The bulk of the air strikes took place out-country, but some hammered enemy supply routes in central South Vietnam. Throughout the 1960s,

Vietcong and North Vietnamese Army forces received supplies over roads that sliced across the Cambodian and Laotian borders.[8]

Seventh Air Force sustained the interdiction campaign throughout 1969 and 1970, but could not neatly coordinate the in-and out-country operations. Even so, interdiction achieved considerable success. While the enemy's movements were not entirely checked, he was kept off balance. This allowed the South Vietnamese forces to shake off the shock of the Tet offensive and stride toward Vietnamization.[9]

Rocket Watch

By 1965, North Vietnamese were concentrating on hit-and-run attacks against outposts, airbases, and urban centers.[10] The attackers favored mortars and rocket launchers, since both could be easily assembled and dismantled. The guerrillas could be packed and gone before being located. Due to dense foliage and darkness, finding these attack teams from the ground was impossible. Airbases like Da Nang proved particularly vulnerable because they lacked covered revetments to protect the parked planes. On 15 July 1967, the enemy rained rockets on that base from as far away as seven miles. The assault killed eight Air Force personnel and caused $1.5 million damage to 43 USAF and Marine Corps aircraft. These hit-and-run mortar/rocket attacks peaked just before the Tet offensive of 30 January 1968. To weed out enemy rocket sites around Da Nang, MACV organized a night watch in February 1968. During the first week, FACs found and directed air strikes or ground sweeps against 32 rocket positions. Around-the-clock rocket watch of Saigon began in March 1968.[11]

Combat Skyspot

Rains, low-hanging cloud cover, and the Vietcong's exploitation of darkness hindered the Air Force's harassment, interdiction, and CAS operations. On clear nights, or when cloud cover was not a factor, flareships, in conjunction with fighters or gunships, could harass and interdict the enemy or provide CAS. Even with ceilings below five hundred feet, FACs could, at times, drop below the clouds and maintain visual contact with the ground. Fighter pilots, flying five times as fast and with one-fourth the maneuverability, had a definite problem with low ceilings and poor visibility. Dive bombing was limited and shallow dive angles did not offer satisfactory results.

Strategic Air Command (SAC) was using a ground-based radar/computer system called Radar Bomb Scoring (designated MSQ-77), which predicted the exact point of impact of a bomb drop. Tests conducted in 1965 used F-100s to deliver live ordnance. Factors such as altitude, wind speed, aircraft speed, temperature, and ordnance characteristics were introduced into the computer. The pilot was given heading, altitude, and airspeed instructions, and was told when to release his ordnance.

Six Combat Skyspot sites were established in Southeast Asia—five in Vietnam and one in Thailand. The system was deployed to Bien Hoa, Pleiku, Dong Ha, Dalat, Binh Thuy, and Nakhon Phanom, Thailand. All sites were operational by the spring of 1967.[12] Under radar control from these locations, Combat Skyspot was used by fighters and bombers during adverse weather or at night. Additional uses of the system included harassment and interdiction of enemy forces and lines of communication, support of special forces, support of rescue and resupply operations, and the plotting of newly discovered targets and directing strikes against them.[13]

To understand the rhythm of the war's course in Vietnam, one must be familiar with the ebb and flow of the annual dry and wet monsoons. The dry monsoon extends from mid-October to mid-May while the rainy season runs from mid-May to mid-October in most of Indochina, but there are variations to this pattern in the northern part of South Vietnam—Military Regions I and II, in particular. High mountains shield the coastal plains from the rains brought by the wet monsoon. These provinces get most of their annual rain during the dry monsoon in the form of a persistent drizzle accompanied by treacherous fog. During these conditions, overland movement was slow and flying was hazardous, even by helicopter.

Nevertheless, the dry monsoon generally meant favorable weather for offensive operations. During the wet monsoon, the North Vietnamese would send troop reinforcements, war materiel, and supplies down the Ho Chi Minh trail to their base areas just north of the demilitarized zone (DMZ) and in Laos and Cambodia. US and South Vietnamese forces attacked enemy troops before they reentered South Vietnam.

Air Operations in Laos

Out-country FAC operations received far less publicity than those in South Vietnam. Even so, Air Force FACs were widely used in Laos along the Ho Chi Minh trail and to some extent for support of Laotian ground troops. They also saw service over North Vietnam, mostly in its southern panhandle near the DMZ.

The steady flow of North Vietnamese troops over the Ho Chi Minh trail into South Vietnam spurred the US government to secure Laotian Prince Souvanna Phouma's approval for USAF reconnaissance flights over Laos. These operations, started in 1964, revealed a continuing enemy buildup. The Royal Laotian Government (RLG) then authorized interdiction programs in both northern and southern Laos. The first of these Air Force strike operations (Barrel Roll) took place on 14 December 1964.[14]

FAC operations in Laos began as the result of a massive enemy attack on the Plei Me special forces camp in the Central Highlands of South Vietnam. The attack, begun on 19 October 1965, lasted ten days. Allied forces flew 696 day and night strike sorties that resulted in 326 known killed and an estimated seven hundred more dead and carried away. A Military Assistance Command-Vietnam (MACV) study team was formed in November to determine the best way to intensify the interdiction effort in Laos. From this study came the Tiger Hound Task Force, which began operations in December 1965. The Task Force was charged with conducting a Laotian interdiction campaign using a combination of airborne FACs and tactical strike aircraft.[15]

This mission of controlling air strikes in Laos carried with it a tremendous responsibility. Political considerations required that rules of engagement be more carefully applied here than in South Vietnam. For instance, napalm could not be expended in Laos unless authorized by the US Embassy in Vientiane. Night attacks on fixed targets were not authorized. Bombing was prohibited except as specifically approved by the Embassy. Flights under FAC control would not expend ordnance if the target was in doubt, if instructions were in question, or if the flight leader so directed. Campfires and civilian structures could not be attacked, and FACs and strike aircraft had to be under the positive control of a ground radar.[16]

On 10 March 1967, Seventh Air Force designated the A-1E, A-26, T-28, C-47, C-123, and C-130A as substitute FAC aircraft for operations outside South Vietnam. Specific guidelines governed their use. T-28s and A-1Es, for example, flew in pairs and acted as FACs for one another. If they flew singly, both crewmen needed to be FAC-qualified before directing their own strikes. The A-26 was allowed to furnish its own controller support if a navigator was in the crew (a FAC flew with the A-26.)[17]

Slow movers could generally work in poorer weather conditions, and they had longer loiter times; fast-mover FACs could range farther afield, react faster, and operate in more hostile environments. Each type had a place in the scheme of the air war. In March 1965, the air activity over the Kingdom of Laos was divided into two separately commanded programs: (1) interdiction of the Ho Chi Minh trail, code-named Steel Tiger; and (2) CAS and interdiction in support of Laotian ground forces, mostly in the northern part of Laos, code-named Barrel Roll.[18]

Interdiction along the Ho Chi Minh Trail

When one looks at a map of Central and Southern Laos, there is a tendency to associate the neatly drawn routes with the two-lane paved or gravel roads found in the rural United States. For the binocular-equipped FAC in his small aircraft, nothing could be further from the truth. Several of the routes had been built by the French. These roads were surfaced with hard-packed gravel and, in some cases, asphalt or concrete.

But the majority of the infiltration route structure was strictly single-lane (in rare cases, two-lane) dirt roads which had been hacked out of the dense jungle. There was no neatly groomed shoulder adjacent to the routes and, in many cases, the trees were so thick and tall that you had to be directly over the road to see it. In several areas of Laos, the road just disappeared into the thick, triple-canopy jungle.

Because of the extensive number of route segments available to the enemy and the fleeting nature of the targets, a "choke point" concept of operations was recommended by the FACs in 1966. The "Choke Point" concept involved FAC-directed air strikes designed to crater and make impassable certain vulnerable route segments. These segments were located in narrow valleys with very steep sides, along the steep sides of cliffs, and at fords of streams and rivers. As long as these choke points were under constant observation both day and night, the concept was effective. But the North Vietnamese, feeling the effects, began to apply countermeasures.

The North Vietnamese deployed increasing numbers of AAA weapons along the route structure. In addition, they increased their use of camouflage to conceal supplies and make fords. But their most effective tactic was to move their supplies at night.[19]

The bulk of air strike control during daylight hours over Laos fell to FACs carrying the call signs of Nail, Covey, and Raven. The Nail FACs were from the 23d TASS at Nakhon Phanom, Thailand; the Coveys from the 20th TASS at Da Nang; and the Raven FACs, designated Detachment 1 of the 56th Special Operations Wing, at Udorn but actually dispersed at several sites throughout Laos. The Nails and Coveys flew O-2s after 1967; the Ravens continued to fly O-1s.[20]

The first Steel Tiger strikes—initiated a month after the start of Rolling Thunder—were directed against enemy personnel and supplies moving into the Laotian panhandle or into South Vietnam through the DMZ. Steel Tiger's mission complemented Rolling Thunder. In both campaigns, political considerations were dominant and air strikes were limited in scope. The United States' primary concern was to avoid involving Communist China and the Soviet Union in the war while maintaining the "neutral" status of Laos.[21]

Air Force and Navy strikes concentrated on cutting roads and bombing "choke points" along routes leading from the Mu Gia and Nape passes, two principal entry points from North Vietnam into Laos. They also attacked trucks, bridges, troops, and storage areas. The Air Force averaged nine to ten sorties per day. By mid-1965, despite poor weather, Air Force and Navy pilots were flying more than one thousand Steel Tiger sorties per month—but not without incident, as demonstrated by the experience of one unnamed FAC.

This particular FAC flew the OV-10, a rigid-wing aircraft that has very little padding and no "cushion effect." These factors combined to produce a painful posterior after a typical four-hour mission. Many OV-10 crews used an unauthorized rubber "donut" inflated just enough to absorb the vibration. This FAC was on his first operational mission, which was usually accompanied by a doubling of the respiratory rate and a firm intention of not going to the hottest spot in your assigned sector just to practice AAA evasive maneuvers.

As the FAC was building his confidence, a flight of Navy A-7 aircraft checked in on his radio frequency. Their task was to strike a ford at the "Dog's Head" in Ban Kari Pass. The Dog's Head was not only the hot spot of the new FAC's sector—it was the hottest area in Steel Tiger. The FAC began weaving his way toward Ban Kari at an altitude previously thought unattainable in a fully loaded OV-10. The lead A-7 pilot described the ground fire they were receiving: "FAC, I've never seen it so bad. This is my third cruise over here and I've never seen flak as thick as this. Man, you ought to see the stuff coming up from the ground."

The FAC's respiratory rate tripled and a cold sweat beaded on his forehead. He arrived over the target and informed his Navy companions that since the ford was visible, "there will only be one marking pass." He then rolled his aircraft and dived toward the target. As he stabilized to fire a marking rocket, the Navy leader began calling out, "FAC, you're getting hosed! It's all around you!"

The FAC fired his rocket and began a "maximum G" pull-off while jabbing at the rudder pedals to randomly change attitude and direction. There was a tremendous explosion just as the "G" forces began to affect his vision. The cockpit filled with smoke and he knew he had been hit. But the aircraft was still controllable and the FAC headed for an isolated area adjacent to the pass.

Another FAC from the bordering sector joined him and inspected the aircraft for damage. There was no exterior damage and no indication of engine malfunction. The "wounded" FAC then found the "hit." He had pulled so many "Gs" coming off the rocket pass that the rubber donut had exploded under the weight of his body. The resultant white cloud of talcum powder and the abrupt change in seating height, coupled with the observations of the Navy strike pilot, logically added up to battle damage. A sheepish but much wiser FAC returned to base to face inquiries about what it was like to take a "near miss" from an exploding large-caliber projectile.[22]

Tiger Hound

As the southwest monsoon subsided in late 1965, the communists stepped up their infiltration. As a result, American and Laotian authorities agreed to concentrate airpower on a segment of the Ho Chi Minh trail most contiguous to South Vietnam. Air Force Col John F. Groom drew up the plans for the new air campaign. Nicknamed Tiger Hound, it began in December 1965. Tiger Hound required more resources than the Air Force had employed in Laos up to that time. An airborne battlefield command and control system (ABCCC) was established. C-47s were used initially, but were replaced later by C-130s. Air Force O-1s and A-1Es, along with Royal Laotian Air Force (RLAF) T-28s, served as FAC aircraft. RF-101s and newly arrived RF-4Cs, equipped with the latest infrared and side-looking radars, also were employed for target detection. UC-123 spray aircraft defoliated jungle growth along roads and trails to improve visibility. The principal strike aircraft were B-57s, F-100s, F-105s, and AC-47 gunships. Substantial Marine, Navy, and Army air forces were also involved in the operation.

Cricket

In January 1966, the Air Force launched another campaign in Laos. Called "Cricket," it involved the use of O-1 and A-1E aircraft, based at Nakhon Phanom Royal Thai Air Force Base (RTAFB) near the Laotian border. The O-1s and A-1Es would fly visual reconnaissance or serve as FACs in the northern Steel Tiger and southern Barrel Roll sectors. In the Barrel Roll area, the primary mission was to support friendly ground units; in Steel Tiger, it was armed reconnaissance. Air Force aircraft ranged outward 300 nautical miles from Nakhon Phanom, concentrating on roads south of Mu Gia pass. Laotian observers flew with some of the FACs to validate targets before F-100s, F-105s, and AC-47s were allowed to strike. The FAC pilots worked with both ground liaison officers and road reconnaissance teams to pinpoint targets inside Laos. Although Cricket was a minor operation, it proved quite effective in destroying or damaging enemy trucks and supplies.

To maintain an umbrella of airpower over the Ho Chi Minh trail, USAF commanders tried new tactics and new aircraft with special equipment. They also inaugurated the practice of having FAC pilots fly over "target boxes" in the same geographic area daily. This procedure enabled the FACs to become familiar with the terrain and aided them in detecting enemy positions. The use of additional ground reconnaissance teams led to the discovery of numerous concealed targets.

The most effective "truck killers" were the AC-119 and AC-130 gunships, the B-57, a few C-123s equipped with special detection devices, and the A-26. Carrying flares and detection devices, these aircraft flew mostly at night when truck travel was heaviest. They also served as FACs, calling in fighters for additional strikes. Other aircraft with a FAC capability included Air Force A-1Es, Navy P-1s, and Laotian T-28s. In 1967, O-2s began replacing O-1s and the Air Force introduced the larger OV-10 aircraft in 1968. Nighttime detection capability was enhanced by the Starlight Scope. During the last two months of 1967, an important advance was made in the ability to detect enemy movement. This was a rudimentary, air-supported electronic antiinfiltration system comprised of "strings" of seismic and acoustic sensors dropped from aircraft. These devices, planted along a number of infiltration roads and trails, picked up the sounds of enemy vehicular traffic. The information was transmitted to a high-flying EC-121, which retransmitted it to an infiltration surveillance center at Nakhon Phanom. The antiinfiltration detection system had a succession of nicknames, Igloo White being best known and most enduring.[23]

Commando Hunt

On 31 March 1968, President Johnson ordered an end to all bombing of North Vietnam above the 19th parallel In November 1968, on the basis of an "understanding" reached with Hanoi, Johnson ended all attacks on North Vietnam. As a result, enemy infiltration down the Ho Chi Minh trail became heavier than ever and Air Force, Navy, and Marine Corps forces launched a new air campaign called Commando Hunt Its major objectives were to destroy supplies being moved down the trail, to tie enemy troops down, and to further test the sensor system's effectiveness. Initial operations were confined roughly to a 1,700-square-mile sector of Laos. The Air Force employed an array of FAC, strike, and reconnaissance aircraft, B-52s, C-130 ABCCCs, and AC-47 and AC-130 gunships. The gunships proved especially valuable in interdicting enemy truck traffic. As the pace of the aerial assault quickened, the number of tactical sorties rose from 4,700 in October to 12,800 in November and 15,100 in December 1968.

Commando Hunt II began in May 1969, coinciding with the beginning of the annual southwest monsoon and the usual reduction in enemy movement over southern Laos. American pilots continued to harass or hamper the efforts of the communists to repair roads and trails washed out by floods. Within North Vietnam, the enemy assembled more manpower, trucks, and watercraft, and stockpiled supplies near the Laotian border. The next infiltration surge through Laos would begin after the monsoon abated. Commando Hunt III, launched as the dry season began in November 1969, witnessed more intense air operations against an expanded southward flow of enemy troops and supplies.

During the annual May to October monsoon in 1971, Commando Hunt operations diminished and the North Vietnamese maintained an above normal level of activity in southern Laos. By late 1971, about 344 antiaircraft guns and thousands of smaller automatic weapons defended vital points along the trail. With the outset of the dry season in late 1971, the communist threat again was formidable. To counter it, the Air Force launched Commando Hunt VII and extended it beyond the Steel Tiger area of southern Laos. However, there were fewer US aircraft available for Laos because of competing requirements in both Cambodia and North Vietnam, where "protective reaction" strikes had been resumed, and because there were budget cutbacks and withdrawals of US air and ground units. When Commando Hunt VII operations were completed at the end of March 1972, US tactical aircraft had flown 31,500 sorties.[24]

Air Operations in Barrel Roll

The northern operations known as Barrel Roll primarily supported friendly government ground forces—the Royal Laotian Army and neutralist troops to be sure, but especially the army of Maj Gen Vang Pao (five thousand CIA-trained tribesmen of the Meo, a mountain people living in Laos).

In the advisory years, the Air Force had deployed Detachment 6, First Air Commando Wing, to Udorn, Thailand. Two of its major objectives were to establish a T-28 flight checkout program for Laotian pilots and to assist with aircraft maintenance. Forty-one airmen with four aircraft began operations at Udorn in April 1964. As support of friendly ground operations increased, Air Force personnel were assigned to work as ground controllers or forward air guides in Laos because few Laotians could speak English and none were familiar with directing air strikes. In early 1965, Detachment 6 began training English-speaking Lao and Meo personnel to direct air strikes from the ground; USAF airmen withdrew from this role.

In addition, the Air Force assigned FACs to Royal Laotian Army units and Vang Pao's forces in an effort to overcome the language barrier between them and the strike aircraft crews. Operating under the designation of Raven, these FACs flew O-1s, U-17s, and T-28s on six-month tours of duty. As necessary, the Air Force deployed a C-47 airborne battlefield command and control center to the area.[25]

The White House felt that Vietnamization was proceeding too slowly and that the South Vietnamese Army would not bridge the gap left by the US troop withdrawals. Airpower bridged that gap, adding another political dimension to the B-52. It became one of the cornerstones of US policy in Indochina, buying time for Vietnamization and Richard M. Nixon. Like Vang Pao, the White House put inordinate faith in airpower.

On 21 February 1973, less than a month after North Vietnam and the United States signed a cease-fire agreement, the Laotians followed suit and bombing operations in Laos were promptly halted. Laos bombing was renewed only two days later, however, at the request of the Vientiane government; the North Vietnamese had already committed cease-fire violations. On 23 February, B-52s launched an attack against enemy positions near Paksong on the Bolovens Plateau. A subsequent cease-fire infringement brought the Stratofortresses back for a strike south of the Plain of Jars in April. With this strike, nine years of USAF operations in Laos came to an end.

The Ravens

Pilots in the "other war" (support for Laotian military operations) were military men who flew into battle in civilian clothes—denim cutoffs, T-shirts, cowboy hats, and dark glasses. They fought with the discarded obsolete aircraft of an earlier era, and they suffered the highest casualty rate of the Indochinese War—as high as 50 percent. Every man had a price on his head—and every man was protected by his own personal bodyguard. Each pilot was obliged to carry a small pill of lethal shellfish toxin, especially created by the CIA, which he had sworn to take if he ever fell into the hands of the enemy. Their job was to fly as the winged artillery of warlord Vang Pao who led an army of mercenaries in the pay of the CIA. They operated out of a secret city hidden in the mountains near the Red Chinese border.

Raven was the call-sign that identified these fliers of America's "Secret War" in Laos, and no name was more fitting. In the early days, when the program was haphazard, a standard form of recruitment was for a Raven to approach a like-minded colleague still in Vietnam. Things became more structured later, but the type of individuals recruited never altered. They were always men who enjoyed a maximum of flying and a minimum of administration—and they tended to be the very best pilots.

Vang Pao provided men, known as Backseaters or Robins, who advised the Ravens on terrain and identified friendly versus enemy areas for them. The Backseaters/Robins were the only targeting authority the Ravens had to consult in northern Laos. (All other Laos targets had to be cleared by American Amb William Sullivan.)[26]

The initial US advisors in Laos assisted the Royal Laotian Air Force (RLAF).[27] Air Force FACs entered the picture in 1964 to aid CAS for the Laotian Army. In 1965, they began training indigenous Laotians as FACs. They occasionally "flew right seat" in Air America aircraft, helping the RLAF strike pilots find and hit enemy targets.[28]

The control of airpower in Laos evolved on a trial-and-error basis. In the early days of the war, it was managed by a half-dozen sheep-dipped,[29] nonrated Air Commandos who flew with Air America pilots in Pilatus Porters. They marked targets by dropping smoke canisters out of the window. Often, they talked fighters onto the target by describing the scenery: "Drop your bombs two hundred yards north of that gnarled tree."[30]

The Ravens were created in 1966 with rated Air Force officers who had at least six months' experience in Vietnam. They suffered growing pains during 1967 and early 1968. There were never enough men or aircraft to manage the ever-increasing use of US air. (There had been only four Ravens for all of Laos until 1966; by 1968, there were only six.

This number slowly grew, but there were never more than 22 Ravens at any one time.)[31]

Early Raven operations flew directly in the face of Air Force doctrine and Gen William W. Momyer, who wanted an all-jet Air Force and was committed to employing state-of-the-art aircraft in Vietnam. There had been an acrimonious interagency debate over whether propeller or jet planes should be used in Vietnam, with the Air Force arguing that jets were better for close air support than slower, prop-driven aircraft. USAF knew this was nonsense but did not want to end up, after what was expected to be a short guerrilla-type war, with an inventory of prop planes. Taking the long view, the Air Force wanted jets to match the Russians; it fought for their use in the Vietnam War.[32]

Sullivan had different ideas for Laos and set about cobbling together a force of propeller aircraft. His earlier job in Washington had given him easy access to Robert S. McNamara, whom he persuaded to initiate Farm Gate. "The gang that tumbled into Nakhon Phanom was a pretty wild bunch," Sullivan remembered fondly. This odd mixture of men and machinery grew to become an entire wing, officially designated as the 56th Air Commando Wing; unofficially, it was called Sullivan's Air Force.[33]

A Raven team normally operated from a forward operating base. While the airman stayed on the ground to handle communications for the Laotian troop commander, the FAC either borrowed an O-1 or flew with an Air America pilot. A Laotian commonly went along to interpret the controller's conversations with the ground commander and the strike pilots.

Air Force colonels who interviewed new pilots for the Raven program had no clear idea of what the mission involved—and much of the data is still guarded today. A large number of the documents and oral histories that relate to the activities of the Ravens will remain classified until after the year 2000.[34]

USAF Controllers in Cambodia

Even though USAF controllers monitored incursions of Operation Daniel Boone reconnaissance teams into Cambodia, they seldom crossed the boundary themselves. An exception occurred in April 1970 when the United States and South Vietnam mounted a campaign into Cambodia against North Vietnamese positions. Seventh Air Force firmed up CAS plans on 27 April. Assigned to South Vietnamese ground units, the FACs adhered to normal rules of engagement. They operated in both aircraft and radio jeeps. The 19th TASS backed up operations in southern Cambodia; 20th TASS in the northeast; 22d TASS in the eastern portion; and 23d TASS in the northwest.[35]

To safeguard the lives and property of noncombatants on this operation, FACs controlled all air strikes. In addition, a special task force (with an ALO and a TACP attached) helped coordinate air support. An O-2A FAC (call-sign Head Beagle) flew out of Di An, climbed to eight thousand feet, and circled south just inside the South Vietnam border. Head Beagle took fighter handoffs from the DASC and passed them on to other controllers. He harmonized all CAS in Cambodia, shifting strikes quickly to points needing them most, and CAS was exceptional throughout the campaign.[36]

Route Packages

USAF and Navy participation in Rolling Thunder was coordinated through "route packages." Elements of Seventh Air Force operated from bases in South Vietnam while Task Force 77 chose a point in the Gulf of Tonkin code-named Yankee Station. Usually, at least two aircraft carriers supported operations over North Vietnam while a single carrier supported operations in the south.

President Johnson reserved the right to select targets and launch times in the north, and American forces were continually given limited objectives. As a result, operational effectiveness was impaired.

Route Package I, assigned to Seventh Air Force, covered an area from the DMZ to just above the 18th parallel Since MACV had initially considered this area an extension of the ground battle zone, operations there were directed by MACV.

Task Force 77 controlled Route Package II, an area from the 18th parallel to just below the 19th parallel, and from the coast to the Laotian border. The most significant target in Package II was the Vinh area and the logistical activities surrounding it. Coastal shipping and traffic were also major target systems. However, all of the major passes leading from North Vietnam into southern Laos were on the southern edge of Route Package I; none were in Route Package II.

The Navy also controlled Route Package III, which was the largest area but which had less significant targets. Barthelemy Pass, however, was a major target because most of the supplies supporting the Pathet Lao and North Vietnamese forces in the Plain of Jars came through that area. Seventh Air Force covered this pass and most of the movements leading into it; the Navy covered the eastern end of the area.

Route Package IV, an active area, was assigned to the Navy. Few of IV's targets were restricted. The most important targets were the rail and road networks and the bridge at Thanh Hoa In addition, Nam Dinh was a major railyard and marshaling area for logistics. Enemy fighters used Bai Thuong, the only all-weather airfield in the area, as a staging field.

The Air Force was responsible for Route Package V, which was twice the size of any other area. It contained most of the railroads in the northwest and the lines-of-communication (LOCs) supporting North Vietnamese forces in northern Laos. Package V was bounded on the east by a line along 150'30" longitude, on the west by the Laotian border, on the north by the Chinese border, and on the south by an imaginary extension of the northeast rail line until it intersected the Laotian border.

By far the most important of all route packages was Route Package VI. Most of the targets were in this area, and enemy defenses there were the strongest. Package VI was divided between the Air Force and the Navy along the northeast rail line. Using the railroad as a dividing line gave the least chance for error if pilots from either Seventh Air Force or TF-77 should stray and be assumed hostile. The package was bounded on the west by 150'30" longitude and on the south by a line just south of Nam Dinh.

Almost all missions into Route Packages V, VIA, and VIB required extensive planning to minimize exposure to probably the most heavily defended area on earth and to achieve a high degree of coordination among support forces. The more complex the defenses, the greater the need for planning.[37]

Strike aircraft taking off from bases in Thailand and from carriers would routinely check in with the ABCCC. The ABCCC could either reaffirm their targets or assign new ones. At the same time, the ABCCC would notify high-speed FACs that strike aircraft would report to their control. From that point, the mission resembled any other FAC-controlled strike.

Dividing North Vietnam into route packages compartmentalized airpower and reduced its capabilities. As expressed by Arthur William Tedder in World War II, "Air warfare cannot be separated into little packets; it knows no boundaries on land or sea other than those imposed by the radius of action of the aircraft; it is a unity and demands unity of command."[38]

Air Strikes on North Vietnam

On 1 November 1968, President Johnson ordered a halt to all bombing north of the DMZ—but a divided American electorate did not reelect him. A few days after the election, President-elect Nixon announced plans to reduce American troop involvement in Vietnam. Nixon kept his promise to implement the plan; by the end of 1969, sixty-nine thousand American troops were out of Vietnam. However, Nixon also responded to renewed Vietcong attacks on Saigon by ordering B-52s to bomb their sanctuaries in Cambodia.

Meanwhile, American airpower was called on to make selective strikes at North Vietnamese targets in response to attacks on unarmed reconnaissance aircraft. In February 1971, stepped-up strikes were launched against SAM sites and their support units. By August, petroleum storage areas were on the target list. In September, a major raid was directed against Dong Hoi (north of the DMZ). The NVAF was ready for the challenge, however: Its older MiG-17 fighters were augmented by newer MiG-19 and MiG-21 interceptors. The North Vietnamese Air Force (NVAF) fighter pilots grew bolder and became more successful in attacking American aircraft, which were still operating under restrictions against pursuing MiGs back to their bases. That restriction was lifted in November 1971.[39]

Notes

1. Lt Col Philip R. Harrison, "Impact of Darkness and Weather on Air Operations in SEA," Headquarters PACAF, Project CHECO, 10 March 1969, 37. These fire arrows could be made of many materials. Metal gas cans filled with gasoline-soaked sand were often used. When ignited, they were easy to see at night.

2. *History of Tactical Air Command (TAC)*, January–June 1966, I, (Washington, D.C.: Office of Air Force History [OAFH]), 276.

3. 504th TASG Manual 55-3, 1 March 1970, 14-2, 14-3.

4. *History of the 504th Tactical Air Support Group (TASG)*, July–September 1970, I (Washington, D.C.: OAFH), 29; 504th TASG Manual 55-3, 1 March 1970, 14-4.

5. Capt Dorrell T. Hanks Jr., "Riverline Operations in the Delta, May 1968–June 1969," Headquarters PACAF, Project CHECO, 31 August 1969, 38.

6. "Operational Test and Evaluation Stabilized Night Observation Device (Eyeglass)," TAC-TR- 67-109, TAC/SAWC, Eglin AFB, Florida, undated.

7. Tactical Air Command, TR-67-274, "OV-10 Category III Test and Evaluation," L-1, L-2. A night observation device with boresighted laser target designator (LTD). The LTD used a laser to direct a light beam onto the target so the proper sensors could track, or "home," on the reflected energy.

8. C. William Thorndale, "Interdiction in Route Package One, 1968, 17–18, Headquarters PACAF, Project CHECO.

9. Kenneth Sams et al., "The Air War in Vietnam, 1968–1969," 35–36, Headquarters PACAF, Project CHECO; Thorndale, 117–19.

10. John F. Kennedy Center for Special Warfare, "The Vietcong," Office of ACS/G-2, USA, 2d rev., November 1965, chap. IV.

11. *History, 504th TASG*, July–September 1968, I, Doc. 6; C. Thorndale, "Defense of Da Nang," Headquarters PACAF, Project CHECO, 31 August 1969, 13–14.

12. Operation plan (OPLAN), Seventh AF, operation order (OPORD), "Combat Sky Spot," 439–67, 10 March 1967.

13. Maj Richard A. Durkee, "Combat Sky Spot," Hickam AFB, Hawaii, Headquarters PACAF, Project CHECO, 9 August 1967, 7.

14. Senate Subcommittee on United States Security Agreements and Commitments Abroad, Testimony of Amb William H. Sullivan, 28 October 1969, in Hearings before the, 91st Cong., 1st sess., *Kingdom of Laos*, pt. 2, 20–22, 367–71, 376–77, 476. Hereinafter cited as Sullivan Testimony.

15. Maj Richard M. Atchison, "The Slow Mover FAC Over the Ho Chi Minh Trail, 1965–1972," Working Papers, 3 February 1975, 4–5, OAFH.

16. Warren A. Trest "Control of Air Strikes in SEA, 1961–66," Headquarters PACAF, Project CHECO, 1 March 1967, 62.

17. Message, Seventh Air Force to Chief, Joint US Military Assistance Group, Thailand (CHJUSMAGTHAI), USAF Command Post, 100840Z March 1967, subject: FAC Aircraft and Crew Requirements.

18. *The Senator Gravel Edition, The Pentagon Papers,* vol. III (Boston: Beacon Press, 1971), 279.

19. Atchison, 8–9.

20. Melvin F. Porter, "Control of Air Strikes–January 1967–December 1968," Headquarters PACAF, Project CHECO, 30 June 1969, 23.

21. Jacob Van Staaveren, "Interdiction in the Laotian Panhandle," in Carl Berger, ed., *The United States Air Force in Southeast Asia, 1961–1973: An Illustrated Account* (Washington, D.C.: OAFH, 977), 101.

22. Atchison, 33–35.

23. Van Staaveren, 104–9.

24. Jscob Van Staaveren, in Gene Gurney, ed., *Vietnam, The War in the Air, A Pictorial History of the US Forces in the Vietnam War—Air Force, Army, Navy and Marines* (New York: Crown Publishers, Inc., 1985), 218–26.

25. Carl Berger, *The United States Air Force in Southeast Asia: An Illustrated Account, 1961–1973* (Washington, D.C.: Office of Air Force History), 121.

26. Christopher Robbins, *The Ravens: The Men Who Flew in America's Secret War in Laos* (New York: Crown Publishers, Inc., 1987), 219. Air Force histories for this period are entitled "The Administration Emphasizes Air Power" (1969) and "The Role of Airpower Grows" (1970).

27. Nearly all these early advisors worked for Air America, a civilian contract air operation. A USAF special air warfare unit (Detachment 6, 1st Commando Wing) deployed to Udorn, Thailand, in December 1962. It comprised 41 men and 4 T-28s. The men flew with Lao pilots and taught them counterinsurgency tactics. In addition, Detachment 6 could help out the RLAF in an emergency by covert action or furnishing aircraft.

28. Robert F. Futrell, *The United States Air Force in Southeast Asia, The Advisory Years to 1965* (Washington, D.C.: OAFH, 1981), 439–45; Sullivan Testimony, 456–57.

29. Sheep-dipped: A complex process in which someone serving in the military seemingly went through all the official motions of resigning from the service. The man's records would be pulled from the personnel files and transferred to a special top secret intelligence file. A cover story would be concocted to explain the resignation, and the man would become a civilian. At the same time, his ghostly paper existence within the intelligence file would continue to pursue his Air Force career: when his contemporaries were promoted, he would be promoted, and so on. Sheep-dipped personnel posed extremely tricky problems when they were killed or captured. There would be all sorts of pension and insurance problems, which was one of the reasons the CIA found it necessary to set up its own insurance company.

30. Charlie Jones (one of the original Butterflies), interviewed by Christopher Robbins, 15 March 1985.

31. Robbins, 49–50.

32. Robert Comer, "Was Failure Inevitable?," in W. Scott Thompson and D. D. Frizzel, eds., *The Lessons of Vietnam* (New York: Crane Russak, 1977), 269.

33. Sullivan's Air Force organized at Nakhon Phanom airport, Thailand, 8 April 1967. Redesignated as Special Operations Wing, 1 August 1968.

34. Robbins, 2.

35. Maj David I. Folkman Jr. and Maj Philip D. Caine, "The Cambodian Campaign, 29 April–30 June 1970," Headquarters PACAF, Project CHECO, 1 September 1970, 11–14.

36. Ibid., 11–15; Lt Col J. F. Loye Jr. and Maj Philip D. Caine, "The Cambodian Campaign, 1 July–31 October 1970," Headquarters PACAF, Project CHECO, 31 December 1970, 23–24, 33–35.

37. William W. Momyer, *Airpower in Three Wars* (Washington, D.C.: OAFH, January 1978), 91–97.

38. Arthur William Tedder, *Air Power in War, The Lees Knowles Lectures for 1947* (London: Hodder and Stroughton, 1947), 91.

39. Anthony Robinson, *Aerial Warfare: An Illustrated History* (New York: Galahad Books, 1982), 287–88.

Chapter 9

The Fast Forward Air Controllers

When the ban on US use of jet aircraft was lifted in 1965, F-100 Super Sabres and F-4 Phantoms began air strikes. These high-performance aircraft carried the close air support load, pounding enemy ground targets. The F-100, with multiple combinations of weapon loads, and the F-4, which could carry up to twelve thousand pounds of ordnance, brought with them a formidable increase in firepower.[1]

Modified versions of two other jets eventually made their way into the war: the F-5 (modified T-38) and the A-37 (modified T-37). Each was highly maneuverable and easily maintained, and most Vietnamese Air Force (VNAF) trainees had trained in the unmodified versions.[2] The A-7D was introduced toward the end of the war, and even the sophisticated F-111 made a brief appearance.[3]

The high-performance jets were not ideal for CAS. The relatively short loiter times due to fuel limits and restricted maneuverability because of large turn radii represented major drawbacks. In addition, the high speeds that resulted in quick response times turned into weaknesses once the jets arrived at the target. Jet pilots encountered difficulty acquiring small, fleeting targets in densely canopied jungles at high speed. Also, the same engines that produced those high speeds consumed excessive fuel at low altitude.[4]

Out-Country Operations, 1964-65

Adm Ulysses S. G. Sharp, commander-in-chief, Pacific (CINCPAC), was impressed with the high-level national interest in the armed reconnaissance program. He gave the maiden mission to the F-105 Thunderchiefs of the 80th tactical fighter squadron at Korat Air Base, Thailand. Sharp selected a section of Route 8 for an armed reconnaissance sweep and the Nape road bridge as a backup target for unused ordnance. A 15-plane force took off from Da Nang on 14 December 1964. Three RF-101s served as pathfinders and damage-assessment craft. Eight F-100s flew combat air patrol to guard against MiG interference. Four F-105s carried 750-pound bombs, 2.75-inch rockets, and 20 mm ammunition. The mission achieved limited results. Short on fuel, the F-105s made a hurried attack on the bridge and missed it.

Navy planes flew on 17 December. Four A-1Hs escorted by eight F-4Bs conducted armed reconnaissance of Routes 11 and 12, with the Ban Boung Bau road bridge as the alternative target. The aircraft failed to damage the bridge but destroyed eight buildings. The next mission sent four F-100s of the 428th Tactical Fighter Squadron along Route 8 on 21 December 1964. Lightly armed, the fighters became disoriented after receiving heavy antiaircraft artillery (AAA) fire, ran low on fuel, and failed to find any secondary target.[5] Reports on the first two USAF missions disturbed Gen Curtis E. LeMay, Air Force Chief of Staff. He sent word to Maj Gen Joseph Moore, 2d Air Division Commander, that he expected better performance.

To prepare for a fourth mission, the 44th TFS deployed six F-105s from Okinawa to Da Nang. Four of them reconnoitered Route 23 on 25 December 1964, with a strike against the military barracks at Tchepone, Laos. The operation went well, though the bombing was inaccurate. During a fifth mission on 30 December, four Navy A-1Hs struck the Tchepone military camp.[6]

On 13 January 1965, the target was the Ban Ken bridge, the most important potential target on Route 7. Aerial photos showed 34 antiaircraft guns (37 mm and 57 mm) in place. The planners scheduled an RF-101 as pathfinder and a second for bomb damage assessment, eight Super Sabres to carry cluster munitions for flak suppression and 16 Thunderchiefs from the 44th and 67th Tactical Fighter Squadrons as strike aircraft. The Sabres flew at low levels to knock the gun sites out with cluster bombs, then eight Thunderchiefs attacked the bridge with 750-pound bombs. This was followed by another eight Thunderchiefs, each loaded with six bombs and two Bullpup air-to-ground missiles. An Air America C-123 served as airborne control for rescue helicopters.

The F-100s pummeled the gun positions, but some continued firing anyway. The first wave of F-105s cut the bridge with their 64 bombs. The F-100s and the second wave of F-105s made multiple runs on the gun sites; one Thunderchief was downed, an F-100 on its fifth pass was shot down, and four other aircraft were damaged. General Moore said the losses were due to poor judgment and suggested that the attackers should have broken off the engagement after the bridge was knocked out.[7]

Flaming Dart and Rolling Thunder

On 24 January 1965, Moore advised Gen William C. Westmoreland that the fastest way to bolster airpower was to make full use of the Air Force resources that were available. Moore believed that jets should be used to fly missions in South Vietnam, that the requirement to carry a Vietnamese observer on operational missions should be dropped, and that helicopters should be removed from air bases to allow an expansion of facilities.[8]

The Joint Chiefs approved using jets in strike roles in South Vietnam if these strikes could not be carried out by Vietnamese A-1s. According to this formula, jet strikes were authorized solely to save American lives or to spoil Vietcong attacks—and then only if a corps commander, the Vietnamese Joint General Staff, and MACV thought the action necessary.[9]

On 7 February 1965, Vietcong mortar squads and demolition teams attacked the small US advisory detachment in II corps, four and one-half miles north of Pleiku. They also struck Camp Holloway, headquarters of the US Army 52d Aviation Battalion (also near Pleiku). The assaults killed eight Americans and wounded 104, destroyed five Army helicopters and two transports, three USAF O-1s, and one Vietnamese O-1. Moreover, the attacks damaged the main building of the advisory detachment.[10]

President Lyndon B. Johnson ordered an instant response and, that afternoon, US Navy, South Vietnamese, and USAF planes hit an enemy military barracks near Dong Hoi in an operation called Flaming Dart. At the same time, Pacific Air Force (PACAF) air transports lifted US Marine Corps light antiaircraft missile units from Okinawa to Da Nang and evacuated US dependents from South Vietnam.[11] On 13 February 1965, Johnson approved measured and limited air attacks in North Vietnam; but the Rolling Thunder air campaign was delayed for two weeks by bad weather and political turmoil in Saigon.[12]

Rolling Thunder was the first of two major American campaigns against North Vietnam. It ran from 13 February 1965 until 31 October 1968, at which time President Johnson imposed a total bombing halt in the North. While Rolling Thunder brought devastation closer to Hanoi, and raised the cost of supporting and supplying the insurgency in the South, critics held that it did not always roll and was not consistently thunderous.

The rules about which targets could be attacked were constantly changing. For a time, decisions as routine as the ordnance to be carried on a mission were made from as far away as the White House. For most of the three and one-half years of the campaign, it was permissible to engage the enemy's growing MiG force in the air but MiGs could not be attacked on the ground. And, even in the air, North Vietnamese fighter commanders often seemed to outthink and outfight their American counterparts.

The enemy had the advantage of fighting over his home ground, often in poor weather (which favored the defender)—at least during the April-to-October monsoon season. He was backed by a staggering array of radar-directed AAA and surface-to-air missiles supplied by the Soviets.

In the south, tactics were devised to make best use of ground-to-air communications and of FACs flying O-1s and O-2s to identify, pinpoint, and mark targets such as Vietcong troop concentrations. Combat jet aircraft exposed themselves to small arms, 37 mm cannon fire, and shoulder-mounted SAMs. Fighter pilots sometimes returned from missions not knowing what had been hit. The struggle in the south was bitter and difficult, but no MiGs challenged US command of the air in the south.[13]

The employment of jets marked the end of the long US advisory phase and the beginning of direct and open American action in the Vietnam war. On 1 March 1965, the new commander in chief of the Vietnamese armed forces, Maj Gen Tran Van Minh, established the Vietnamese Air Force air request network as the primary source of immediate air support for all military operations. He further removed the restriction that only a Vietnamese FAC could mark targets for air strikes.[14]

Commando Sabre

Stiffening enemy defenses in the panhandle of North Vietnam and southern Laos made it extremely dangerous for the "slow mover" FACs. On 17 May 1967, therefore, Seventh Air Force Commander, William W. Momyer approved Operation Commando Sabre—a test of the F-100F's ability to fly armed reconnaissance and FAC missions.[15]

Several features favored the F-100F. Good speed and maneuverability helped it survive in high-threat areas. The jet was equipped with two rocket launchers for target marking and a 20 mm cannon that was well suited for armed reconnaissance. External fuel tanks (and in-flight refueling) stretched operating time and, finally, the view from both front and back seats was fairly good.

F-100 "Misty"

The Commando Sabre mission (call-sign Misty) was assigned to Detachment 1 of the 416th TFS, 37th Tactical Fighter Wing, at Phu Cat Air Base, Vietnam, on 28 June 1967. Seventh Air Force furnished the detachment with liberal guidelines and authority to freely experiment.[16] Misty FAC volunteers had to be flight leaders with at least one hundred strike missions in Southeast Asia and one thousand total flying hours. The initial duty tour was 120 days or 75 missions, whichever came first. Twelve of the first 16 volunteers from F-100 units in South Vietnam lacked controller experience. The remaining four (fighter-qualified controllers from the 504th Tactical Air Support Group) would instruct the others, using F-100Fs borrowed from in-country fighter squadrons.[17]

Training

Initially, the Misty volunteers practiced air refueling and operating at various airspeeds and altitudes.[18] Next, they learned how to locate gun emplacements, bunkers, camouflaged trucks, and trails. Instruction in FAC communications, visual reconnaissance procedures, and strike control followed. The Misty controllers discovered that the F-100F's greater speed dictated adjustments in procedures because they had less time to locate targets. The jet FAC had to do in seconds what the O-1 or O-2 FAC would take a minute to complete.

Two days of ground training included the rules of engagement, escape and evasion, map-reading, tactics, and enemy order of battle. The Misty volunteers flew the first six missions as observers while the instructors in the front seat went through FAC procedures. The students alternated between front and rear seats until the twelfth mission, when they received their flight check. Full qualification was obtained after 20 sorties.[19]

Tactics

Except for deviations dictated by greater speed, jet reconnaissance and strike control tactics were the same as the slow tactics. The Misty FAC set a minimum of 4,500 feet in high-threat areas, descending lower solely to investigate suspicious targets.[20] He preferred to fly at 540 MPH (450 knots indicated air-speed [KIAS]) or above—seldom under 450 MPH (400 KIAS). Whenever cloud cover fell below seven thousand feet, the Misty discontinued reconnaissance and strike control because his silhouette against the clouds aided enemy gunners. Unless absolutely necessary, the controller never made more than a single pass over a potential target. Nor did he go in immediately after a strike to perform battle damage assessment; he returned later for that purpose.[21]

As the only FACs who could survive in certain hostile areas, the Misties stressed reconnaissance over strike control. Having found it difficult to locate jungle roads and trails from 4,500 feet, they secured permission to "recon" at 1,500 feet. In rare instances, they also flew below hilltop level and into valleys to identify targets.

In reconnoitering roads and trails, the FAC generally flew a series of "S" maneuvers back and forth across the road—never presenting a predictable pattern. Upon spotting something suspicious, he continued on until he was out of range. He then turned in a wide circle, dropped as low as possible, and came back at right angles to the road.[22] Even when flying low, the controller had difficulty finding well-camouflaged trucks. The infiltration routes contained numerous points where vehicles could hide under trees. In fact, a truck could move down the entire length of the Ho Chi Minh trail and never be detected unless something went wrong—a breakdown in an open area, poor camouflage, or traveling at the wrong time of day.

Once the Misty FAC located a target, he called for a slow FAC to come in. If enemy defenses were too strong for the slow FAC, the Misty controlled the air strike. He contacted the fighters and furnished them the rendezvous point. Join-up usually occurred above twenty thousand feet. After discussing target information and tactics, the FAC helped the fighter pilots locate the target. He then marked it, firing an extra rocket at each end of the target area. Since marker-rocket motors differed in performance and there were sudden shifts in F-100F airspeed, the Misty often launched several rockets, using the closest one as the reference for directing air strikes.

When the fighters had completed their passes, the controller let the area "cool off" before going in to assess bomb damage.[23]

Effectiveness and Expansion

Misties met with little opposition during their first weeks of operation, but this "honeymoon" ended abruptly on 5 July 1967. A FAC drew heavy fire while directing a flight of F-105s against truck traffic in the North Vietnamese panhandle near Quang Khe (close to the coast in Route Package I). Antiaircraft artillery fire became common after that.[24] Nevertheless, the Misties fared better than expected. In July 1967, they flew 82 missions and directed 126 strikes against targets that stemmed almost exclusively from their own reconnaissance. They discovered 150 truck parks, bridges, fords, and spots suitable for road interdiction[25] in hostile areas where most other FAC aircraft could not go. The results grew more impressive as the fast FACs sharpened their ability to locate targets.

Commando Sabre FACs first tasted large-scale action in September and October 1967. All through the summer, the North Vietnamese had pounded positions at Con Thien, Gia Linh, Camp Carroll, and Dong Ha with artillery barrages from across the DMZ. To blunt these attacks, a six-week campaign called Operation Neutralize started on 12 September.[26] O-2A FACs controlled air strikes south of the DMZ while the Misties worked north of it.[27] Operation Neutralize statistics showed that strikes flown by fighters under Misty control were twice as effective as those flown without them.[28] General Momyer was impressed with the Commando Sabre operation. On 13 November 1967, he extended it into the Steel Tiger area of Laos—an area that was too deadly for slow FACs.[29]

Steel Tiger

When Momyer ordered Commando Sabre into Steel Tiger, his staff weighed the pros and cons of moving the Misty detachment from Phu Cat to Da Nang. Flying out of Da Nang would increase the time for the Misties to operate in their assigned area by 45–50 minutes. In addition, they could receive up-to-date intelligence from the 366th Tactical Fighter

Wing there. This contrasted with the stale intelligence (36-hours old) at Phu Cat, which impelled the Misties to lean heavily on their own reconnaissance. Moreover, Misty FACs could coordinate more easily with the fighter crews at Da Nang, who flew out-country strikes. Despite these advantages, however, Seventh Air Force took no action at this time. It did move the detachment later— in May 1969—but to Tuy Hoa, not Da Nang.[30]

The Misties found the AAA fire lighter in their Laotian operating areas than over southern North Vietnam. They therefore "reconned" at 1,500 feet and went down to five hundred feet in some areas. Area Echo in Steel Tiger, adjacent to the North Vietnamese border, contained the Ho Chi Minh trail's two major passes—Mu Gia and Ben Karai. The Misties concentrated on the roads leading away from these passes.[31]

Starting 1 July 1968, the Misties engaged in Operation Thor, a one-week rerun of Operation Neutralize. On 14 July, they joined in a 30-day US effort to stop supplies from flowing through Route Package I. The Misties concentrated the fighter strikes against roads that, if plugged, would impede the movement of supplies. Misty reconnaissance and strike control helped to slow daytime truck traffic in southern North Vietnam to a trickle. But the enemy worked furiously at night to open the roads, and the chokepoints had to be hit repeatedly.[32]

On 7 March 1968, Misty FACs discovered an active SAM site in the southern portion of North Vietnam. They controlled 14 strike flights while being fired upon by numerous AAA guns, and they successfully avoided one SAM launch. Smoke and devastation made it impossible to determine how many SAM positions were destroyed. Bomb damage assessment (BDA) included one 57 mm AAA site silenced, two SAMs and two SAM transporters destroyed, three pieces of SAM support equipment destroyed or damaged, 36 trucks destroyed or damaged, 16 secondary explosions, and seven fires.

Two weeks later, a Misty crew discovered a convoy of 150 to 175 trucks that were unexpectedly "uncovered" as a result of improved weather conditions. These trucks were lined up bumper-to-bumper on a hilly secondary road in the northern portion of Route Package I. The Misty FACs stopped the convoy by damaging the lead trucks with strafing passes and marking rockets while calling for strike aircraft. Controlled by four Misties, strike aircraft destroyed or damaged 79 trucks.[33]

The first of five successful rescue combat air patrols (RESCAP) that were controlled by Misty crews was flown in June. During the late afternoon of 8 June, an F-105 Thunderchief was downed by AAA south of Dong Hoi. The pilot ejected in a heavily defended area but managed to evade North Vietnamese soldiers while unsuccessful attempts were made to rescue him that afternoon. The following morning, Misty crews reinstated the RESCAP and directed strikes against the many active AAA sites. An F-4C was hit by AAA and the crew ejected over the Gulf of Tonkin, where they were picked up by helicopter. By late afternoon, threatening AAA sites had been either destroyed or silenced and a rescue helicopter had picked up the downed pilot.[34]

Night Operations

While planning the RESCAP operation, Seventh Air Force decided to evaluate the F-100F in a night role. On 11 June 1968, two veteran Commando Sabre pilots from the 3d TFW were selected to conduct the test from Bien Hoa—Capts Donald W. Sheppard and James E. Risinger. These pilots flew one night mission on 13 June and another the next night. Impressed with the aircraft's potential for night reconnaissance, they recommended further testing. Accordingly, Seventh Air Force planned to operate at night in Route Package I. For illumination, the SUU-25 flare dispenser with eight flares was fitted to the F-100F.

The Misties flew 46 night sorties in Route Package I between 12 July and 18 August. The FACs discovered that the enemy liked to travel during moonless nights and in bad weather. Massed in hidden parks along the highways, his trucks did not move until after dark. They would push through Route Package I the first night and converge at staging areas where they would spread out under the thick jungle overhang and try to make it into Laos the second night. To counter attacks on choke points, the communists waited until a major movement was ready. And even then, they opened only essential roads.

Misty night controllers also discovered the mystery of a missing bridge. Route 101 crossed the Song Troc River at Phoung Choy, a major bottleneck 21 miles northwest of Dong Hoi. Day reconnaissance showed no bridge spanning the river at this point; nevertheless, trucks were seen rolling down the highway. The puzzle was solved one night when a Misty FAC saw the North Vietnamese float a huge pontoon bridge from a cave several thousand yards away and place it across the river. The Misties also learned that they could scarcely see the soft-glowing blue headlights of enemy trucks from above five thousand feet.[35]

Seventh Air Force stopped jet night FAC activity in Route Package I on 16 October 1968; problems had begun to outweigh achievements. Even under flarelight, it was extremely difficult to detect the smoke of marker rockets. Moreover, flares could not be accurately aimed and their light eliminated the element of surprise. Also, the F-100F Super Sabre carried too few flares. Further, the F-100F's navigation systems (TACAN/ADF) had proved unreliable below ten thousand feet in Laos and North Vietnam. (The FAC frequently had to rely on pilotage[36] for orientation, rendezvous, and target location.)[37]

Other elements also figured in the decision to discontinue jet night FAC activity. The chance of midair collision increased during darkness and the Misty controller had to clear strike aircraft into the target area one at a time. Because the FAC needed to fly higher for safety, the quality of his reconnaissance suffered. Further, the starlight scope was bulky and unwieldy, its operation was disturbed by the cockpit lighting, and its narrow field of vision disoriented the operator. A final factor contributing to the decision was that the use of the F-100Fs for night FAC duty limited their day activity.[38]

On 30 November 1968, Seventh Air Force opened up Steel Tiger to Commando Sabre operations and began Misty night operations over Laos. There was a compelling need for around-the-clock coverage of the enemy's road network. The Misties would fly night missions only when ground fire grew too intense for the slower FAC aircraft. Along with ABCCC control and radar flight-following, they required an approved working altitude, ranging from ground level to twelve thousand feet.[39] All these conditions could not be met, however, and the Misties flew on waivers.

On 19 February 1969, Misty operations in Laos became a twilight affair. The first of two sorties took off one hour before sunrise; the second, one hour after sunset. Keeping to a minimum altitude of three thousand feet, the Misty FACs used flares and the starlight scope; they employed minimum maneuvering.[40] Twilight operations ended in December 1969, owing largely to a shortage of jet aircraft.[41]

Coordination with Slow Movers

Jet and slow-mover FACs cooperated because they often worked in the same areas. Each kept track of the other by constant radio contact. Since the jet's speed allowed only a swift glance at suspected targets, he turned to the slow mover for closer inspection. Similarly, when the slow mover encountered heavy AAA fire, he called the "fast FAC."

Enlarging the Commando Sabre Role

Commando Sabre lent itself easily to auxiliary roles: search and rescue, artillery spotting, weather reconnaissance, hunter-killer, and photo reconnaissance.

Search and Rescue. About 25 percent of the first 93 Misty FACs were shot down at some time, but most were recovered. Commando Sabre's efforts to aid downed jet FACs led to a deeper involvement in search and rescue (SAR). Upon receiving word of a lost aircraft, the ABCCC called for Misty help. A Misty controller then searched for the missing crew members. After locating them, he would occupy the enemy with machine gun and rocket fire while the rescue helicopter picked up the airmen, staying on the scene until the rescue was concluded.[42]

Artillery Spotting. Before 1967, slow-mover FACs in South Vietnam had done much artillery spotting and fire control for the Army. From 1967 onward, however, an increase in Navy offshore shelling of coastal targets in North Vietnam fueled the need for artillery adjustments. This job fell to the Misties, since the area was too dangerous for slow-movers. Hence, a few days before Operation Sea Dragon began on 1 June 1968, several Commando Sabre pilots visited the cruiser SS *Saint Paul* to discuss their support. As Sea Dragon unfolded, Air Force-Navy coordination went very well and Misty controllers adjusted artillery fire with accuracy. Their Sea Dragon exploits behind them, Misty FACs found themselves in much demand by the Navy for artillery spotting.[43]

Weather Reconnaissance. Weather played a key part in the success of tactical air operations. When a target was under the influence of bad weather, the strike was aborted unless the aircraft had all-weather equipment or was under control of ground radar. Seventh Air Force required FACs to keep an almost continual watch over weather conditions in the target areas, and the Misties proved very adept at weather reconnaissance. This was largely due to their high speed, which allowed them to experience the target area weather just as the fighters would. Misty controllers filed weather reports routinely, along with mission reports. If faster action was dictated, they called in the report while en route to home base.[44]

Hunter-Killer Teams. The Air Force had first tried the hunter-killer concept in the Korean War. Its debut in Southeast Asia linked a slow-mover FAC with a fighter. Greater exploitation came later, with the jet FAC. During April 1969, hunter-killer teams of Misties and F-100 fighter-bombers from Phu Cat flew test missions in the Laotian panhandle. The results outran expectations.[45]

Hunter-killer teams operated only with Seventh Air Force and Royal Laotian Government approval, and only in areas free of friendly troops. During a typical mission, the Misty "hunter" rendezvoused with the strike aircraft and flew to a reconnaissance area. The "killer" jet trailed three miles behind and five thousand to seven thousand feet above the FAC, who kept a running commentary on his position. If the strike aircraft lost sight, the FAC turned on his lights or lit his afterburner. Once the hunter pinpointed targets, he flew the marking pass and the "killer" pilot attacked. The hunter-killer team worked best when the "killer" pilot was a former jet FAC; he knew Misty tactics, the area, and the names of reference points.

A common problem for the hunter-killer team was the struggle of the ordnance-laden "killer" aircraft to keep up with the Misty. The killer pilot generally flew at higher altitudes where the thinner air permitted greater airspeed. Looking down, however, he had difficulty seeing the hunter aircraft whose camouflage blended with the landscape beneath. Bad weather and the hunter's constant maneuvering to confuse the enemy compounded the identification problem.[46] Nevertheless, Seventh Air Force enthusiastically endorsed the hunter-killer team as one of the best means for catching the enemy by surprise.

Photo Reconnaissance Photo reconnaissance crept into Misty operations when the rear-seat pilot started taking pictures of selected targets with a hand-held camera. However, the cramped cockpit made it hard to maneuver the camera for good coverage.[47] In the summer of 1969, the Misties engaged in a photo experiment with RF-4Cs (call sign Yo-Yo) of the 460th tactical reconnaissance wing at Tan Son Nhut. The Misty FAC located targets and the RF-4C photographed them and rushed the film back for processing. This experiment did not work as hoped, chiefly because Misty units and Yo-Yo units were located on separate bases—an arrangement that precluded effective coordination. In addition, the photo results were filtered through three distinct intelligence channels before arriving at Seventh Air Force Headquarters for analysis.

Meanwhile, the Misties modified a specially built camera fitted with a pistol grip and a plug for an electrical connection. This allowed the rear-seat pilot to take quality pictures. In fact, this "armpit" camera secured the first clear photos of the water route over which the enemy floated petroleum-filled pigskins from the DMZ to Tchepone.[48]

Phasing Out

When the Commando Sabre program was started in 1967, plans already existed to phase out the F-100 by 1970. Seventh Air Force therefore framed plans early in 1968 for an F-4 fast-FAC program.[49] Several problems dogged the Misty operations. The F-100F lacked a radar-warning receiver that would detect imminent SAM or AAA attacks, and it lacked electronic countermeasure pods to counter them. The Misty FAC sensed no danger until alerted by the ABCCC, ground radar, or other aircraft. Even then, he was in no position to direct strikes against the SAM/AAA sites unless he could see them.[50] In addition, the underpowered F-100F was vulnerable to ground fire during evasive maneuvers.[51] Perhaps the greatest limitation, however, was the insufficient number of aircraft on hand. The Misties scarcely knew daily how many F-100Fs they could muster, since the number varied with fighter training demands.[52]

Despite these drawbacks, Commando Sabre underlined the worth of the jet FAC and forged the basic tactics that were carried over to F-4 FAC operations. On 14 May 1970, when the last Misty mission flew, the F-4 program was well underway.

F-4 "Phantom" FACs

On 1 January 1968, Seventh Air Force received authorization to try the F-4 Phantom in a FAC role. The 12th Tactical Fighter Wing readied an F-4D for testing in Steel Tiger and Route Package I. The test aircraft carried two 370-gallon external fuel tanks, two rocket launchers, and a 20 mm gun pod. A Misty FAC rode in the Phantom's rear seat during the test. By 20 March, 10 missions had been completed. Though impressed with the overall F-4D performance, the Misty FACs

F-4D

noted several shortcomings. The engine intakes obstructed the view from the back seat; a 60-degree bank was required to restore it. More air refueling was required for the F-4D to remain on-station as long as the F-100F—and the F-4D had a lower turn rate and a larger turn radius than the F-100F. Also, the F-4D was a bigger target and its twin J-79 engines provided a smoke trail for enemy gunners.

Still, the pluses of the F-4D outweighed the minuses. Two engines allowed an airspeed of 400-450 knots to be maintained, reducing the chances of being shot down. Navigation aids and radar warning equipment were superior, and it was equipped with an airborne intercept radar for in-flight refueling rendezvous. In addition to regular FAC armament, the aircraft could carry a wide variety of ordnance. Lastly, it was located with the F-4 strike aircraft it controlled.[53]

Before settling on the F-4D as a controller, Seventh Air Force evaluated the F-105F "Thunderchief" (Wild Weasel) in June 1968; it was unsatisfactory in the FAC role. The view from its rear seat was extremely poor, it maneuvered marginally whenever airspeed slipped below four hundred knots, and it burned too much fuel. Furthermore, exposing the F-105F, a costly and limited resource, to increased ground fire in the FAC role could not be justified. General Momyer therefore directed that "a couple of F-4s from the 366th" (at Da Nang) be used to start a program.[54]

Stormy FACs

The 366th Tactical Fighter Wing and the Misty FACs had the F-4 controller program readied by 12 August 1968. Student pilots assigned to it were volunteers of flight-leader caliber with at least 20 combat missions in Route Package I and not less than nine months remaining to serve in-theater. Duty tour with the 366th detachment (call-sign Stormy) was 90 days or 50 missions—later rising to 125 days or 75 missions. The first two volunteers, F-4 aircraft commanders, flew five sorties from Phu Cat in the rear seat of the F-100F. They then occupied the front cockpit of the F-4 on three missions with a Misty instructor in the back seat, completing training on 26 August. On 2 September, they flew their maiden FAC missions in Route Package I.[55]

Stormy operations resembled those of Commando Sabre;[56] but Stormy FACs were collocated with their strike units, which allowed them to receive their intelligence firsthand. The Stormies flew two sorties per day, performing reconnaissance at 4,000-4,500 feet and at 400-knot minimum airspeed. To assess bomb damage, they made a single pass at five thousand feet and five hundred knots.[57]

The unceasing demand for night surveillance of enemy roads and trails swayed Seventh Air Force to conduct a Stormy night experiment in Laos. Beginning on 24 October 1968, F-4Ds flew one sortie each night. Enthusiastic controllers pushed for more, but Seventh doubted the program's soundness because moonless or cloudless nights severely hampered reconnaissance. In addition, when trucks on the ground turned off their lights, the Stormies had difficulty finding them again. To Seventh, armed night reconnaissance seemed preferable since targets could be hit at once. Safety was a gnawing concern as well, because the blacked-out strike aircraft and the Stormies risked colliding (of the first eight night sorties the Stormies flew, six near-misses occurred). Also, the Stormies' day/night schedule sliced deeply into FAC training time. These concerns led Seventh Air Force to halt the Stormy night program temporarily.[58]

In April 1969, night Stormy operations were resumed in Laos. This time, the Stormies flew two sorties a night. They used the starlight scope, and they received flare support from C-123 "Candlesticks" and C-130 "Blindbats." Day tactics governed, but the FAC kept his dive angle on marking passes to no steeper than 30 degrees.

The Stormy operation changed with experience. In May 1969, the sortie rate climbed to three per day and the number of FAC pilots grew to ten. The small F-4D detachment moved directly under the 366th Wing's Deputy Commander of Operations (DO) in July, improving coordination with the fighter squadrons in the wing.[59] Like the Misties, the F-4Ds worked with the RF-4Cs of the 460th Wing and were affected by the same spotty coordination and slow film-processing.[60]

The Stormies handled strike control for tactical fighters supporting the 1970 incursion into Cambodia and continued to shoulder the bulk of the FAC load there.[61]

Wolf FACs

Other F-4 units became interested in the stormy operation. Early in October 1968, Capt Richard G. Mayo (a Stormy FAC) briefed wing operations officers of Seventh Air Force at Bangkok, Thailand. As a result, Col Slade Nash, Eighth Tactical Fighter Wing DO, requested permission to employ an F-4D FAC element in his wing. He assured Seventh Air Force the aircraft were available and could be used without straining other missions. He received authorization on 26 October.[62]

In the Eighth Tactical Fighter Wing, the F-4 FAC Section (called Wolf) worked directly for the DO with a status comparable to the wing fighter squadrons. To ensure a smooth flow of information, the Wolf office was located in the Intelligence Division. Maj Benjamin R. Battle, the first Wolf commander, handpicked every pilot for the initial program. The first five Wolf crews, volunteers from all the fighter squadrons, represented a cross-section of experience.[63] All pilots had at least three months of out-country combat experience, came highly recommended by their commanders, and were approved by the DO.[64]

Training began on 12 November 1968. By month's end, five crews were qualified. Each crew member flew 10 sorties in the F-4. Two were in the backseat behind Major Battle (or his operations officer), the remainder in the front seat with an instructor in the rear cockpit. The Wolf controllers received night orientation flights in the O-2A and the C-130 Blind Bat.

To take advantage of this new fast-FAC concept, the Eighth TFW hosted a "FAC-IN" on November 25-26 to exchange ideas and information and to standardize procedures. Misty (F-100), Stormy (F-4D), Covey (O-1), Nail (O-2), Snort (OV-10) and Blind Bat (C-130) FACs were represented. Many ideas and recommendations to improve mission effectiveness were discussed, and problems affecting FAC operations were forwarded to higher headquarters.[65]

In December 1968, Wolves started flying day missions of three and one-half hours in Steel Tiger. The first crew arrived early in the afternoon; the second, two hours later. Seventh Air Force authorized a third sortie in January 1969 to spread the patrol into the early evening hours.[66]

The communists felt the jet FACs' sting and replied with stepped-up ground fire. Flying below five thousand feet quickly became hazardous and fatiguing. The jet controller maneuvered constantly during visual reconnaissance. He invited battle damage if he stayed below four thousand feet very long, doubled back to circle a target, slowed down, or flew a predictable pattern for more than 10 seconds. Wolf FACs were accordingly advised to do visual reconnaissance during their first 45 minutes in the area (when they were fresh), then mix the remaining time with reconnaissance and strike control.

Col Dave Yates, former Wolf and Tiger FAC, describes the life of a Forward Air Controller in the Vietnam war:

> The advantage we had (over the F-100 and the A-4) was power; we had a lot of it in the F-4—and two people. Two people was a tremendous advantage when you had to write down all the data of an air strike, sometimes on the side of your canopy in grease pencil.
>
> When I got to Wolf 'FACing,' in a much larger area, [I found that] you were not considered experienced until you had 60 missions. We flew with an old head with over 60 missions on our first 40 missions. We worked four or five different areas. When the war opened up, in the last five months of my tour, we carried maps for northern Laos MRI, Packs I through IV, and even Pack VI. The hottest place we went to was Military Region I after the North raided South Vietnam, north of Da Nang to the DMZ. The heavy SAMs, the AAA fire, and the SA-7s we encountered were the heaviest I had ever seen.
>
> In the last four months of my tour, we lost five Wolf crews of the seven we had. There was no "exposure" rule at Ubon and I got hit four days straight and was counseled for "bad form." I was shot down on my 37th mission as a Tiger (on 6 May 1970) and was one of the reasons Korat had the rule about being over-exposed (three hits or 40 missions and you were out). The statistics, for Wolfs at least, were [that] you had an 85 percent chance of being shot down in 100 missions.
>
> A Wolf mission started at 3 a.m., takeoff at 7 a.m., and flew four or five hours. Then we spent two hours to debrief and then developed targets for the next day. We arranged the schedule so you flew the next later mission each day. You flew the 7 a.m. takeoff one day, the

next day you flew the 10 a.m. takeoff. We took off at three-hour intervals throughout the day. You would go through that schedule until you covered the whole day and then start the cycle again after a day off. A work day was 14-16 hours, so the day off was a pretty quick drunk, then sleep.[67]

The soaring demand for Wolf controllers forced the fighter crews to orbit longer, waiting for the FAC to be brought in. To ease this delay, Seventh Air Force let strike aircraft be their own FACs in areas of the eastern Laotian panhandle that were free of friendlies. However, the Wolf FAC still made sure the target was positively identified and enemy defenses pinpointed. A review of attack procedures followed and the strike leader took charge. This freed the Wolf FACs for extra reconnaissance and strike control.[68]

Targets for all-weather strikes were selected from reconnaissance during good weather; the groundwork for bad-weather strikes was laid by a series of missions run while the weather was good. The radar site at Hue Phu Bai plotted fighter flight paths and the pilot verified his position. When the weather turned bad, flights under this radar control could strike these areas with a high degree of confidence. Good radar coverage of Route Package I and parts of Laos as far north as Mu Gia Pass was available. During the 1968–72 campaign, long-range navigation (LORAN)[69] became the preferred technique for all-weather bombing in Laos and Route Package I.[70]

LORAN techniques offered two advantages: the accuracy was better than ground-directed radar, and a formation could bomb at the same time as the leader for better bomb spacing. A formation of four to eight aircraft could bomb with only one or two Wolf aircraft having LORAN equipment. Thus, in bad weather on 21 September 1971, using LORAN as a guide, one hundred and ninety-six F-4s in two waves struck five targets 35 miles above the DMZ. More than two thousand 500-pound bombs and three thousand cluster-bombs were dropped on petroleum and logistical storage areas and military barracks.[71] This strike was a significant advance in the use of large numbers of fighters against targets that would normally not have been struck due to bad weather. Seventh Air Force reported excellent target coverage with major damage to the target area. This mission developed and confirmed the all-weather techniques that were used against targets in Route Package VI in 1972.

Tiger Forward Air Controllers

The success of the Misties, Stormies, and Wolves impressed the 388th Tactical Fighter Wing, Korat AB, Thailand; in January 1969, it sought approval to use some of its F-4Es as FACs in Barrel Roll.[72] Wing intelligence pointed out that the beefed-up enemy defenses had rendered a large part of that area risky for the O-1 Raven controllers. After securing Seventh Air Force's approval in February for one FAC sortie a day in Barrel Roll, the 388th gave its new venture the call-sign "Tiger" and sent volunteers from its 469th TFS to Ubon to check out with the Wolf FACs. By 19 March, the Tigers were in operation.[73]

The Tiger FACs were the first jet controllers to see duty in the Barrel Roll area of Laos. Their commander found that being a member of the Barrel Roll Working Group 74 helped cement good relations with the Raven FACs. Basing the Tigers with the strike crews of the 388th Wing also smoothed coordination. One F-4E feature proved a boon in Barrel Roll—the inertial guidance system that automatically determined the plane's position. For example, when the sole TACAN channel in Laos was lost with the fall of Lima Site 36 (northeast of the Plain of Jars) on 1 March 1969, Tiger visual reconnaissance and strike control continued—even in marginal weather. Moreover, the thrust and range of the F-4E surpassed those of earlier F-4 models (and it carried an internal cannon).[75]

The Tigers made their mark in March 1969 during Operation Rain Dance when General Vang Pao's forces went on the offensive against communist troops on the Plain of Jars. USAF and RLAF fighters attacked the roads and trails leading into the Plain. Between 17 March and 7 April, the Tigers flew two sorties per day on reconnaissance, strike control, weather recce, and BDA missions.[76]

By July, the Tigers were so immersed in strike control that they seldom did visual reconnaissance. To remedy this,

F-4E

Seventh Air Force hiked the sortie rate to four missions a day. In October, the entire FAC program suffered when tanker support was reduced. (It was restored three months later, in January 1970.) Misties, Stormies, Wolves, and Tigers continued directing air strikes, forcing the enemy to build bypasses around closed portions of his roads. Such achievement exacted its price—five F-4Es suffered heavy battle damage from September to December 1969.[77]

> Korat F-4s were the E models. The E was nose-heavy and you had to fly fast, maybe 50-100 knots [faster] than in a D, to stay alive and not dig-in during turns. The advantage of the F-4D was its turn capability with the same power—and the airplane was lighter. But then you strapped a gun-pod on, so you ended up with increased drag. There were tradeoffs. There was a definite difference between doing reconnaissance at 450 knots and 500 knots. I preferred the D.
>
> In the Tiger tour, we worked a rather small area of Barrel Roll in northern Laos. There were very few active routes and we were limited away from slow-moving controlled areas where there were troops-in-contact. This kept us in the heavy-shooting areas. We went to the same areas every day, with a few incursions into other areas. Occasionally, when we had a big mission, we would go into North Vietnam ahead of everyone else to take a look around and mark targets.

THE FAST FORWARD AIR CONTROLLERS

You were permitted to use the gun as a Tiger FAC for two reasons: troops-in-contact and a SAR effort. In fact, I was shot down in a troops-in-contact situation while directing strikes of F-105s. We did have a slow FAC working with us, and we never talked to anyone on the ground. In SARs, we did talk to the survivors and put in strikes.

In the Tiger FAC program, we did a mixture of FAC and armed reconnaissance missions. Along with our ability to work close to the ground, find targets, and stay alive single-ships, we also had the ability to shoot the gun, which happened to be the weapon of choice for troops-in-contact and SARs. When you worked with someone and they went down, the first thing they needed was to have the area around them cleared. You would locate the downed crew and clear the area with a couple of bursts and convince the enemy that the fighters overhead were armed.[78]

Falcon/Laredo FAC/Reconnaissance Teams

In February 1969, shortly after Seventh Air Force authorized the Tiger program, the 432d Tactical Reconnaissance Wing at Udorn developed a significant fast FAC concept. It called for an RF-4C to orbit an assigned area searching for targets and photographing enemy positions. Another fast FAC (F-4D) carried out visual reconnaissance at the same time. When the controller spotted something suspicious, he requested photo coverage from the RF-4C.

RF-4C

The photo reconnaissance crew (call-sign Atlanta), upon locating a lucrative target, called in the FAC to control strikes against it. The scheme also included photo coverage of FAC-directed attacks.[79] The 432d Wing proposed the plan to Seventh Air Force on 19 March 1969 and received quick approval.[80]

The 432d TRW established the Falcon FAC unit at Udorn in April, structured after the Wolfs at Ubon. The first five crews, having received checkouts from Stormy and Misty controllers, flew their maiden missions in Steel Tiger on 8 April.[81] They became the first jet FACs to work for a tactical reconnaissance wing. They and the Atlanta photo recce crews formed a close-knit team. A chief advantage for the Falcons was access to fresh intelligence from rapidly developed photos.[82]

The Vulcan cannon on the RF-4C was replaced by a glass nose enclosure that housed camera equipment. The "clothes rack" on the top of the fuselage behind the rear cockpit indicates that this RF-4C was also equipped with the ARN-92 long-range-navigation (LORAN) system.

A general operational pattern emerged from the first joint Atlanta/Falcon mission on 26 April 1969. As soon as the Atlanta RF-4C landed at Udorn, its film was speedily processed and rushed to the Wing Intelligence Division for evaluation and target selection. At a joint preflight briefing, Falcon and Atlanta air crews pinpointed targets and discussed surveillance tactics.[83] Both aircraft took off together. The Falcon headed for a tanker, the Atlanta to the target area for a look at the weather. Upon receiving a weather briefing from the Altanta crew, the Falcon FAC determined the sequence for hitting the targets. The Atlanta took prestrike photos of the first target and, as the fighters attacked, moved on to photograph other targets. The photo recce crew then returned to take poststrike pictures of the targets. If the mission was mainly for visual reconnaissance, the Falcon FAC planned it and the Atlanta crew flew as an escort.

The Atlanta/Falcon team yielded more strikes per sortie than other jet controller programs. In fact, its BDA tripled Seventh Air Force averages. This success rested largely on the Atlanta's picture-taking, which reduced visual reconnaissance time. Hence, the Falcon FAC could concentrate on strike control.[84]

The increase of enemy activity in Barrel Roll (July-September 1969) swamped the Tiger controllers. They asked for assistance from Atlanta/Falcon teams and the 432d Wing replied with four sorties daily. Then, as the Laotian government counteroffensive (About Face) gained momentum, the Atlanta/Falcon effort centered in Barrel Roll. Two sorties a day continued there, even after About Face was completed; four sorties returned to Steel Tiger.[85]

Laredo FACs (F-4Es from the 432d TRW) developed a variation of the Misty hunter-killer concept. Dubbed "Snare Drum," this operation employed formations of 16 to 20 fighter-bombers. In September 1969, Laredo controllers led three of these special missions. The Air Attaché in Vientiane reported that one of them (comprising 20 aircraft) decimated one thousand enemy troops who were massed in the target area.[86]

The Atlanta/Falcon teams found targets not detected before. For example, their dawn-to-dusk coverage in Steel Tiger and Barrel Roll uncovered 102 new targets in November 1969 and another 172 the next month. The crews often risked going in below four thousand feet—and, as a result, suffered 21 cases of battle damage between October and December.[87] Seventh Air Force then ordered the FAC/Recce crews to remain above 4,500 feet—but they still located more targets than other FAC units.

Night Owls

All jet FAC units had at one time or another tried night programs with differing degrees of success. Nonetheless, Seventh Air Force in October 1969 again opted for night FACs to block enemy truck traffic at selected points along the roads leading from the Mu Gia and Ban Karai passes It therefore established an F-4D controller unit (call-sign Night Owl) in the 8th Tactical Fighter Wing at Ubon. These FACs led fighter-bombers (loaded with laser-guided bombs) to the chokepoints. They would remain in the area, dropping flares and bringing in more air strikes to stop road repair teams.

Most Night Owls were equipped with a laser target designator to provide laser illumination and guidance for five hundred-, one thousand-, and two thousand-pound laser bombs.[88]

Night Owl operations began on 18 October after a four-night test. The Night Owl aircraft carried two flare dispensers, three rocket launchers, and three cluster bombs. The FAC dispensed flares at random in an effort to deny the enemy an opportunity for road repair.[89]

> For the Owl FACs, the LORAN was a pretty effective way of finding targets. When they 'canceled' fast-FACs but still wanted the mission flown, they gave me a backseater that was not trained in FACing but was an expert with a LORAN bird. He could find targets. He could get to an area and he had all the numbers and data he needed, although the LORAN botched up the back seat—he was not able to look forward and see people [who were] shooting at us.[90]

The danger to the Night Owls outweighed any requirement to slow road repair, however. The FACs could not work in marginal weather or in the mountains. In the first month, two F-4Ds crashed, with crews aboard, while making marking passes during bad weather; moreover, the AAA fire intensified. These and other dangers induced Seventh Air Force to conclude the Night Owl operation in January 1970.[91]

From the first Misty sortie in July 1967, the jet FAC program proved it could control strike aircraft in heavily defended areas. By 1970, the program's refinements included hunter-killer teams, photo recce/FAC support, weather reconnaissance, day and night operations, and artillery spotting. At the same time, jet-FAC/strike pilot coordination improved through briefings, conferences, and exchange programs.[92]

Statistically, jet-FAC duty ranked among the most hazardous in Southeast Asia—yet volunteers were always available. Between July 1967 and July 1970, 42 jet-FAC aircraft were shot down. This loss rate of 4.37 per one thousand sorties far surpassed that for other flight duty. Seventy percent of the losses took place below 4,500 feet, where AAA fire was devastating (30 aircraft down). Jet-FAC losses soared during the last six months of 1969 (14 planes) and on through early 1970. Nevertheless, Seventh Air Force deemed the program too vital to terminate.[93]

Fast-FAC Expansion

When air strikes against North Vietnam resumed in April 1972, the fast-FAC operation expanded significantly. The major effort was directed against enemy lines of communication and defensive positions in Route Package I. The operation compiled an impressive record of bomb damage assessment between April and November 1972, when a FAC conference produced standardized pilot selection and training programs.

The conference also produced target priorities for the renewed bombing campaigns, the two primary objectives being interdiction of the enemy's lines of communication and a "Gun Kill" program designed to reduce the enemy's defensive capability to protect his roads. Of the 3,594 targets destroyed, 1,322 (37 percent) were fleeting targets (trucks, tanks, missile transporters) whose mobile characteristics required immediate strike. Eighteen percent of the targets destroyed and 25 percent of those damaged represented enemy defenses (SAM/AAA/Heavy field guns for coastal defense). When only night operations were considered, the results were even more significant: Fleeting targets represented 64 percent of those destroyed and 91 percent of those damaged. These figures rise to 81 percent in the destroyed category and 100 percent in the damaged category for fast-FAC-directed strikes.

Between April and November 1972, 24 USAF aircraft were lost in Route Package I. Twelve of these losses were fast FACs—a disproportionate number of losses. Losses due to AAA represented over half of the total and nearly 67 percent of the fast-FAC totals. (The fast-FACs experienced prolonged exposure to AAA.)

The most significant changes in the renewed air offensive involved the advent of the two-ship FAC operation and the Pave Wolf concept of the Eighth TFW. The Pave Wolf program equipped the fast-FAC with Paveway laser illuminator capability, with which he could act as target illuminator for laser-guided ordnance throughout his time on station. Paveway-equipped aircraft were used on 30 to 50 percent of the Wolf FAC sorties. Use of the laser produced a 50 percent BDA increase per sortie. In addition, instant BDAs were made by the FAC laser operators (the F-4 weapons systems officers [WSO]).

The fast-FAC mission was a key element in the employment of tactical airpower in a conventional conflict. The conference recommended that the fast-FAC program be retained after Vietnam. Additionally, the conference recommended a formal training course with the ultimate objective of maintaining two or three trained and current FAC aircrews in each fighter squadron.[94] These suggestions were not followed after US hostilities ended in early 1973; the fast-FAC concept went the way of the FAC concept in general.

Forward Air Controller Comparison

There were several marked similarities between the Fast-FAC Program in Vietnam and the Mosquito Operation in Korea. In Korea, the function for which the airborne FAC was initially conceived was strike control—matching high-performance aircraft with fast-moving targets. To this was added the responsibility for performing constant visual reconnaissance over the entire front line. Because of poor communications in Korea and no effective ABCCC capability, the FAC was normally delegated the additional responsibility of calling for strike aircraft for immediate CAS. Given these three functions (visual reconnaissance, strike aircraft procurement, and strike control), the airborne FAC became the focal point of the tactical air control system. Because he monitored all ground activity, discovered virtually every target, and procured aircraft for all immediate CAS strikes, the airborne FAC gave the TACS flexibility and accuracy.

The same could be said of the fast-FACs. They performed the same functions, but against well-camouflaged and fleeting targets. Jet-FACs also procured aircraft through the more sophisticated ABCCC.

The Mosquito program's success resulted from a fortuitous set of circumstances. Initiative and a willingness to experiment were characteristics of the Mosquito squadron's original staff. Their equipment was improper and inadequate, but they found enough adaptable equipment to maintain the program. Without the T-6, for example, the Mosquito program would probably never have lasted. The same might be said of the original Misty pilots and the F-100F aircraft.

In Korea, General Partridge and his staff at Fifth Air Force were enthusiastic about the program. They provided top-notch personnel and equipment to the Mosquito squadron. General Momyer and his staff at Seventh Air Force had a similar enthusiasm for the Misty FAC program and, later, for fast-FACs in general.

In Korea, the fact that there was a front line made possible on immediate assessment of the effectiveness of the Mosquito-controlled air strikes. Ground was gained if the air strike was successful. This kind of analysis provided a graphic demonstration of the Mosquitoes' effectiveness. The absence of a front line in Vietnam made assessment of combat effectiveness more nebulous. One must develop inferences and other means to evaluate the effectiveness of an interdiction program in a high-threat environment. Nevertheless, judging from fast-FAC BDA alone, the program must be considered a success.

Fast-FAC operations proved the ability of jet-FACs to accomplish the mission in a high-threat environment. One reason for the success of fast-FAC operations was the fact that aircrews performed reconnaissance on the same area daily. Their familiarity with the roads and defenses proved invaluable in locating concealed targets. Another reason for success was the amount of time available in the interdiction area. Because of fuel requirements, a heavily loaded aircraft could not perform armed reconnaissance very long. The F-100F did not consume fuel as rapidly as strike aircraft, but F-4s consumed fuel rapidly at low altitude. Still, it was more economical to refuel a single FAC aircraft than an entire flight of strike aircraft.[95]

Both the Mosquito operation and the Fast-FAC program had vital missions. The necessary organization, equipment, and training were developed for both, enabling them to fulfill those missions.

Notes

1. Tactical Air Command, *Cost Effectiveness of Close Support Aircraft* (Langley Air Force Base (AFB), Va.: USAF, TAC, 1965), 2.

2. The F-5A flew its first strike in October 1965; the A-37 was introduced in July 1967.

3. William W. Momyer, "Close Air Support Tactics and Techniques," (Washington, D.C.: Office of Air Force History [OAFH]), 139–41.

4. Myron W. Crowe, *The Development of Close Air Support*, thesis (Maxwell AFB, Ala., Air War College, June 1968), 45; O. D. Cunningham, *Close Air Support Aircraft*, special study (Maxwell AFB, Ala., Air Command and Staff College),16 May 1960. This 1960 study concluded that high-performance aircraft were not best suited for the CAS mission.

5. Robert F. Futrell, *The United States Air Force in Southeast Asia: The Advisory Years to 1965* (Washington, D.C.: OAFH, 1981), 256–57.

6. Message, Second Air Division (2d AD) to 23d ABG, 24 December 1964 and to 80th tactical fighter squadron (TFS), 25 December 1964, and chief of staff, United States Air Force (CSAF), to PACAF, 24 December 1964; Robert T. Helmka and Beverly Hale, "USAF Operations from Thailand," 1964–1965, Headquarters PACAF, Project CHECO, 10 August 1966, 81–82.

7. Message, Detachment 2, 18th Fighter Tactical Wing, to 2d AD, 18 January 1965, 2d AD to PACAF, 17 January 1965, Thirteenth Air Force to PACAF, 27 January 1965, and 2d AD to CSAF, 15 March 1965; Helmka and Hale, 61–65, 123.

8. Message, 2d AD to PACAF, 28 January 1965.

9. Ibid., Joint Chief of Staff to commander-in-chief Pacific (CINCPAC), 27 January and 4 February1964; *History of Second Air Division (2d AD)*, January–June 1965 (Washington, D.C.: OAFH, 1965), II, 29.

10. Report of Investigation, "Pleiku Incident," by board of officers to investigate incident at Military Assistance Command-Vietnam (MACV) compound and Camp Holloway, Pleiku, Republic of Vietnam (RVN), 16 February 1965.

11. *History, 2d AD*, January–June 1965, 22–26.

12. Futrell, 266.

13. Robert F. Dorr, *McDonnell Douglas F-4 Phantom II* (London: Osprey Publishing Limited, 1984), 54–55.

14. Monthly Evaluation Report, MACV, March 1965, annex B, OAFH, 23.

15. *History of Commando Sabre Operations*, April–June 1969 (Washington, D.C.: OAFH, 1969), vi.

16. Lt Col John Schlight, "Jet Forward Air Controllers in SEAsia 1967–1969," Headquarters PACAF, project CHECO, 15 October 1969, 2–3, 10–11; Report, Seventh Air Force, "Commando Sabre Operations," 31 July 1967.

17. Maj A. W. Thompson, "Strike Control and Reconnaissance (SCAR) in SEA," Headquarters PACAF, Project CHECO, 22 January 1969, 41–44.

18. Schlight, 3–4.

19. Maj Merrill A. McPeak, Director/Plans, 31 tactical fighter wing (TFW), interviewed by USAFHRA staff , 22–23 March 1971. McPeak was an F-100F Misty FAC at Phu Cat, South Vietnam (20 December 1968–31 May 1969) and Tuy Hoa, South Vietnam (1 June 1969–15 November 1969).

20. *History of 37th Tactical Fighter Wing (TFW)* (Washington, D.C.: OAFH, 1967), 21; Schlight, 1967–69, 4.

THE FAST FORWARD AIR CONTROLLERS

21. *History, Commando Sabre*, July–September 1967, 23.

22. July–September 1968, 14–23, January–March 1969, 12–13, April–June 1969, 10.

23. *History, Commando Sabre*, October–December 1968, 16. The pilot and pilot-observer of the F-100F learned to work well together. The rear-seat observer did most of the searching during VR, plotting and recording the targets sighted. Using the hand-held camera, he also snapped pictures of permanent and semipermanent targets such as truck parks and bridges. After both crew members verified potential targets, the rear-seater requested strike aircraft from the ABCCC. The pilot handled the rendezvous, marked the target, and controlled the strike while the pilot-observer monitored. One man could do the entire job but two made it a great deal easier.

24. Schlight, 6.

25. *History, Commando Sabre*, 31 July 1967; Schlight, 5.

26. *Operation Neutralize: The Pattern is Set*, Headquarters PACAF, Project CHECO, June 1969, 1–2.

27. Schlight, 7–8.

28. *Operation Neutralize*, 20–21, 24–25, 34; Lt Col Herbert Brennan, Assistant DCS/Operations, 366th TFW, interviewed by Warren A. Trest, 30 September 1967.

29. *History, 35th TFW*, October–December 1967, 1; *History, Commando Sabre*, July–December 1968, vi.

30. One reason was that the 366th TFW had set up its own F-4 FAC detachment (the Stormies) at Da Nang.

31. *History, 37th TFW*, October–December 1967,1, 15.

32. Schlight, 14, 15.

33. *History, 37th TFW*, January–March 1968, 20–21.

34. Col Stanley M. Mamlock, *Use of the Jet Fighter Aircraft as a Forward Air Control Vehicle in a Non-Permissive Environment*, Maxwell AFB, Ala., Air War College study, April 1970, 62–63.

35. *History, Commando Sabre*, July–September 1968, 30–38; Capts Donald W. Sheppard and James E. Risinger, 3d TFW, letter to Director/Tiger Hound and Tally Ho Division, Seventh Air Force, subject: Inflight Evaluation of PVS-3 Night Starlight Scope, 16 June 1968.

36. Navigation by reference to checkpoints.

37. Staff Summary Sheet, Seventh Air Force, "Misty Night Missions," September 1968; 37th TFW to Seventh Air Force, 14 December 1968, letter, subject: "Commando Sabre Night Operations, October 1968."

38. Night ground fire downed one Misty aircraft on 16 August and another the next night. These losses influenced the decision to discontinue night operations.

39. 37th TFW to Seventh Air Force, 1 October 1968, and 9 April 1969, letter, subject: Special Operational Historical Report, 9 April 1969, 1–2.

40. *History, 37th TFW*, April 1969, 1–2, and *Commando Sabre*, January–March 1969, 12, April–June 1969, 9, October–December 1969, 9.

41. *History, Commando Sabre,* January–March 1970, 7.

42. Lt Col Benjamin R. Battle, interviewed by USAFHRA staff, 8 April 1971. (Battle was the first Wolf FAC Commander, Eighth TFW, Ubon, Thailand.

43. *History, Commando Sabre,* July–September 1968, 25–26; *History, 37th TFW,* October–December 1968, 19.

44. *History, 37th TFW,* October–December 1968, 18.

45. Schlight, 29–30.

46. *History, 37th TFW,* "Misty," April–June 1969; Schlight, 32; McPeak, interview.

47. Thompson, 44.

48. *History, 366th TFW,* July–September 1969, 20–22.

49. *History, 31st TFW,* April–June 1970, 37, 39; *History, Commando Sabre,* 1 April–15 May 1970, 1, 6; Seventh Air Force Deputy Commander/Operations to Seventh Air Force DCS/Plans, letter, subject: Misty FAC Operational Requirement, 15 March 1968.

50. Schlight, 9; 37th TFW to Seventh Air Force, letter, subject: Commando Sabre Operations, 12 August 1968.

51. *History, Commando Sabre,* 31 July 1967.

52. Col Heath Bottomly, memorandum to Gen Norman O. Sweat, Deputy Director/Plans, Seventh Air Force, 5 January 1968.

53. TACLO Activity Report 17, 15 September 1968, 4–5; 366th TFW to Seventh Air Force, letter, subject: End of Training Comments/Recommendations of 366th TFW, 20 August 1968; 37th TFW to Seventh Air Force, letter, subject: Report of FAC Training, 37th TFW, 20 August 1968.

54. Staff Summary Sheet Tactical Intelligence Division, Seventh Air Force, "Increased FAC Sorties for Operation Thor," 30 June 1968, OAFH; Schlight, 23.

55. TACLO Activity Report 18, Seventh Air Force TAC et al., 16–30 September 1968; 366th TFW to Seventh Air Force, letter, 20 August 1968; 37th TFW to Seventh Air Force, letter, subject: Report of FAC Training, 37 TFW and 366 TFW, 26 August 1968; *History, 366th TFW,* July–September 1968, 20.

56. Each F-4D could carry two 370-gallon fuel tanks on its outboard stations, an SUU-23 gun pod for the 6-barrel, 20 mm cannon on the centerline, two LAU-59 rocket pods at the inboard stations, and a wing root the point at which the wing joins the fuselage) camera. The pilot also carried a 35 mm Pentax hand-held camera.

57. 366th TFW, OPlan 10-68, 15 September 1968, Project CHECO, 24–25.

58. Message, 366th TFW to Seventh Air Force, November 1968, subject: Stormy Night Operations.

59. *History, 366th TFW,* April–June 1969, 21–27 and July–September 1969, 20.

60. *History, 366th TFW,* July–September 1969, 20–22.

61. Ibid., April–June 1970, 14, and July–September 1970, 27.

THE FAST FORWARD AIR CONTROLLERS

62. End of Tour (EOT) Report, Col Charles C. Pattillo, commander, Eighth TFW, July 1968–May 1969, and Col Slade Nash, Deputy Commander/Operations and Vice Commander, Eighth TFW (October–December 1968.

63. *History, Eighth TFW*, October–December 1968, I, 22.

64. Battle interview; Nash, EOT Report; *History of the Eighth Tactical Fighter Wing*, October–December 1968 (Washington, D.C.: OAFH), 22.

65. *History, Eighth TFW*, October–December 1968, vol. I, 23–24. The Eighth Wing later used a navigator FAC in the rear seat of the F-4D. He underwent the same training as the pilot FAC, except for flying the aircraft.

66. Pattillo, EOT Report, 23; Nash, EOT Report, 17. The Wolf F-4Ds added an ALQ-87 ECM pod and LAU-3 rocket pods to its inboard stations. For night work, a SUU-42 flare pod (16 flares) replaced the left outboard fuel tank, and a 600-gallon fuel tank went on the centerline.

67. Col Dave "Scud" Yates, interviewed by author, 24 August 1994.

68. *History, Eighth TFW*, January–March 1969, 23–25, 73–74; Battle interview.

69. ARN-92 LORAN-equipped F-4Ds were available in limited numbers in the Eighth TFW, Ubon Air Base, Thailand.

70. Momyer, 219.

71. Working paper for Corona Harvest Report, "USAF Air Operations Against North Vietnam, 1 July 1971–30 June 1972," Headquarters PACAF, Project CHECO, 42–43.

72. Message, 388th TFW to Seventh Air Force, January 1969, subject: F-4E Tiger FAC Program; *History, 388th TFW*, January–March 1969, 42.

73. Pattillo, EOT Report; *History, 388th TFW*, January–March 1969, 42–43.

74. Other members came from Seventh Air Force, Air Attaché, Laos, Task Force Alpha, the Royal Laotian Government, and the Royal Laotian Air Force.

75. *History, 388th TFW*, January–March 1969, 42–44, July–September 1969, I, 61; 88th TFW, Oplan, 1 March 1969, 301–69; EOT Report, Col A. K. McDonald, commander, 388th TFW, December 1968–June 1969; EOT Report, Maj John F. O'Donnell, 388th TFW Tactics Office, subject: Tiger FAC Program. The F-4E FAC configuration kept outboard stations clean. The left inboard station carried rocket pods and the right one held a Nellis camera pod with fore-, aft-, and side-looking 16 mm cameras. A KB-18 camera nestled in the right forward missile bay; a 600-gallon fuel tank on the centerline.

76. *History, 388th TFW*, April–June 1969, I, 52–53.

77. Ibid., October–December 1969, I, 49–50, and January–March 1970, 84.

78. Yates interview.

79. Ibid., April–June 1969, I, 13; 432d TRW to Seventh Air Force, letter subject: Falcon FAC Report, 24 May 1969.

80. Message, Seventh Air Force to 432d TRW, 190501Z, Mar 69, subject: Request for Approval of F-4 FAC Program; *History, 432d TRW*, April–June 1969, I, 13.

81. Message, Seventh Air Force to 432d TRW, 230656Z May 69; *History, 432d TRW*, April–June 1969, I, 13; Message, Seventh Air Force to 432d TRW, subject: FAC Certification.

82. Message, Seventh Air Force to 432d TRW, 240200Z Apr 69, subject: RF-4C Visual Reconnaissance Program; *History, 432d TRW*, April–June 1969, I, 13–14.

83. "History, Current Operations Division, 432d TRW," April–June 1969, OAFH, 1–3, 14; Schlight, 31–32.

84. Schlight, 31–32.

85. *History, 388th TFW*, July–September 1969, I, 63; *History,432d TRW*, July–September 1969, I, 18–20; *History, Eighth TFW*, April–June 1969, I, 24; Col Walter L. Bevan Jr., Director/Combat Ops, Seventh Air Force, to 432d TRW Commander, letter, 3 July 1969; Message, 388th TFW to Seventh Air Force and 432d TRW, 250915Z July 1969, subject: Tiger FAC/Atlanta VR Barrel Roll. The Falcon's call sign in Barrel Roll became Laredo; the Atlanta's, Bullwhip. The Laredos directed 146 strikes during operation About Face.

86. *History, 432d TRW*, July–September 1969, I, 25. Political sensitivity in Laos ruled out the use of B-52s in Barrel Roll at the time.

87. Ibid., October–December 1969, I, 19–20, and Doc. 34, January–March 1970, I, 18.

88. *History, Eighth TFW*, January–March 1970, I, 103–4. Paveway II—a laser device for directing ordnance to the target after release from the aircraft. Specially equipped F-4Ds with laser designators were used in the Night Owl, Wolf, and Laredo programs.

89. *History, Eighth TFW*, October–December 1969, I, 55–57, and *History, 497th TFS*, October–December 1969, 9–13; Schlight, 33–34.

90. Yates interview.

91. *History, 497th TFW*, October–December 1969, 9–13, and *History, Eighth TFW*, October–December 1969, i, 56, January–March 1970, I, 103–104.

92. Schlight, 34; *History, Eighth TFW*, April–June 1970, I, 31, and July–September 1970, I, 23, April–June 1970, 1, 17, and July–September 1970, 1–2.

93. *History, Commando Sabre*, 1 April–15 May 1970, 6–13, *History, 31st TFW*, April–June 1970, I, 39, and History, Eighth TFW, April–June 1970, I, 31–33.

94. *History, Seventh/Thirteenth Air Force*, January–December 1972, vol. II, appendix v, support doc (Washington, D.C.: OAFH), 45; Minutes, "Fast FAC Conference," OAFH, 1–15.

95. Maj Charles M. Summers, "Interdiction Concepts and Doctrine: 1954 through 1968," thesis (Maxwell AFB, Ala., Air Command and Staff College), May 1969.

Chapter 10

Vietnamization and American Withdrawal

President Richard M. Nixon brought a new approach to the war: pursuit of victory while withdrawing ground troops. To accomplish this, he continued the dishonest policy of his predecessor, Lyndon B. Johnson. As a result, Nixon generated distrust, drove some elements of the antiwar movement into terrorism, and degraded the nation's armed forces. Early in 1969, the commitment of American combat troops was reduced and the air war was stepped up by subterfuge. The ploy most commonly used was the "protective reaction strike": American aircraft loaded with bombs and rockets would fly over North Vietnam, Cambodia, and Laos; at the first sign of hostile intent—detecting a radar being switched on, for example—they would unload their ordnance.

Much of South Vietnam was heavily bombed, efforts to bomb the Ho Chi Minh trail were increased, and North Vietnam was regularly attacked up to 50 miles north of the demilitarized zone (DMZ). The bomb tonnage dropped on Southeast Asia from 1969–72 surpassed the American bombing effort in both major theaters in World War II.[1] During this period, attention turned to close air support (CAS) missions.[2]

The objective of the 1968 Improvement and Modernization Program (Vietnamization) was to stabilize the war. The military rationale implicit in the "Nixon Doctrine" rested on the assumption that US airpower, technical assistance, and economic aid could provide sufficient support for South Vietnamese ground forces to keep the Saigon, Phnom Penh, and Vientiane regimes in power against determined attacks by their enemies.[3] The military forces of Laos and Cambodia showed little substantial strength, however, and even the Army of the Republic of Vietnam (ARVN) did not demonstrate extended self-sufficiency against the enemy's best forces. The official American hope was that enough time could be gained to permit these armies to consolidate into effective fighting forces. It was assumed that "Vietnamization" would succeed in

South Vietnam, and that similar transformations could occur in Cambodia and Laos if military disaster was averted long enough.

Vietnamization was a slow and often faltering process in South Vietnam; elsewhere in Indochina, it was even slower and less promising. ARVN's rebuilding program was made possible by the protection offered by US ground forces between 1965 and 1970. That protection was not available in Cambodia and Laos, where the local armies compiled a very poor performance record.[4]

Vietnamization and Close Air Support

In 1963, most of the training provided to Vietnamese Air Force (VNAF) personnel was accomplished in the United States. This method was very expensive, however, and the Advisory Group continually strove to expand in-country training. As a result, in-country training at the VNAF Air Training Center increased by five hundred percent between 1963 and 1968. The basic airman in the VNAF was an enlistee, not a draftee, and was a junior high school graduate. When he completed basic training, he was given an aptitude test and assigned to an appropriate technical school. Following technical training, he was assigned to a VNAF wing where he entered on-the-job training to a higher skill level.

The VNAF officer cadet was required to have a first baccalaureate degree, which was equivalent to a US high school diploma. This educational requirement, along with very strict physical standards, made it difficult for the VNAF to recruit the high number of pilot cadets it needed.[5]

The Military Assistance Command-Vietnam (MACV) estimated that Vietnamization of the war would take five years. In April 1969, however, Defense Secretary Melvin Laird directed that the schedule be accelerated to less than three years. Faced with a deadline of December 1971, USAF and VNAF leaders moved to bolster the Vietnamese structure and personnel associated with the close air support system. They emphasized four areas: (1) accelerate VNAF efficiency through early unit activation and transfers; (2) assign Vietnamese to US units; (3) move training for VNAF personnel from the

United States to South Vietnam; and (4) improve VNAF equipment.

The VNAF forward air controller program realized some gains under American tutelage. The VNAF also made some progress in its aircraft inventory. By December 1970, the VNAF had grown to nine tactical air wings, 40,000 personnel, and approximately 700 aircraft (A-1Hs, A-37s, F-5s, AC-47s, O-1s, and AC-119s). The original plan called for building a VNAF force of 45 operational squadrons; by early 1973, the actual number was 54.[6] In terms of numbers of aircraft, it had emerged as the fourth largest Air Force in the world—behind Communist China, the United States, and the Soviet Union.[7] Nevertheless, serious problems continued to plague the VNAF. The FACs, for instance, lacked sound training and received less-than-enthusiastic support from the ARVN.

There were two categories of VNAF FACs: those trained and certified by the VNAF and those trained and certified by the US Air Force. All combat-ready observers were qualified to control VNAF air strikes, but the emphasis in their training had been in controlling propeller-driven aircraft. The VNAF did not have the capability to train FACs for the control of US fighter strikes.[8] But the Improvement and Modernization Program was determined to make the VNAF self-sufficient; there was a need to upgrade and certify VNAF FACs and ALOs.

The joint plan called for three stages of training. During the first, the USAF ALOs at corps, division, and province levels would develop the capacity of the VNAF ALOs to direct tactical air operations and to advise the ARVN commanders on air support of their troops.[9] During the second stage, the emphasis would be on training and certifying VNAF FACs to USAF standards. In the third stage, the VNAF would assume the ALO and FAC functions completely. There were no target dates, but the turnover was to be as fast as possible.[10]

Command and control arrangements for CAS increasingly came under Vietnamese control after 1969. Assessing the role of CAS in the war remains elusive because the standards of evaluation were imprecise. One measure was its impact on the way the war in South Vietnam was fought. Within this context, CAS operations seemed to have a profound effect. Of course, CAS alone could not guarantee that enemy assaults would always be turned away. Experience in prior wars showed that tactical air units could have only a temporary effect. There is some evidence that friendly ground forces did not maintain contact with the enemy as vigorously as in previous wars,[11] but CAS played such a prominent role in South Vietnam that it affected the basic assumptions about the conduct of the war.

By early 1970, there had been substantial progress in the FAC and ALO upgrade program. Against an authorization of 152 crews on 31 March 1970, the O-1 "liaison squadrons" had 139 observers qualified as FACs for VNAF strikes and 140 combat-ready pilots.[12] Forty-two pilots and 39 observers had also qualified as FACs for US and Australian air strikes, with 10 more in training.[13] From 505 strikes flown by VNAF FACs during January 1969, the number rose to 1,083 during December. During the same period, the percentage of FAC sorties flown by the VNAF increased from 10 percent to 26 percent.

Vietnamization of the FAC program and the tactical air control system had not been completely accomplished by 1971. The VNAF depended on USAF advisers until US force withdrawals compelled reliance on their own resources. Similarly, when ARVN commanders could no longer call upon Americans, they turned to the VNAF.[14] On 11 May 1971, Air Force controllers were ordered to stop performing FAC duties in support of ARVN ground operations. This prompted the Vietnamese Air Force to move toward full acceptance of its role.[15]

When joint USAF-VNAF control of the tactical air control center stopped in June 1971, the Vietnamese Air Force used its TACC to coordinate air activity. Three months later, all of its direct air support centers (DASC) were self-sufficient and positioned with ARVN tactical operations centers in the military regions. The radio request network, which was patterned after the US Air Force's, also began to work.[16] Problems remained, however.

A few diehard ARVN commanders complained of unresponsive air support and distrusted the young, low-ranking VNAF FACs. Many Vietnamese pilots continued to look down on controller duty; the more experienced ones shunned it. The TACS sometimes sent too much air support to some FACs while cutting others short. There was poor target planning, with the DASC holding back sorties until a forward air controller had found a target. Nevertheless, coordination was a far cry from the chaos of two years earlier. By 1972, it had become clear that the Vietnamese Air Force could do its job adequately.

Before the 1968 Improvement and Modernization Program began, the Air Force believed that four liaison squadrons could meet VNAF FAC needs. During 1968, however, the number rose to seven; in 1971, to eight. The first seven units (25 O-1s each) were combat-ready by 30 June 1972; the eighth by the end of 1972.[17]

In March 1972, the Vietnamese Air Force conducted over 90 percent of all in-country tactical air strikes. The Tactical Air Control Parties (TACP) worked at ARVN division level. At the DASCs, the US Air Force maintained token advisory elements (called tactical air support divisions) for dovetailing American air support with the VNAFs. These advisers, and the few remaining Air Force TACPs, were disbanded in 1973. The Vietnamese Air Force now ran the whole show.

The South Vietnamese Air Force

The South Vietnamese Air Force was created in July 1955 with 32 planes inherited from the French. As the level of combat increased, the United States began supplying aircraft of all types. Initially, the only strike aircraft in VNAF were propeller-driven A-1s. The first jets, a squadron of F-5 Freedom Fighters, entered the inventory in 1967. In 1968, the first A-37 light-attack jets were turned over from the US Air Force. The major goals for 1971 were to increase the rate at which helicopter units were turned over to VNAF and to add a squadron of C-123 providers to improve VNAF's airlift capabilities.[18] To help fill a gap in VNAF's ability to operate at night, AC-47 gunships were replaced by the more effective AC-119s in 1972.[19] VNAF's personnel strength in 1968 was less than twenty thousand; by the end of 1971, its strength was about fifty thousand.

VNAF attack sorties increased slowly—from two thousand per month in 1968 to about three thousand per month by the end of 1971. Sorties within South Vietnam dropped sharply when air activity in Cambodia began in April 1970, suggesting that VNAF was operating close to its maximum capability. VNAF's sortie rate remained unchanged during the February 1972 escalation by US fighter-bombers in South Vietnam.[20] Though the aircraft inventory was augmented rapidly, there was no suggestion that VNAF could take over all the functions performed by US airpower when the Americans totally withdrew.

During low US activity, the VNAF flew most of the fighter-bomber attack sorties within South Vietnam. In November 1971, for example, VNAF flew 2,745 sorties while US aircraft flew only 218.[21] One should not infer that Vietnamization of the air war progressed at anything like the rate of Vietnamization on the ground. These figures apply to South Vietnam when ground fighting there was low; moreover, they take no account of B-52 activity, for which the VNAF had no equivalent.

The role envisaged for VNAF by US policy makers was affected by several considerations. Though VNAF pilots were very effective in daylight bombing (many had been flying combat for ten years, while the tour of duty for US pilots was often only one year), their nighttime and all-weather capabilities lagged behind. A training program in radar bombing was designed to overcome this deficiency, but maintenance of the more sophisticated avionics was a problem for the Vietnamese.[22]

The jets delivered to VNAF—the A-37 (developed specifically for counterinsurgency) and the F-5 (developed for Third World Air Forces)—lacked the capability to suppress surface-to-air missiles and to institute sophisticated electronic countermeasures. Because of this, they were not suited for operation in areas of significant antiaircraft defense. Their ordnance-carrying capacity and range were relatively low. Thus, the VNAF was prepared primarily for in-country activity in support of troops in combat. It could not conduct any significant long-range strategic operations or offer close support to troops far from the borders of South Vietnam.

With A-1s, A-37s, and gunships, it was possible to conduct interdiction within South Vietnam and on sections of the Ho Chi Minh trail so long as ground defenses remained minimal. Some token participation in the trail bombing was announced late in 1971: "The Vietnamese Air Force will be flying over the more benign areas near the southern panhandle. They will be flying with us, using AC-47s and AC-119s and maybe a few fighter-bombers too. . . . But they will never be able to build up the capability to do all that the United States Air Force has been doing in Laos."[23]

Since VNAF was being geared to fight an air war in which complete air superiority was assumed, this superiority had to be maintained by US aircraft operating from Thailand and from carriers.[24] VNAF's limited air-to-air capability rested on a squadron of twenty-five F-5 Freedom Fighters (supplemented after 1973 by the newer F-5E). In this category of jet fighters and interceptors, VNAF was more than matched by the North Vietnamese Air Force, whose inventory included 91 MiG-21s in addition to 166 MiG-17s and MiG-19s.[25]

According to one military spokesman, "austerity was the name of the game in Vietnamization."[26] The South Vietnamese economy made VNAF incapable of substituting for US airpower. By December 1971, the US Air Force had reduced its inventory of fighter and strike aircraft in South Vietnam to 277 (from a high of 737 in June 1968). The number of USAF personnel in-country also declined dramatically—from the 1968 peak of 54,434 to 28,791 at the end of 1971. By then, the Vietnamese Air Force was responsible for 70 percent of all air combat operations.[27]

Cambodia

The situation in Cambodia worsened as the US forces were deeply involved in carrying out an orderly, phased withdrawal. By April 1970, about 115,000 American servicemen (60,000 Army, 55,000 Marine) had been withdrawn from South Vietnam. The flow of replacements to remaining American units was also greatly curtailed. Roughly one-fourth of the Army's combat forces and one-half of the Marine combat units in Vietnam were included in the initial phase of American withdrawal.

Concurrent with these troop withdrawals, substantial reductions in US tactical air and B-52 operations were ordered. These reductions, coupled with Defense Secretary Melvin Laird's October 1969 order to Gen Creighton Abrams to cease all offensive operations by American ground forces, meant that US air strikes had become in reality Abrams' strategic reserve in Vietnam. He used them skillfully and with devastating effect. The probability of offensive operations by US ground forces in Vietnam seemed remote.[28] President Nixon's decision to send forces into Cambodia was made late in April 1970, after a week of furious consultations[29]

In August 1969, the Cambodian parliament elected a new government headed by Lt Gen Lon Nol, the Army Chief of Staff. During the next several months, Nol and Prince Norodom Sihanouk tried unsuccessfully to secure international assistance in removing the North Vietnamese troops and the Vietcong from Cambodian soil. In March 1970, while Prince Sihanouk was visiting Europe, the Cambodian government boldly demanded withdrawal of all North Vietnamese. On 18 March, Lon Nol announced the overthrow of Prince Sihanouk and the establishment of the Khmer Republic. Sihanouk subsequently formed a government-in-exile in Peking. The Lon Nol government soon found itself threatened by an estimated 40,000 North Vietnamese and Vietcong troops; Lon Nol appealed for arms assistance. By 20 April 1970, enemy forces had taken control of large areas of the country and had cut roads within 15 miles of Phnom Penh. This apparent threat triggered an American-South Vietnamese invasion of Cambodia to root out and destroy communist forces there. The operation was essential to safeguard the withdrawal of American forces from South Vietnam under Nixon's Vietnamization policy.

The operation began on 24 April when USAF and VNAF tactical aircraft launched strikes against enemy targets in Cambodia. On 29 April and 1 May, 48,000 South Vietnamese and 42,000 American troops drove across the border. The initial tactical air strikes, like the operations of the ground troops they were supporting, were limited to areas within 18 miles of the South Vietnamese-Cambodian border. In addition to the numerous tactical sorties, there were hundreds of B-52 strikes against enemy positions inside Cambodia. By 29 June, all American and most South Vietnamese troops had withdrawn from Cambodia. They had killed more than 11,300 enemy troops and captured 2,300 others.

On 30 June 1970, the day after the allied withdrawal, Air Force tactical aircraft began flying air strikes against enemy forces west of the Mekong River, which were menacing the town of Kompong Thom. When attempts by Lon Nol's forces to advance overland to the town failed, USAF crews turned their attention to roads leading from enemy-occupied Laos toward Kompong Thom. This interdiction attempt failed, however, because flat terrain permitted enemy troops to bypass cratered segments of the highway. Aerial efforts to defend Kompong Thom finally bore fruit; between 31 July and 9 August 1970, 182 fighter-bomber and 37 gunship strikes forced the enemy to fall back. But language problems developed during this operation.

Some Cambodian officers understood English, but few Americans could speak the local languages. Since the nearest thing to a common tongue was French, in a carryover from colonial days, the Air Force used French-speaking volunteers to fly with FACs and serve as interpreters. The Cambodians also made an effort to find and assign English-speaking officers as forward air guides with infantry units, thereby permitting direct communication between Cambodian ground commanders and Air Force FACs.[30]

The Cambodian operation, termed an "incursion" by the Nixon administration, triggered massive antiwar sentiment and civil disorders in the United States, culminating in the Kent State tragedy on 4 May 1970. The cross-border Cambodian action also marked the beginning of a series of congressional resolutions and legislative initiatives that severely limited the executive power of the president. Congress forbade the use of American advisers in Cambodia and limited US military aid to Cambodia. By the end of 1970, Congress had prohibited the use of funds for any American ground troops operating outside Vietnam.

Repercussions from the Cambodian operation became a major factor in accelerating the withdrawal of US forces. Congressional defense budget reductions and lowered draft calls made it mandatory that US troop strength in Vietnam be rapidly reduced. Meanwhile, General Abrams felt a strong sense of camaraderie with the Air Force as the ground forces were reduced. The bond became even stronger as Abrams had to rely more and more upon B-52 strikes and tactical air support.[31]

Lam Son 719

In February 1971, the South Vietnamese Army, with heavy US air support, invaded Laos in the region of the Ho Chi Minh trail. This invasion provided a dramatic lesson that illustrates three important points about the trail. First, the fact that an attempt at ground interdiction was made at all reflects the difficulty of impeding the flow of men and supplies down the trail by air action alone. Second, the stiff resistance with which enemy forces met the invasion was an indication of the value they attached to this supply line. Third, the fact that the incursion, which reached as far west as Tchepone, did not significantly reduce the volume of supplies underscored the effectiveness of this diffuse system of jungle paths.

The objectives of the 1971 Laotian operation were to seize the logistic complex at Tchepone, interdict the trail, and destroy the logistic facilities in the area. A successful campaign, it was hoped, might buy as much as two years since the enemy would need about one year to rebuild his logistic structure to support an offensive in the following dry season (October 1972–May 1973). Many US strategists considered trail interdiction a prerequisite for the success of Nixon's Vietnamization policy.[32]

The ground operation would have to be conducted solely by South Vietnamese troops. Moreover, no American advisers were permitted to accompany ARVN units into Laos. US forces were, however, allowed to support Lam Song 719 with tactical air, helicopters, and long-range artillery operating from South Vietnamese bases.[33]

The Lam Son invasion of Laos was launched on 8 February 1971. South Vietnamese troops—drawn from ranger, airborne, and ARVN infantry divisions—fought for the first time without US advisors. The Air Force operated a tactical air control system from the DASC collocated with the US XXIV Corps forward command post at Quang Tri. It also provided most of the O-2 and OV-10 FAC aircraft. English-speaking Vietnamese flew with the Air Force FACs and aboard C-130 command posts to bridge language difficulties. Other participating USAF aircraft included F-100s, F-4s, AC-119s, AC-130s, and B-52s Also supporting the operation were RF-4Cs for reconnaissance, A-1Es for rescue missions, and KC-135s for air refueling. C-130, C-123, and C-7 transports airlifted more than 30,000 tons of supplies during the invasion. Faced with mounting personnel and equipment losses, Lt Gen Hoang Xuan Lam, commander of the invasion forces, decided to cut short the operation. In the hasty retreat that followed, with many personnel being evacuated by helicopter, the South Vietnamese abandoned large quantities of armor, tanks, trucks, and other military hardware. Intense enemy ground fire shot down or seriously damaged scores of helicopters, leading to panic among many ARVN troops. Under massive tactical and B-52 air cover, virtually all South Vietnamese troops were extricated by 24 March. A number of ground reconnaissance units fought a rear guard action as Lam Son 719 officially ended on 6 April. American air support had been massive: More than eight thousand tactical air sorties and 20,000 tons of ordnance.[34]

Domestic reaction was not as sharp as in May 1970 during the Cambodian incursion. Nevertheless, during and well after the operation, efforts to limit the president's discretionary power to conduct military operations escalated in the Congress. Pressure from the media also intensified. Six weeks of demonstrations in Washington against US involvement in the war culminated on 1 May 1971 with a deliberate effort to bring the federal government to a halt. Meanwhile, a successful pacification program was evolving under MACV and the South Vietnamese government. Military operations in support of pacification focused on attacking the enemy's Achilles' heel—his logistic system.

As 1972 approached, MACV and the Vietnamese Joint General Staff worked overtime to get the nation's defenses in a better state of readiness to meet the next North Vietnamese invasion. It was expected to come in January or February 1972, and to hit hardest in the northern provinces of South Vietnam.

An important element of the Vietnamization program entailed a large expansion of the regular South Vietnamese forces, which increased by almost one-third (from 825,000 to over a million), while Saigon's paramilitary forces almost tripled in size (from 1.3 million to 4 million). Most of the paramilitary increase was in the People's Self-Defense Forces, which were armed with primitive weapons and had no organized units.

The program for the regular forces included a strenuous effort to build greater capabilities for air, naval, artillery, logistic, and other support activities. This effort involved training thousands of pilots, mechanics, navigators, engineers, and others needing advanced skills. Large numbers of US aircraft, naval vessels, armored vehicles, and artillery pieces were turned over to the South Vietnamese.

The US advisory structure was also being rapidly reduced. By mid-1972, advisors were assigned only at ARVN's corps, division, and province levels. But the advisory effort enjoyed the highest priority for quality personnel, a status it had not always enjoyed.[35] The Nixon administration was also attempting to get serious negotiations underway with North Vietnam.

Interdiction in Route Packages I and II

The air war over North Vietnam can be characterized as two main campaigns (Rolling Thunder and Linebacker) with a 42-month bombing halt separating the two. The campaigns had essentially the same objective—to reduce to the greatest extent possible North Vietnam's capability to support the war against South Vietnam. That was to be accomplished through three basic tasks: (1) the destruction of war-related resources already in North Vietnam; (2) the reduction or restriction of North Vietnamese assistance from external sources; and (3) ultimately, the interdiction or impeding of the movement of men and materials into Laos and South Vietnam. Each air campaign concentrated on these objects.[36]

In preparation for a new offensive in 1972, the North Vietnamese continued to pour forces into the area above the DMZ. Special strikes against them, which began in a very limited way, expanded. On 30 December 1971, 1,000 sorties were flown against 41 targets in Route Package I. From January 1971 until March 1972, Americans conducted more than three hundred strikes south of the 20th parallel These missions in southern North Vietnam were controlled by the fast-FACs. In addition to striking SAMs, AAA, and MiG airfields, many missions targeted supply concentrations in the central parts of Route Packages I and II. By the size of these concentrations of supplies, it was apparent that the South Vietnamese could be overrun by a superior force in the northern provinces if those supplies were not reduced. But these special strikes became principally a political tactic rather than a military maneuver. As a military action, they were insufficient to substantially reduce the buildup. They were used instead to threaten the North Vietnamese with resumed bombing above the 20th parallel if they did not stop their obvious preparations to mount a major offensive.[37]

The 1972 Spring Offensive

Despite public expressions of confidence in the progress of Vietnamization, the US government recognized that, without US airpower, the South Vietnamese Armed Forces would have only a minimal chance of staving off defeat if the North attacked in force. For that reason, US airpower did not dwindle as fast as ground forces during the American withdrawal. The tactical airpower available for a major contingency did decrease, however, even in the face of the enemy buildup.[38]

By the spring of 1972, the Nixon administration still hoped to end the war through negotiations. The United States therefore kept a tight rein on its principal bargaining card—airpower. Hanoi, on the other hand, was thinking in terms of another military offensive. By late 1971, evidence had begun to accumulate that Hanoi was planning a large-scale invasion of South Vietnam. Gen John D. Lavelle,[39] who in August 1971 had succeeded Gen Lucius Clay Jr., requested the recall of certain USAF units to the theater (Operation Constant Guard). North Vietnam had assembled a force of about 200,000 men for a push into the South.[40] On 30 March 1972, the North Vietnamese launched a large, three-pronged invasion spearheaded by tanks and mobile armor units.

Once the invasion began, the need for massive tactical airpower support for South Vietnam became critical. Few people had expected the NVA to throw almost their entire strength into the attempt to defeat South Vietnam outright. NVA's use of armor in such massive numbers and in some of the locations chosen was also a surprise. The ARVN was on the verge of collapse and needed aid desperately; the aid came in several forms.

Most of Constant Guard's aircraft were F-4s, but others were F-105s and EB-66s. In the largest single unit move in TAC history, an entire fighter wing, the 49th tactical fighter wing (TFW), deployed to Takhli, Thailand. Another extensive deployment was the buildup of the carrier fleet from three to six carriers off the coasts of Southeast Asia. The Marines also deployed a large contingent of fighter-bombers to Da Nang and Bien Hoa during the second phase of the air buildup. The Strategic Air Command buildup assumed awesome proportions as B-52s and KC-135 tankers were deployed to several bases in Thailand and the western Pacific.

The third phase of US air deployments in 1972 was closely tied to the continued drawdown in South Vietnam. The 366th TFW and the USMC Marine Air Group (MAG) 15 redeployed, with almost all assets going to Thailand. An entirely new base, Nam Phong, was opened to bed-down the Marines. American personnel in Thailand at the end of July totaled nearly fifty thousand, most of them airmen. There were nearly 850 US planes in the country, creating the strongest striking force the United States ever had in Southeast Asia.[41] This bolstered force attacked enemy units with 12,000 sorties per month.

Linebacker

Against the massive invasion of South Vietnam, President Nixon ordered renewed bombing of North Vietnam by both tactical aircraft and B-52s. On 8 May 1972, he authorized the mining of harbors and river inlets in North Vietnam to prevent the rapid delivery of replacement arms, munitions, and other war essentials from the Soviet Union and Communist China. This latest interdiction campaign against North Vietnam continued throughout the summer and early fall of 1972.[42] During this offensive, fast-FACs were often diverted from their primary missions in Route Package I to lead search-and-rescue (SAR) missions for downed American crew members in Route Packages V and VI.

By June 1972, the North Vietnamese had begun withdrawing from some of their advanced positions. By summer, the battles of An Loc and the highland regions were largely over. Attention then turned to the northern provinces, where the regular North Vietnamese Army (NVA) had seized considerable amounts of South Vietnamese territory. Peace talks resumed in Paris on 13 July. In the ensuing weeks, Saigon's forces, heavily supported by US and VNAF air strikes, continued their offensive against the 200,000 enemy troops who had seized control of large portions of the countryside.

While the North Vietnamese offensive continued, US ground forces proceeded with their withdrawal. The last American combat troops departed the country in August 1972, leaving only about 40,000 American support personnel in South Vietnam. The period had seen a significant demonstration of at least marginally successful Vietnamization. During the heavy fighting in 1972, General Abrams emphatically stated, "By God, the South Vietnamese can hack it!" He remained confident of the ARVN's ability to stop the NVA, albeit immeasurably helped by heavy US air support and US advisors on the ground.[43]

On 23 October 1972, when it seemed the Paris talks were leading to an agreement to end the war, the United States again halted air operations above the 20th parallel Soon after, however, the negotiations stalled amid indications that Hanoi might renew its offensive in South Vietnam. Nixon therefore ordered a resumption of air strikes above the 20th parallel. There followed a final 11-day bombing campaign, nicknamed Operation Linebacker II, which became the heaviest aerial assault of the war. The Air Force dispatched F-105s, F-4s, F-111s, and—for the first time, B-52s—over the heavily defended enemy capital and the adjacent port of Haiphong. The tactical aircraft flew more than one thousand sorties, the B-52s about 740—mostly against targets previously on the restricted list: rail yards, power plants, communications facilities, air defense radars, Haiphong's docks and shipping facilities, fuel storage, and ammunition supply areas.

During the strikes into Route Package VI, US support forces ran at a ratio of about four to one.[44] The plan for all linebacker force compositions centered around the type and degree of threat expected at the target area. As a rule, high SAM threat areas called for chaff, ECM, and SAM-suppression aircraft. The support package grew larger when combat air patrol flights (MIGCAP) and escorts were added for protection against MiGs.[45] The number of aircraft varied with each mission, depending upon the targets, the extent of the threat, and whether common support aircraft could be used to cover separate missions with closely scheduled times-on-target. A typical linebacker mission involved about 30 strike aircraft and as many as 80 support aircraft.

Linebacker planners had to overcome the formidable North Vietnamese air defense system during both day and night bombing operations. The USAF daily attacks were divided into two distinct, highly compressed operations: a daylight force comprised solely of F-4 and A-7 strike aircraft, and a nighttime force that incorporated F-111 strikes and B-52 sorties. The night B-52 strikes and the daylight tactical strikes had separate support packages. Naval air strikes around Haiphong were coordinated with the Air Force effort.[46]

The North Vietnamese responded by launching most of their inventory of about one thousand SAMs and opening up a heavy barrage of AAA fire against the attackers. Of 26 aircraft lost, 15 were B-52s that were downed by SAMs. By 28 December 1972, the enemy defenses had been all but obliterated. During the last two days of the campaign, the B-52s flew over Hanoi and Haiphong without suffering any damage.

On 30 December 1972, Nixon announced that negotiations between Dr. Henry A. Kissinger and North Vietnam's representative, Le Duc Tho, would resume in Paris on 8 January 1973. While the diplomats talked, American air attacks were restricted to areas below the 20th parallel Linebacker Operations from May 1972 through January 1973 are summarized below.

	USN Attacks	USMC Attacks	USAF Attacks	Total	Sorties	B-52 Sorties
May '72:	3,920	23	1,919	5,862	10,982	1
Jun '72:	4,151	34	2,125	6,310	12,121	271
Jul '72:	4,175	8	2,310	6,493	12,879	308
Aug '72:	4,746	38	2,112	6,896	13,316	572
Sep '72:	3,937	102	2,297	6,336	13,233	411
Oct '72:	2,674	84	2,214	4,999	11,368	616
Nov '72	1,716	79	1,606	3,401	8,909	846
Dec '72	1,383	119	1,548	3,050	7,894	1,381
Jan '73:	863	50	716	1,629	6,731	535[47]

Linebacker provided USAF an excellent opportunity to demonstrate the totality of its strike capability. Linebacker I, which had lasted for six months, was an interdiction campaign directed primarily against the North Vietnamese supply system. Linebacker II was aimed at sustaining maximum pressure through the destruction of major target complexes in the vicinity of Hanoi and Haiphong.[48]

On 15 January 1973, the United States announced an end to all mining, bombing, shelling, and other offensive action against North Vietnam. A nine-point cease-fire agreement was signed on 23 January. In addition to the cease-fire, the agreement provided for the return of all American and allied POWs within 60 days, establishment of a commission to supervise truce and territorial disputes, the right of the Vietnamese people to determine their own future peacefully, a promise of US economic aid, and an affirmation of the neutrality of Laos and Cambodia. The United States tacitly recognized the presence of about 100,000 North Vietnamese troops still entrenched in northern South Vietnam.[49] Linebacker was deemed a success: The targets selected were destroyed, the stalled peace talks were jarred back into motion, and the final agreements were signed in January 1973.[50]

The United States continued to fly combat missions in Cambodia throughout the first half of 1973. A Wolf FAC piloted by Maj Jerry Cox, with Capt Wade "Mother" Hubbard in the back seat, was shot down on 26 May 1973 near Kratie, Cambodia. Rescued within four hours, they are considered the last combat loss and recovery of the war in Southeast Asia. Major Cox was interviewed by the author on 27 July 1994. Herewith, his account of the shootdown:

> Gary (Lester) and I were at Ubon Air Base, Thailand, with the 308th Tactical Fighter Squadron. Kissenger and the boys in Washington had "ended the war in Southeast Asia," but we were still flying missions in Cambodia. On 26 May, Wade Hubbard and I were flying an F-4D as an escort for Wolf 05 (we were Wolf 06). We were working an area in southern Cambodia along Route 13, which extended from the highlands of South Vietnam through Laos to the town of Kratie, Cambodia.
>
> Our role was to protect the FAC we were working with. We had bombs on board, and we had a laser guidance system known as the ZOT—a laser designator located in the rear cockpit of the F-4. The back-seater would direct laser energy at the target while a companion aircraft dropped a bomb that followed the signal to the target.
>
> We had gone to the tanker for a full load of fuel and were back in the target area before noon. It was a beautiful day for flying. We had put a 2,000-pound bomb on a wooden bridge near Kratie and were back to confirm the hit when we experienced a severe thump. The right floorboard in the front cockpit blew out as debris and smoke came in. I thought we had been hit just once, but we had actually been hit four times.
>
> I was thinking, "OK, we have to get the airplane to a safe area." Knowing that Udon was two hundred miles to the northwest, I turned the F-4 in that direction as the cockpit instruments began to fail. Both fire lights were on, and the heat indicators were maxed out at 1,000 degrees. The plane's systems began to fail and the cockpit filled with smoke. The Ram-dump didn't clear the smoke, but I figured if I kept the sun in the top of the cockpit, my wings would be level.
>
> I hit the panic button, which jettisoned the external fuel tanks and bombs. I could hear John Miller on the radio, but did not know whether my transmissions were being received. I dialed an emergency squawk on the IFF, but was not sure that the system was working. I told Mom what was going on, and that I intended to fly as far as the F-4 would go or until it blew up. Hubbard said, "I'll stay with you."

As it turned out, we didn't fly very far. All the cockpit gauges failed and the rudder peddles fell out of the airplane. John Miller was telling me to jump out as he described the condition of the F-4 from an external view. The fire continued to grow worse in the front cockpit, but being caught on the ground in Cambodia was not a comforting thought. POWs never came back. What was happening was near panic on one side of my mind, slow motion on the other.

The control stick burned loose and was detached from the airplane. I dropped it down the hole that was now boiling flame by my right leg. John Miller was yelling, "Get out, get out—you're going to hit the ground." I told Hubbard, "OK Mom, we have to jump out now," as I pulled the lower ejection handle. The rear seat should eject first, followed by the front seat in four-tenths of a second.

Mom ejected, but my seat failed to eject. The front cockpit was completely engulfed in flames. Molten metal was spattering against me as the F-4 burned itself up. I felt a sharp pain in my right arm and looked down to see a large blob of molten metal slide down into my glove. I pulled the manual release handle and somehow managed to push the canopy enough for the 600 MPH airflow to rip it and me out of the airplane.

When the ejection seat stabilized, I went from a very chaotic environment to an almost serene one. Wind force had pushed the oxygen mask over my eyes, but I managed to pull it down so I could see. Then the Martin-Baker seat exploded into a parachute. I looked up and saw some rips in it just before large swinging motions caused it to become violent. I reached behind me and pulled loops that cut four shroud lines, spilling air out of the back and stabilizing the chute.

I saw my airplane in flames, other F-4s flying around, and, in the distance, Hubbard. Below, I saw the Mekong and a village about a mile to the east. My problem then became one of getting as far away from the village as possible. I pulled on the front risers and gained about a half-mile by gliding west. When I hit the top canopy of jungle, I sailed through cleanly. I then found myself hanging about 40 feet from the ground in the second canopy with my chute tangled in a tree.

I took a couple of deep breaths, then took out the tree-lowering device and wrapped it around the chute harness. Now I had to release the shoulder risers. I was apprehensive, to say the least. I released the right riser and dropped a couple of feet. When I released the left, I hit the tree and lost my grip. I fell the 40 feet to the ground and discovered the true meaning of pain. I thought I had broken my back.

My fear of being caught was tremendous. I got up on my knees, the seat kit still strapped on. The slow motion part of my mind kicked in, even though I was near panic. I took off the chute gear, opened the seat kit, and cut the survival kit loose. I took the compass out of the survival kit and waited for the needle to settle on north. After sending a radio message that I was on the ground, I gathered up my gear and headed west. After walking about one kilometer, I stopped to assess where I was. I sent another radio message and again got no response.

I could hear airplanes circling overhead, but the aircrews couldn't see me under the jungle canopy. I moved a bit further west and found a place to hide. If I stood up, I could see 40 or 50 yards in every direction. I had a badly burned right leg and was losing a great deal of fluid. I was in a great deal of pain from the fall, but I knew I had to get some sort of covering on my leg. And, realizing that my .38-caliber revolver was no match for an AK-47, I decided against a shoot-out with the bad guys.

I waited for the Jollys to come from Ubon. It did not seem to be going the smooth way the Air Force always talked about. I have said that I'd take luck over skill anytime, and that was the case when an OV-10 flew overhead. I grabbed my survival radio and told him where I was. He found me quickly, then just as quickly found Hubbard. About 40 minutes later, I heard the helicopters. One asked for smoke. I popped a smoke signal, but the smoke traveled on the ground about 50 meters before rising up through the canopy. I told the chopper guy I was about 50 meters west of the smoke, but he didn't hear me.

I gathered up my gear and moved as fast as I could to the chopper's area. I saw a paramedic lower himself to the ground, but he couldn't hear me. I scared him when I fell out of the brush behind him and I thought for an instant he might shoot me. He recognized me as the man he was after, however, and didn't pull the trigger.

A forest penetrator was lowered from the helicopter and we strapped ourselves in for the trip back through the canopy. I lost still more skin on that trip. The paramedic got into the chopper, then turned me around backward and yanked me in. I was on the floor, holding on to the penetrator for dear life. Another paramedic kneeled down and spoke in my ear: "OK major, you can turn loose now."

Four hours had transpired from shoot-down to pick-up. When a paramedic looked at my leg, he painted it with a vile, blackish substance. What had been a numb leg now became a violently painful one. Back at Ubon, I was not in the best of all possible conditions. Mom Hubbard, however, hadn't even a scratch. He became famous for being the only person ever to jump out of the back seat of a ZOT airplane.[51]

The last US air strike occurred in Cambodia on the morning of 15 August 1973. When Capt Lonnie O. Ratley returned the A-7 Corsair to its home base in Thailand, he marked an end to the nation's longest war.

It had been a war of attrition and the United States had achieved only a stalemate. By any measurable terms, the United States came out of Vietnam in far worse shape than when it entered—and that is one of the definitions of defeat. The costs—in lives, careers, broken homes, inflation, and taxes—were great. The effect of the war was seen daily in almost every home in America. It was a cruel lesson in fighting the wrong war in thewrong place at the wrong time.

Notes

1. Geoffrey Perret, *A Country Made by War: From the Revolution to Vietnam—the Story of America's Rise to Power* (New York: Random House, Inc., 1989), 527–28.

2. John J. Sbergo, "Southeast Asia," in Cooling, Benjamin Franklin, ed., *Case Studies in the Development of Close Air Support* (Washington, D.C.: Office of Air Force History [OAFH]), 464.

3. Sir Robert Thompson's concept of achieving a "stable war." *US News & World Report*, 1 November 1971.

4. Raphael Littauer and Norman Uphoff, eds., *The Air War in Indochina* (Boston: Beacon Press, Air War Study Group, Cornell University, 1972), 186–87.

5. "Vietnamese Air Force forward air controller operations in South Vietnam, September 1961–July 1968," Headquarters PACAF, Project CHECO Support Documents, Annex I, 1.

6. Ralph Rowley, "Tactics and Techniques of Close Air Support Operations, 1961–1973," thesis (Maxwell AFB, Ala.: Air War College1976), 128–33.

7. Gene Gurney, *Vietnam: The War In The Air* (New York: Crown Publishers, Inc., 1985), 207.

8. Lt Col Albert H. Wuerz, Chief of TACS programs, Operations Plans, AFGP, interviewed by J. T. Bear, 15 February 1970.

9. Training Plan, VNAF/7AF/AFGP, subject: "VNAF TACS ALO/FAC Upgrading Plan," March 1969.

10. Wuerz interview.

11. Lt Gen Julian J. Ewell, Papers, 80, US Army Military History Institute (AMHI).

12. James T. Bear, "VNAF Improvement and Modernization Program," Headquarters PACAF, Project CHECO, 5 February 1970, 39.

13. Maj Jack H. Taylor, AFGP/ODC, interviewed by J.T. Bear, 8 April 1970.

14. Bear, VNAF Improvement and Modernization Program, 34–35, 39; Brig Gen Walter T. Galligan, Director/TACC, Seventh Air Force, to Deputy Director/TACC, Seventh Air Force, letter, subject: Vietnamization of the SEA TACS, 7 July 1970.

15. Maj David H. Roe, et al., "The VNAF Air Divisions Reports on Improvement and Modernization," Headquarters PACAF, Project CHECO, 23 November 1971, 10–11.

16. *History, Pacific Air Command (PACAF)*, July 1969–June 1970 (Washington, D.C.: OAFH), 154o, 154p; Roe, 80; debriefing , Lt Col Russell B. Ruonavaara, 10 May 1972 [Ruonavaara was Ops Off, 20th TASSq (April 1971–April 1972)].

17. "USAF Management Summary for SEA," 19 February 1971, 55, 13 March 1970, 2–46, 2–47, 2–51, 2–52, 17 December 1970, 54, OAFH; I DASC to Chief, Air Force Advisory Team 1, letter, subject: Phase-out of US FACs in ARVN System, MR-1, 10 January 1971.

18. For a history of VNAF, see "Vietnamization's Impact on the Air War," Vietnam Feature Service (TCB-089), January 1971.

19. John L. Frisbee, "USAF's Changing Role in Vietnam," *Air Force Magazine*, September 1971, 44.

20. *Washington Post*, 11 February 1972.

21. *Ithaca Journal (AP)*, 8 December 1971. (The DOD figure for US sorties that month was actually 366.)

22. Littauer and Uphoff, 175.

23. Quoted in Craig R. Whitney (unknown title), *New York Times*, 12 December 1971.

24. Kenneth Sams, "How the Vietnamese Are Taking Over Their Own Air War," *Air Force Magazine*, April 1971, 30.

25. William Beecher (unknown title), *New York Times*, 26 January 1971.

26. "How the Vietnamese Are Taking Over," 29.

27. Rowley, 64.

28. Bruce Palmer Jr., *The 25-Year War, America's Military Role in Vietnam* (Lexington: University Press of Kentucky, 1984), 99–100.

29. Henry A. Kissinger, *The White House Years* (Boston: Little, Brown & Co., 1979), 258–59.

30. Carl Berger, "Air War in Cambodia" in Gene Gurney's, *Vietnam: The War in the Air* (New York: Crown Publishers, Inc., 1985), 249–50.

31. Palmer, 102–03.

32. "Laos: April 1971," Staff Report, Subcommittee on US Security Agreements and Commitments Abroad, Committee on Foreign Relations, US Senate, 3 August 1971, 9, 22. See also "Igloo White," *Air Force Magazine*, June 1971, 48.

33. Palmer, 109.

34. Jacob Van Staaveren, "The Air War Against North Vietnam," in Gene Gurney, *Vietnam, The War in the Air* (New York: Crown Publishers, Inc., 1985),114–16.

35. Palmer, 115.

36. "Linebacker II USAF Bombing Survey," Headquarters PACAF, Project CHECO, April 1973, 1.

37. William W. Momyer, *Airpower in Three Wars* (Washington, D.C.: OAFH), 217.

38. Capt Charles A. Nicholson, "USAF Response to the Spring 1972 North Vietnamese Offensive: Situation and Redeployment," Headquarters PACAF, Project CHECO, 10 October 1972, 65.

39. Gen John Lavelle was recalled from his post in April 1972, charged with having authorized certain "protective reaction" strikes beyond those permitted by the rules of engagement. He was succeeded as Seventh Air Force commander by Gen John W. Vogt.

40. Van Staaveren, 154.

41. Nicholson, 65–66.

42. Rowley, 64–65.

43. Palmer, 121–122.

44. Corona Harvest, "USAF Air Operations Against North Vietnam, 1 July 1971–30 June 1972," Headquarters PACAF, 8 June 1973, 150.

45. Calvin R. Johnson, "Linebacker Operations: September–December 1972," Headquarters PACAF, Project CHECO, 19.

46. Karl J. Eschmann, *Linebacker: The Untold Story of the Air Raids Over North Vietnam* (New York: Ivy Books, 1989), 30.

47. *History, Military Assistance Command, Vietnam,* January 1972–March 1973, I (Washington, D.C.: OAFH), B–19.

48. Col William F. Shackelford et al., "Eleven Days in December: Linebacker II" study (Maxwell AFB, Ala.: Air War College, 1977), 101.

49. Van Staaveren, in Gurney, 154–59.

50. Eschmann, 203.

51. Col Jerry Cox, interviewed by author, 27 July 1994.

THIS PAGE INTENTIONALLY LEFT BLANK

Chapter 11

A Perspective on Close Air Support

Among military men, it is commonplace to speak of interservice operations as difficult to execute. Differences in equipment, doctrine, attitudes, and outlook inhibit and complicate harmonious interaction. Past success, however, has shown that these difficulties can be overcome with determination, effective procedures, and proper training. In no area of interservice operations has this phenomenon been more pronounced than in close air support (CAS).

The history of CAS since World War I is marked by tragedies such as lives lost, unduly protracted conflict, and victory deferred because both air and ground officers have too often failed to benefit from experience garnered and recorded by earlier generations. This repeated pattern of behavior gives credence to the observation that the only thing we learn from history is that we do not learn.

Interservice Cooperation

The Joint Chiefs of Staff define CAS as air action against hostile targets that are close to friendly forces. These operations require meticulous coordination for each air strike, but close support can better be understood when placed in the broader context of Air Force roles and missions as a whole. Strategic airpower seeks to influence the war by destroying the enemy's military, political, and economic base for waging war. Tactical airpower seeks to influence the battle indirectly by interdiction and directly by CAS. Interdiction involves air strikes at some distance from the point of engagement to prevent or inhibit the flow of men and material to the battle front. CAS, on the other hand, involves direct intervention at the forward edge of battle. In World War I this could mean strafing a line of trenches with machine gun fire. In World War II, it might mean bombing an enemy gun position on a reverse slope masked from friendly artillery. In Vietnam, it could mean flying cover for a column of trucks. All successful air operations, however, whether strategic or tactical, rest ultimately upon air superiority; the freedom to operate, even if only locally and temporarily, without effective interference from the enemy.

Tactical airpower has three functions: (1) It must be ready to fight for air superiority, intercepting and destroying enemy aircraft that seek to drive off friendly air or harass ground units; (2) at the same time, tactical airpower must be prepared to isolate the battlefield through interdiction strikes; and (3) tactical airpower must provide close support assistance to ground troops in the battle. Which role airpower will perform at any given time depends upon the shifting tides of battle.

In each major conflict in which the United States has engaged in the twentieth century, procedures were eventually developed to deliver close support with considerable success. The question is not one of asking if effective close support is possible; the real issue is why such procedures are not put into effect at the very outset of engagement.

Probably no factor colors the performance of CAS more than the attitudes brought to it by the air and ground personnel involved. Airmen, especially since the US Air Force achieved independence in 1947, tended to see every bid by the Army to attain a larger share of control in close support as a threatening encroachment upon their hard-won and long-delayed autonomy. While the airmen's insistence upon retaining ultimate control is certainly valid, their zeal for autonomy has inhibited effective execution of the CAS mission. Another basic attitude shaping Air Force practice is the belief that tactical air should give the interdiction mission a higher priority than close support. In terms of damage imposed weighed against risk, the interdiction mission has usually outweighed close support in the Air Force view.

Unfortunately, the effects of interdiction are indirect, delayed, and long-range, and thus difficult to measure against the losses and frustration of the ground commander. The character of close support makes aircraft especially vulnerable to ground fire. To identify an enemy target with assurance and be sure that he is not hitting friendly troops, a pilot is under pressure to come down to lower altitudes. The lower he flies, the greater the risk. The increased risk often makes a dubious trade-off for the damage inflicted. This makes interdiction, in Air Force eyes, more profitable than close support. From the perspective of the ground force, the problem presents an entirely different face. Whenever aircraft fail to arrive in response to a ground request, the reaction is almost certain to be irritation.[1]

Improved command at the top will not solve the problem of close support without similar developments at the lower end of the chain of command. The British showed the way in North Africa and the Americans perfected their system after moving into Italy. The challenge was how to help the fighter pilot locate targets with sufficient precision to make the kill without harming friendly troops. The problem had a two-fold solution: Pilots, serving as FACs on the ground in radio-equipped jeeps, relayed requests from the ground troops and talked aircraft onto targets. When the terrain prevented this, airborne controllers in light liaison planes performed the same service.

Whether ground-based or airborne, the essence of the FAC lay in his ability to meld the point of view of the ground troops with a knowledge of the capabilities and limitations of airplanes. By the end of World War II, a reasonably effective system for providing CAS had been established and codified as official doctrine in Field Manual 31-35, "Air Ground Operations," issued in 1946. It was based largely on the experience of Ninth Air Force in working with the 12th Army Group in Europe. This was an important body of experience, but it failed to provide guidance to the Navy and Marine Corps.

Competition in close support from Marine Corps aviation in Korea proved painfully embarrassing to the Air Force because of the Marines' superior performance. Marine flyers were specialists in close support; it was their mission, they were trained for it, and their equipment was optimized for the role. By the time the shooting stopped in Korea, Air Force organization and procedures were also highly effective. One might reasonably assume that this would provide a basis for the distillation of improved doctrine and a determination in the Air Force not to repeat the neglect of close support that had followed World War II. Unfortunately, this was not the case.

When US forces again went into action in Southeast Asia, the Air Force was once more unprepared to provide the kind of close support the ground units required. The Army still argued that ground commanders should have operational control of aircraft assigned to the close support mission. A new generation of leaders, with little knowledge of the past, fought over the same old issues. These leaders eventually perfected a workable organization with appropriate procedures, but there were years of delay and a great deal of friction that might have been avoided if the experiences of World War II and Korea had been remembered. In Vietnam, dedicated and conscientious individuals had to establish a viable organization and sound procedures just as their predecessors had to do.

Again, the end of the Vietnam War saw forward air controllers (FAC) and the CAS mission languish from low priorities and lack of funds. Little was accomplished for nearly 20 years. America's involvement in the Grenada and Panama invasions did not generate a need for CAS or FACs. Ground support in these actions was provided by C-130 gunships and Army attack helicopters.

In the 1991 Gulf War, the need for FACs was somewhat limited. The desert environment created a problem opposite to that encountered in Vietnam: targets were too easy to find. The Air Force found that many "previously killed" targets were being struck a second and third time. To prevent this, the "Killer Scout" program was conceived. Killer Scouts were experienced F-16 and A-10 pilots whose mission was to identify previously destroyed targets in their assigned areas. They also validated "live" targets and assisted fighter pilots in distinguishing these from "dead" ones. Again, as in previous wars, the Killer Scouts were "invented" to solve a problem created by the environment in which the war was fought.

The current joint doctrine for close air support is outlined in a number of sources, including Tactical Air Command Pamphlet (TACP) 50-28 and Army Field Manual (FM) 90-20. The concept, known as *J-Fire*, outlines the requirements for air support, a joint tactical air strike request format, a format for briefing CAS pilots, the structure of communications networks, and weapons data.

J-Fire is applicable to the tactical forces of the Army, Marine Corps, Navy, and Air Force. It is a US unilateral-only document, but it includes NATO formats. Intended primarily for use by members of battalion-level combat units, it contains procedures and information for coordinating artillery/mortar fire, CAS, and naval gunfire. It describes the duties of all liaison elements, and it contains risk-estimate distances for weapons employment.[2]

Devising workable structures and effective procedures to ensure a smoothly functioning close support system has been the principal challenge, but other elements were involved—notably, the three classes of equipment required to effectively accomplish the mission: aircraft, ordnance, and communications.[3]

Aircraft

Ground officers urged the development of specialized aircraft to perform CAS. Continual development of high-performance aircraft after the mid-1950s widened the gap between the characteristics best suited to the support function and those appropriate for air superiority. Higher speeds of the more sophisticated aircraft impair the ability of an observer to identify targets on the ground and increased fuel requirements means reduced loiter time, which means longer periods when ground troops lack air support. The advocates of specialized aircraft have also argued that low-performance aircraft, suited for CAS, are less costly and could be procured in large numbers—but all these arguments in favor of low-performance aircraft presuppose air superiority.

Characteristics of importance in any FAC aircraft include these: excellent cockpit visibility; communications equipment sufficient for simultaneous voice contact with friendly ground forces, strike aircraft, and controlling agencies; the ability to operate from short, unimproved airfields under austere maintenance and support conditions, and the capability to accurately and positively mark targets for strike aircraft. This capability should be adequate for use by the most advanced ordnance delivery system of the strike aircraft. For example, if strike aircraft have laser seekers or carry laser-guided ordnance, then the FAC aircraft should have a laser target designator. In addition, FAC aircraft should have the ability to detect, identify, track, and mark targets at night. It should also provide crew protection against small arms fire and a system for rapid emergency crew egress under uncontrolled flight conditions.[4]

The high-wing L-5 had excellent visibility, but its inability to carry adequate communication equipment and its lack of defensive armament limited its value as a FAC aircraft when it was used early in Korea. At the same time, pilots of high-performance F-80 jets found it difficult to identify ground targets. This led to use of the sturdy T-6, which was slow enough to give pilots time to search the terrain and heavy enough to carry communications equipment that permitted talk with ground commanders and fighter aircraft. But the low-wing T-6 had less visibility than the high-wing L-5.

When US troops became engaged in Vietnam, the question of finding a suitable aircraft for close support surfaced again. The L-5 had become the L-19, rechristened O-1, and the jets were F-100s and F-4s—but the story was the same. The O-1 was easy to maintain and afforded good visibility, but it was underpowered, unarmed, and lacked adequate capacity for communication. The more modern F-100s and F-4s guzzled fuel, lacked loiter time, and were too fast for observers to see fleeting targets.

In 1969, four years after US units began fighting in Vietnam, the Air Force finally discovered the OV-10. This twin-engine plane carried four machine guns and four rocket pods, which allowed it to provide immediate response as a forward air controller. It was designed to pursue a fleeting target that would disappear before a jet fighter could arrive, but the OV-10 could not survive against North Vietnamese jets. While it proved to be highly effective, it was largely limited to in-country operations in areas made safe by a protective umbrella of friendly jets.[5]

In March 1977, the Air Force introduced the A-10 "Thunderbolt II" into the inventory and A-10 units today

A-10 "Thunderbolt II"

provide much of the FAC support. Armed with a 30 mm "Avenger" seven-barrel cannon, the A-10 can also carry a variety of munitions to support close air support. Funding was terminated in 1983; the last of 713 A-10s was delivered in March 1984.[6]

Ordnance

Any consideration of ordnance for close support must account for the relationship between the ordnance and the aircraft carrying it. Five-hundred-pound bombs were available when US troops went into combat in Korea, but the F-80 jets were not equipped with pylons to carry them. The air superiority mission had a higher priority. The Air Force designates a pilot an ace after five kills in air-to-air combat, where high speed and maneuverability are essential. Pylons and ordnance slow a fighter and limit its maneuverability. Five air-to-ground support operations might well be of crucial importance to the success of the battle on the ground, but they will never make a pilot an ace.

Conventional ordnance, such as five hundred-pound bombs, machine guns, and napalm, was the ordnance of choice until late in the Vietnam War when all jet fighters could carry a variety of weapons. The introduction of laser-guided bombs and advanced air-to-surface missiles increased the accuracy of fighter attacks and made CAS more efficient. Long-range navigation systems (LORAN) and ground-based radar direction enabled fighters to attack targets at night and in marginal weather. Advanced navigation and bombing systems that use global positioning system (GPS) data make today's fighters far more effective in conventional ordnance delivery than even the F-4s were 20 years ago.

Communications

Communication is another material factor in CAS. Because coordination of air and ground operations is vitally important, communication is of central concern. Today, communication means electronics.

Remarkable technical strides had been made in radio by the outbreak of World War II, but radio still suffered from serious defects. Air Corps planes participating in the Louisiana maneuvers had to convert their radios to Army frequencies to permit air-ground coordination. In doing this, they lost their ability to communicate at long range. Disoriented pilots found themselves unable to communicate with their airbase. In short, the evidence pointed to surprising delays in recognizing the importance of providing easy communications between all echelons and services that were expected to cooperate.

Lack of money to develop adequate communications equipment was the reason offered to explain the shortcomings in this area. But when funds are lavished on the armed forces in wartime, it is harder to explain the delays to upgrading communications capabilities. In the Southwest Pacific during World War II, Army units with high-frequency radios could not communicate with Navy fighters equipped with very high-frequency radios until suitable equipment was obtained late in the war.

After the experience of three wars, the problem resurfaced during the *Mayaguez* incident in 1975. When Cambodian Communists attacked a US freighter, rescue operations disclosed that the problem of interservice communication still had not been resolved.[7]

Personnel

The availability of qualified pilots is another dimension of the problem in CAS. Because the production of trained pilots has borne a relationship to the number of aircraft available, a shortage of pilots has seldom been the weak link in the early days of a conflict. When pilots are used as ground FACs, however, the situation changes drastically. With appropriate training, individuals without pilot wings can do the job.

The confidence level of the pilot is raised when he knows that he is being directed by one who may be swapping roles with him in a few days. There is also much to be said for having pilots know the ground personnel they are supporting.

A substantial case can also be made for using other trained personnel. With the cost of training a modern jet pilot at one to two million dollars, it may not be cost effective to assign pilots to ground controller duty. To be fully effective, a controller must operate closely with the ground unit being served. Would it not be better military economics to risk pilots in fighter-bombers rather than on the ground performing a role that might be performed by a less expensive officer? The British practice in World War II was to use Army officers rather than pilots as ground controllers. Their success suggests a precedent worth investigating.

Perhaps the most important question remains to be answered: Is CAS by high-performance Air Force aircraft a viable mission in an era of precision-guided munitions? The historical record cannot answer that question, but it can provide the context within which new experience may produce a solution.

Airpower in Regional Conflicts

The advances in military technology since World War II have given American presidents a substantial independence from

Congress and the public in waging war. The development of airpower—its present responsiveness to centralized control, its remoteness from the tide of the ground battle, and its vast destructive force—has created an opportunity for American presidents to conduct war without reference to the wishes of the body politic. The reason is simple: War from the air is not very tangible to the average American.

Air warfare is cheap in terms of American lives. Two men flew an F-4 Phantom fighter-bomber that carried 12,000 pounds of explosives. Six men formed the flight crew of a B-52 Stratofortress that lifted 108 five-hundred-pound bombs to 30,000 feet. The dollar cost of an air war is not perceptible to the citizenry. The relatively low cost of air action tends to become lost in huge defense budgets. Furthermore, presidents can swiftly escalate an air war without arousing much public attention. Airpower can be turned on and off, up or down, with a simple order from the White House. Air warfare is perceived by the American public only intermittently, whenever a presidential administration varies a pattern of raids.

Official accounts of US air activity in Vietnam naturally laid heavy stress on the close-support function. A rather surprising picture emerged. Close air support constituted a small fraction—below 10 percent—of US fixed-wing air activity in Vietnam.[8] In view of the large-scale US air effort, US ground forces would expect to get all the CAS they wanted. Had there been a need, close support could easily have been increased. The real question, however, was different. Given that less than 10 percent of the sorties satisfied the close-support requirement, what were the other 90 percent being used for? They fell into the wide and diffuse category of interdiction,[9] supported largely by the Fast-FAC program in the out-country war.

Current High-Risk Strategy

The United States has a consistent history of underestimating in peacetime the forces that it will require in war. The Persian Gulf War, for example, ultimately required a third more fighter forces than the strategy had estimated. It required most of

USAF's best aircraft and the largest coalition air fleet since World War II. RAND corporation analysts, studying regional conflict, discerned a pattern of imperfect US forecasts: peak US deployments needed to fight in Korea, Vietnam, and Iraq "exceeded planner's prewar expectations by a factor of two in critical areas."

The danger of global war has diminished, but there has been a corresponding increase in the probability of regional conflict. It is clear that the new world order is characterized by instability, regional power struggles, and violence that were restrained when the superpowers exerted more influence.

A few years ago, it was considered almost eccentric to worry about North Korea as a military threat; nobody is smirking today. A few years ago, before the breakup of the Warsaw Pact and the collapse of the Soviet Union, the prospects of near-term conflict in Europe were rated as virtually nil; few would make that judgment today, having seen the relentless animosity unleashed in the Balkans and the tensions at play among the new nations of the former USSR. Nor does it take a hyperactive imagination to conceive of trouble originating in—or spreading from—the old Soviet Union.

Beginning in 1976 and continuing into the 1980s, the Air Force officially was building toward a force of 40 combat-coded fighter and attack wings. A somewhat arbitrary goal, it represented a compromise between official requirements and available budgets. The requirement actually indicated by analysis was about 44 wings. In 1987, the Air Force dropped its goal to 37 wings—but said it would concentrate on supporting those wings properly. In February 1991, the Pentagon announced plans to again reduce USAF fighter structure—this time to 26 wings. In March 1993, the Pentagon's annual budget announcement said the base force would be reduced to 24.3 fighter wings, the only major force-structure change announced by Secretary of Defense Les Aspin. The Bottom-Up Review, in late 1993, dropped the fighter force structure to its lowest point yet—20 combat-coded fighter and attack wings. Fiscal Year 1994 was a benchmark: The active duty fighter fleet slipped below 1,000 aircraft. A-10 forces comprised one active duty squadron and one reserve squadron (about 48 aircraft).

RAND said, "Historically, the Air Force has deployed an average of ten fighter wings (about 30 squadrons) to the three major post-World War II conflicts: Korea, Vietnam, and Iraq" (Korea-July 1953 [10.4 Wings], Vietnam-December 1968 [10.6 Wings] and Desert Storm-February 1991 [10.6 Wings]).[10]

Future Trends

The Air Force has embarked on a major campaign to make space systems a key part of its fighting force. The focal point of this effort is Air Force Space Command's Space Warfare Center at Falcon AFB, Colorado. The origins of the center and its mission date to early 1991 and the Persian Gulf War. Shortly after the war ended, Gen Merrill A. McPeak, Air Force Chief of Staff, announced that USAF should seek to control and exploit both air and space.

In the Gulf War's aftermath, analysts focused on major deficiencies in the service's ability to make high-quality space information available to aircrews and ground unit commanders. Brig Gen David L. Vesely was the Space Warfare Center's (SWC) first chief. According to him, there was little tactical warning in the Gulf War. The reconnaissance data that arrived was of little use—and during mission execution, information flow was almost nonexistent.

The principal mechanism for increasing the service's operational use of space is an initiative known as TENCAP (tactical exploitation of national capabilities). The program dates to the early 1970s, but only recently has it gained serious attention. TENCAP is divided into six programs (code-named Talon). GPS information is integrated into military survival radios, making it easier to rescue downed airmen and providing satellite targeting data to cockpits in near real time.

The intelligence community acknowledged the need for greater operational input and Gen Charles A. Horner, former commander of US Space Command, developed an integrated priorities list for intelligence systems.

In the mid-1980s, another stimulus arose from Air Force efforts to provide near-real-time information to the cockpit. The Soviet Union deployed mobile nuclear missiles, presenting

Air Force officials with a huge targeting problem. To solve it, the Air Force launched a number of highly classified initiatives to deal with strategic relocatable targets (SRT). Before the SRT program evaporated with the Cold War, it had revealed the difficulty of linking satellite data to airborne systems. Today's mobile missile targets are difficult to detect. During the Gulf War, for example, the Air Force was frustrated in its efforts to locate Iraqi Scud launchers.

TENCAP has an ambitious agenda. Its goal is to harness space-based assets to service pilots in fighters, bombers, and airlift cockpits (Talon Shooter), battlefield command and control (Talon Command), mission planners (Talon Ready), and special operations forces (Talon Night). In addition, the program is investigating support systems such as communications (Talon Touch) and new technologies (Talon Vision).

The first TENCAP product to make the transition to the acquisition community is a six-layer system that provides near-real-time intelligence updates for aircrews en route to a target. The multisource tactical system (MSTS) provides multispectral imagery from satellites, digital charts and elevation maps, satellite intelligence (including signals intelligence) on air- and ground-based threats, and real-time data from the Global Positioning System.

The system debuted on a C-141 transport during exercise Bright Star '94 in Egypt. It was demonstrated on C-141, C-130, and KC-135 aircraft on relief missions over Bosnia-Herzegovina. For now, multisource tactical system (MSTS) is more appropriate for heavy-lift aircraft, which have sufficient space for the unit's twelve-inch computer monitor. The program office hopes that advances in flat-screen technology—now being pursued separately under the Talon Vision program—will make the gear suitable for fighters.

The Air Force is separately studying the feasibility of putting a high-speed mini-super-computer on board fighters under the Talon Lance project. The computer would work 10 to 30 times faster than existing aircraft processors and would reduce the load of raw data for pilots to handle.[11]

When this system is successfully introduced, perhaps in eight years, it may eliminate the need for traditional airborne

FACs. CAS target information from ground commanders, or interdiction target information from a command network, could be fed through satellites and broadcast directly to fighter cockpits. Codes would ensure that the information was coming from a valid source. Inertial navigation systems onboard fighters would use positioning data from the GPS. Target location would also be GPS-derived. The pilot would depart an initial point (IP), also selected through the GPS system. His heads-up-display (HUD) aiming index would automatically be positioned over the target location on the ground. Before beginning his attack, he could verify the target with a photograph broadcast directly to the cockpit. This photo could come from either satellite imagery or a remotely piloted vehicle. With this information, a successful attack would be possible without voice communication or target marking.

Col Dave Yates gives his views on the proper use of FACs and his thoughts concerning their future:

> I do not think it's the smartest thing in the world to work for the Army commander who needs you. If the theater commander has charge of everybody and knows that air superiority and SEAD (suppression of enemy air defenses) are accomplished before interdiction and close air support, that allows the system to work. If you gave close air support back to the Army, somebody still has to be the air component commander who knows about air in particular. The theater commander must understand the use of this artillery piece called air. Army commanders grow up from grunts and Air Force commanders grow up from fighter pilots. They do not know much about each other. We need to grow up together again.
>
> I do not know [whether FACs have a future role]. As long as we can put up remote sensors, maybe not. That is where it's going with technology in the next 10 years. The Army commander will be able to put [up] little remote airplanes that give him viewing sensors to locate targets. Those targets are identified and their coordinates are passed via satellite to an F-16. The F-16 goes to an IP (a point from which to plan an attack), which is pointed out by the same satellite. He pops up and rolls in for his attack and the diamond on his HUD (heads-up display) is on the target. If he also had a picture sent to him, which will be here in a few years, he could identify the target. All this information is coming through data links and if the fighter pilot knows the ground commander sent it, he can drop on that target.
>
> Will the manned FAC still have a mission? I do not know. Remote vehicles are doing nearly everything today. Remote vehicles are going

to do air-to-air before long. We are right now finding targets via sensors, photo, IR, and airborne sensors at long range and passing this data through satellites, down to a fusion center and up to airplanes in the air. No words are passed. We are now at the point we can actually do that. Sensors go off on a launch warning and an F-16 within range is alerted. Will there always be FACs? I do not know, but we are [having] less need for them. The FAC in desert Iraq was much different [from] the FAC in the trees of Vietnam.[12]

Conclusion

Airpower is economical, flexible, and unobtrusive. In this capsule statement are contained many of the aspects of airpower that make its use so attractive. The direct costs of delivering a ton of ordnance by air are lower than for other methods. The air war delivered about the same tonnage of munitions as the ground war in Indochina while accounting for no more than one-third of the total cost. More important, the number of American lives lost in the air was less than 10 percent of the total.

The deployment of airpower is flexible and can be very unobtrusive. Aircraft can be based far from the scene of action. They need not take war correspondents or television crews with them on their missions. Their destinations may remain obscure, their targets unpublicized. Airpower can be turned on and off quickly and quietly; no mobilization or draft calls need disturb the peace of the voters.

Escalation is an easy—even attractive—course of action. Because airpower is remote and indirect, and because it is relatively economical, it appears reasonable to apply more airpower when success is elusive. If the ultimate objectives remain out of reach, policy makers are likely to escalate the air war, applying "more of the same medicine." Escalation is easier when there is no fear of retaliation in kind by the other side. So, in the use of airpower against a weaker nation, there need be no thought of possible retribution.

The costs of war accumulate, but its successes do not. One can win a battle, even many battles, and yet lose the war. This dictum applied with special force to airpower in Indochina. The ultimate goal of the struggle there was political, not military.[13] Yet airpower is far from being an instrument of political persuasion. It can force people to move, even remove them from the scene, but it cannot win allegiance from them or establish the legitimacy of a regime. Even as an instrument of coercion, it is deficient because its effects are intermittent. It can disrupt economic, social, and political activity, but it cannot enforce desired behavior like ground forces can. Military gains obtained through airpower are difficult to translate into political objectives. The CAS mission is an exception, however; its effects are short-term and immediate. Friendly lives are at risk and tactical military objectives can either succeed or fail based on airpower's effectiveness.

According to Col Charles Varvi, who served as a FAC in both Korea and Vietnam, there is no more important mission for a fighter pilot, especially in a troops-in-contact situation, than close air support. Colonel Varvi began his FAC career as a peacetime Mosquito pilot in 1954 Korea. When he retired in 1982, he had flown the T-6G, the O-1, the OV-10, and the F-4D/E.

In comparing Korea and Vietnam, Colonel Varvi said the two conflicts were very different. "In Korea, you generally had a line with the friendlies on one side and the enemy on the other. You could have a ground FAC moving with a battalion or division even though the lines were fairly fluid. But in Vietnam, there were no lines; it was airlifting GIs into the jungle and extracting them by helicopter. I think the airborne FAC in that environment was essential while a ground FAC was extremely limited."

He was enthusiastic about the F-4 as a FAC aircraft, "especially in an extremely hostile environment like Laos, where the Ho Chi Minh trail was lined with all kinds of weapons. It had a two-man crew, it was fast, it could climb in the blink of an eye, and it carried a wide range of ordnance. I thought it was an excellent airplane for that role."

Asked about his view of the FAC's role today, Colonel Varvi said he thinks the mission remains basically the same. "The things that influence the FAC mission are the type of terrain you are flying over, the kind of battle you are fighting, and what the threat is. Technology today gives us the capability to remove very specific targets. The potential today is enormous. Whether to turn over this mission [forward air control] to the

Army is a matter of Air Force and Army doctrine. If the Air Force doctrine of air superiority, interdiction, and CAS has not changed, then the Air Force needs to retain the mission."

"The bottom line of the FAC mission was to help the troops on the ground. You know, it's unfortunate that a fighter jock cannot hear the conversation between the FAC and the ground commander. There are times the ground commander pleads for help. When fighters show up, they do not hear these conversations. They hear the FAC, but the fighters do not hear the desperation in the voice of troops asking for help. I told my pilots there was only one time I wanted to see them hang it out for God and country, and that is when they were being controlled by a FAC in a troops-in-contact situation. I believe there is no more important mission for a fighter pilot."[14]

Notes

1. I. B. Holley, "A Retrospect on Close Air Support" in Benjamin F. Cooling, *Case Studies in the Development of Close Air Support* (Washington, D.C.: Office of Air Force History [OAFH], 1990), 535–38.

2. Tactical Air Command Pamphlet (TACP) 50-28, *J-Fire*, July 1989.

3. Holley, 542–45.

4. Corona Harvest Report, "Command, Control, Communications," Volume I (August 1970), 2-52-53.

5. Holley, 545–46.

6. Michael J. H. Taylor, *Jane's World Combat Aircraft* (Jane's Information Group, London, 1988), 295.

7. Holley, 549–51.

8. Official data for 1968, 1969, and 1971. During these periods the percentages of total attack sorties devoted to close air support were, respectively, 8 percent, 5 percent, and 6 percent. Summaries, Military Assistance Command, Vietnam (MACV) Office of Information, Saigon.

9. Neil Sheehan, *The War in Indochina*, Raphael Littauer and Norman Uphoff, eds., Air War Study Group, Cornell University Press (Boston: Beacon Press, 1972), 55.

10. John T. Correll, "The High-Risk Military Strategy," *Air Force Magazine*, September 1994, 37–40.

11. David J. Lynch, "Spacepower Comes to the Squadron," *Air Force Magazine*, September 1994, 66–70.

12. Col David Yates, vice-commander, Air Warfare Center, Eglin AFB, interviewed by author, 24 August 1994.

13. Adm U.S.G. Sharp, commander in chief, Pacific wrote: "In coordination with our military operations, the task of nation building in

South Vietnam, the ultimate goal of our struggle, received its full share of attention." Report on the War in Vietnam (United States Government Printing Office, 1968), 9.

14. Col Charles Varvi, interviewed by author, 9 August 1994.

Bibliography

All the armed services have published histories of their Korean and Vietnam War service. The Air Force archives of the USAF Historical Research Agency (AFHRA), Air University (AU), Maxwell Air Force Base (AFB), Alabama, contains the single most important set of documents on the Korean and Vietnam air wars.

Headquarters US Air Force, Far East Command, Far East Air Forces, and Fifth Air Force organized studies during and after the Korean war. These studies provide a core of data and analysis (often conflicting) on CAS operations. Most of them are now part of the individual command records stored at the Historical Research Agency.

The private papers of many of the senior officers of Far East Command/United Nations Command provide important information and personal attitudes toward the CAS question. For the US Air Force, see the collections at the Historical Research Agency for Gen Earle Partridge, commanding general of Fifth Air Force (1950–1951); Lt Gen George Stratemeyer, commanding general of Far East Air Forces (1950–1951); and Gen Otto Weyland, vice commander and commanding general, Far Eastern Air Forces (1950–1954). The oral memoirs of Generals Partridge and Weyland add division detail to their diaries and correspondence.

The operations of the Air Force's tactical air controllers (airborne) are described and analyzed in a number of sources. Of particular value is William Cleveland's "Mosquitoes in Korea, 1950–1953," published by the 6147th Tactical Control Group Association.

For the Vietnam era, two general classifications of Air Force documents are particularly pertinent: "Corona Harvest" collections and Project CHECO Reports (contemporary historical examinations of current operations). These collections examine the full range of Air Force experiences in Southeast Asia.

Interviews and end-of-tour reports by the participants in the war proved to be a valuable source of information. Certain research studies (available at the Air University Library, Maxwell AFB, Alabama) by officers at the professional service schools provide important information about CAS in Southeast Asia. Finally, guides to both civilian and military periodical literature offer hundreds of published articles about CAS. Most of these proved of only marginal use in this study, however.

Unit histories and Korean War era studies were all classified "Secret" until 1984 when they were declassified under the 30-year rule. Unit histories from both wars contain the pertinent letters, memos, and messages that shaped the unit history during the reporting period (either quarterly or twice a year, depending on the command level of the unit). Corona Harvest, Project CHECO Reports, Vietnam era unit histories, interviews, end-of-tour reports, and studies were classified up to Top Secret until 1993, when an accelerated declassification program made much of this material available. By January 1994, all material cited here had been declassified.

Cited References

Books

Air Force in Southeast Asia: The Tactics and Techniques of Night Operations, 1961–1970. Washington, D.C.: Office of Air Force History, 1973.

Anderton, David A. *The History of the US Air Force.* New York: Crescent Books, 1981.

Ballard, Jack S. *The Development and Employment of Fixed-Wing Ships.* Washington, D.C.: Office of Air Force History, 1982.

Berger, Carl, ed. *The United States Air Force in Southeast Asia: An Illustrated Account, 1961–1973.* Washington, D.C.: Government Printing Office, 1977.

Cleveland, William M. *Mosquitos in Korea.* Portsmouth, N.H.: The Mosquito Association, Inc., 1991.

Cooling, Benjamin Franklin, ed. *Case Studies in the Development of Close Air Support.* Washington, D.C.: Office of Air Force History, 1990.

Dorr, Robert F. *McDonnell Douglas F-4 Phantom II.* London: Osprey Publishing Limited, 1984.

Eschmann, Karl J. *Linebacker: The Untold Story of the Air Raids Over North Vietnam.* New York: Ivy Books, 1989.

Futrell, Robert F. *The United States Air Force in Korea.* New York: Duell, Sloan and Pearch, 1961.

———. *Ideas, Concepts, Doctrine: A History of Basic Thinking in the United States Air Force, 1907–1960.* 2 vols., Maxwell AFB, Ala.: Aerospace Studies Institute, Air University, June 1971.

———. *The United States Air Force in Southeast Asia: The Advisory Years to 1965.* Washington, D.C.: Government Printing Office, 1981.

———. *The United States Air Force in Korea: 1950–1953.* Washington D.C.: Government Printing Office, 1983.

Goldberg, Alfred. *A History of the United States Air Force: 1907–1957.* New York: D. Van Nostrand Co., Inc., 1957.

Gurney, Gene, ed. *Vietnam, The War in The Air.* New York: Crown Publishers, Inc., 1985.

Higgins, Marguerite. *Our Vietnam Nightmare.* New York: Harper & Row, 1965.

Hoopes, Townsend. *The Limits of Intervention.* New York: David McKay Co., 1969.

Johnson, Lyndon B. *The Vantage Point.* New York: Popular Library, 1971.

Kissinger, Henry A. *The White House Years.* Boston: Little, Brown & Co, 1979.

Littauer, Raphel, and Norman Uphoff, eds. *The Air War in Indochina.* Cornell University: Air War Study Group, 1972.

Momyer, William W. *Airpower in Three Wars.* Washington, D.C.: Department of the Air Force, January 1978.

———. *The Vietnamese Air Force, 1951–1975.* No publisher data, Air University Library, Documents Section, M-S 42229-41, 10 September 1975.

Palmer, Bruce, Jr. *The 25-Year War, America's Military Role in Vietnam.* Lexington: University Press of Kentucky, 1984.

Perret, Geoffrey. *A Country Made by War.* New York: Random House Inc., 1989.

Public Papers of the Presidents of the United States: John F. Kennedy,1961. Washington, D.C.: Government Printing Office, 1962.

Rees, David. *Korea: The Limited War.* New York: St. Martin's Press, 1964.

Robbins, Christopher. *The Ravens: The Men Who Flew in America's Secret War in Laos.* New York: Crown Publishers, Inc., 1987.

Robinson, Anthony. *Aerial Warfare: An Illustrated History.* New York: Galahad Books, 1982.

Rowley, Ralph A. *USAF FAC Operations in Southeast Asia, 1961–65.* Washington, D.C.: Office of Air Force History, January 1972.

Stewart, James T. *Airpower: The Decisive Force in Korea.* New York: D. Van Nostrand Co., Inc., 1957.

Thompson, W. Scott, and D. D. Frizzel, eds. *The Lessons of Vietnam.* New York: Crane Russak, 1977.

USAF FAC Operations in Southeast Asia, 1961–65. Washington, D.C.: Office of Air Force History, January 1972.

Westmoreland, William C. *A Soldier Reports.* Garden City, N.Y.: Doubleday and Co., 1976.

Articles and Periodicals

Andrews, Walter. "OV-10s Five-Minute Response," *Armed Forces Journal.* 6 September 1969.

Beecher, William. (Unknown title). *New York Times.* 26 January 1971.

Berger, Carl. "The Air War in Cambodia." In *Vietnam, The War in the Air.* Edited by Gene Gurney. New York: Crown Publishers, Inc., 1985.

Butz, J. S., Jr. "Forward Air Controllers in Vietnam—They Call the Shots." *Air Force and Space Digest,* May 1966.

Correll, John T. "The High-Risk Military Strategy." *Air Force Magazine,* September 1994.

Evans, Douglas K., Maj, USAF. "Reinventing the FAC: Vietnam, 1962." *Air Force Magazine,* February 1980.

Frisbee, John L. "USAF's Changing Role in Vietnam." *Air Force Magazine,* September 1971.

Henderson, F. D. "Cleared in Wet!" *Air Force Magazine,* August 1968.

Holley, I. B. "A Retrospect on Close Air Support." In *Case Studies in the Development of Close Air Support.* Edited by Benjamin Franklin Cooling. Washington, D.C.: Office of Air Force History.

"Igloo White." *Air Force Magazine.* June 1971.

Ithaca Journal, 8 December 1971.

Johnson, Earl D. "Department of the Army." *Air Force Magazine,* October 1953.

Kennett, Lee. "Developments to 1939." In Cooling.

Lynch, David J. "Spacepower Comes to the Squadron." *Air Force Magazine,* September 1994.

Millett, Alan R. "Korea, 1950–1953." In *The Evolution of the Airborne Forward Air Controller: An Analysis of Mosquito Operations in Korea.* Edited by J. Farmer and M. J. Strumwasser. Santa Monica, Calif.: RAND, 1967.

Milton, T. R., Maj Gen, USAF. "Air Power: Equalizer in Southeast Asia," *Air University Review* XV (November-December 1963).

Sams, Kenneth. "How the Vietnamese Are Taking Over Their Own Air War." *Air Force Magazine*, April 1971.

Sbergo, John J. "Southeast Asia." In Cooling.

Sheehan, Neil. "The Air War in Indochina." In *The Air War in Indochina*. Edited by Raphel Littauer and Norman Uphoff. Cornell University: Air War Study Group, 1972.

Thompson, Robert. "A Stable War." *US News & World Report*, 1 November 1971.

Van Staaveren, Jacob. "Interdiction in the Laotian Panhandle." In *The United States Air Force in Southeast Asia: 1961–1973*. Edited by Carl Berger. Washington, D.C.: Government Printing Office, 1977.

———. "The Air War Against North Vietnam." In Gurney, Gene.

"Vietnamization's Impact on the Air War." *Vietnam Feature Service*, January 1971.

Washington Post, 11 February 1972.

Weyland, Otto. "The Air Campaign in Korea," *Air Force Magazine*, August 1954.

Whitney, Craig. (Unknown title). *New York Times*. 12 December 1971.

Official Documents

<u>Contemporary History of Effective Combat Operations (CHECO) Reports</u>

Atchison, Richard M. *The Slow Mover FAC Over the Ho Chi Minh Trail, 1965–1972*. 3 February 1975.

Bear, James T. *VNAF Improvement and Modernization Program*. 5 February 1970.

Brynn, Edward P. *Reconnaisance in SEAsia, July 1966–June 1969*. 15 July 1969.

Durkee, Richard A. *Combat Skyspot*. Headquarters PACAF, 9 August 1967.

Folkman, David I., and Philip D. Caine. *The Cambodian Campaign, 29 April–30 June 1970*. 1 September 1970.

Hanks, Dorrell T. *Riverline Operations in the Delta, May 1968–June 1969.* 31 August 1969.

Harrison, Philip. *Impact of Darkness and Weather on Air Operations in SEA.* 10 March 1969.

Helmka, Robert T., and Beverly Hale. *USAF Operations from Thailand, 1964–1965.* 10 August 1966.

Johnson, Calvin R. *Linebacker Operations: September–December 1972.* June 1973.

Loye, J. F., and Philip D. Caine. *The Cambodian Campaign 1 July–October 1970.* 31 December 1970.

Nicholson, Charles A. *USAF Response to the Spring 1972 North Vietnamese Offensive: Situation and Redeployment.* 10 October 1972.

Overton, James B., Maj, USAF. *FAC Operations in The Close Air Support Role in South Vietnam.* 31 January 1969.

Porter, Melvin F. *Control of Airstrikes–January 1967–December 1968.* 30 June 1969.

Roe, David, H., Maj, USAF, et al. *The VNAF Air Divisions Reports on Improvement and Modernization.* 23 November 1971.

Sams, Kenneth. *Operation Harvest Moon.* Headquarters PACAF. 31 January 1969.

Schlight, John, Lt Col, USAF. *Jet Forward Air Controllers in SEAsia, 1967–1969.* October 1969.

Seig, Louis. *Impact of Geography on Air Operations in SEA.* 11 June 1970.

Thompson, A. W., Maj, USAF. *Strike Control and Reconnaissance (SCAR) in SEA.* 22 January 1969.

Thorndale, C. William. *Interdiction in SEAsia, November 1966–October 1968.* March 1969.

———. *Defense of Da Nang.* 31 August 1969.

Trest, Warren A. *Control of Air Strikes in SEA, 1961–1966.* 1 March 1967.

United States PACAF. *Operation Neutralize.* June 1968.

Corona Harvest Reports

Command and Control, 1969.

Command, Control, Communications. Volume I, August 1970.

Out-Country Air Operations, Southeast Asia. 1 January 1965–31 March 1968. May 1968.

Out-Country Report. September 1966.

USAF Activities in Southeast Asia, 1954–1964. Undated.

USAF Air Operations Against North Vietnam. 1 July 1971–30 June 1972. 1973.

RAND Reports

Edelman, J. I., et al. *Airborne Visual Reconnaissance in South Vietnam.* RM-5049-ARPA, RAND. September 1966.

Farmer, J., and M. J. Strumwasser. *The Evolution of the Airborne Forward Air Controller; An Analysis of Mosquito Operations in Korea.* RM-5430PR, October 1967.

Graham, William B., and Amron H. Katz, *SIAT: Single Integrated Attack Team, A Concept for Offensive Military Operations in South Vietnam.* 4400-PR, 1964.

Unit Histories

Commander in chief, Pacific Command. 1961.

Commando Sabre Operations. April–June 1969; July–September 1967, July–September 1968; July–December 1968; January–March 1969; April–June 1969; October–December 1968; October–December 1969; January–March 1970; April–June 1970.

Deputy of Operations, Fifth Air Force. December 1951.

Director of Plans, USAF. July–December 1961; July–December 1963.

Eighth Tactical Fighter Wing. July 1968–May 1969; October–December 1968; January–March 1969; October–December 1969; January–March 1970; April–June 1970; July–September 1970.

Fifth Air Force. July–December 1952.

Military Assistance Command, Vietnam. 1965.

Office of Engineering, Fifth Air Force. May–November 1950.

PACAF. January–June 1964; July 1964–June 1965; January–December 1966; July 1969–June 1970.

Second Air Division. January–June 1964; July–December 1964; January–June 1965.

Second Echelon Division. November 1961–October 1962.

Seventh/Thirteenth Air Force. January–December 1972 and support documents.

Special Air Warfare Center. April–December 1962; January–June 1963; July–December 1963.

Tactical Air Command. 1 July–30 November 1950. Volume I; July–December 1964; January–December 1965.

Thirteenth Air Force. January–June 1963; July–December 1963.

18th Fighter-Bomber Wing. October 1951–July 1953.

27th Fighter-Escort Wing. March 1951.

31st Tactical Fighter Wing. April–June 1970.

35th Tactical Fighter Wing. October–December 1967.

36th Fighter-Bomber Group. July 1951–March 1952.

37th Tactical Fighter Wing. July–September 1967; October–December 1967; January–March 1968; July–September 1968; October–December 1968; April–June 1969.

49th Fighter-Bomber Group. February 1951.

366th Tactical Fighter Wing. April–June 1969; July–September 1969; April–June 1970; July–September 1970.

388th Tactical Fighter Wing. January–March 1969; April–June 1969; July–September 1969; October–December 1969; January–March 1970.

401st Tactical Fighter Wing. July–December 1964.

432d Tactical Reconnaissance Wing. April–June 1969; July–September 1969; October–December 1969; Current Operations Division. April–June 1969.

497th Tactical Fighter Wing. October–December 1969.

504th Tactical Air Support Group. July–December 1968; July–September 1969; October–December 1969.

6132d Tactical Air Control Group. July–August 1950; September–October 1951.

6147th Tactical Control Squadron (Airborne). July 1950–July 1951 and supplements.

Letters

Anthis, Gen Bollen H. To Gen Jacob E. Smart, 25 November 1963.

Bertram, Lt Col William E. To commander, 27th Fighter-Escort Wing, 15 March 1951.

Bevan, Col Walter L., Jr. Director of Operations, Seventh Air Force. To 432d TRW Commander. Subject: Not given, 3 July 1969.

Commander in Chief, Far East. To commanding general, Eighth Army, XVI Corps, FEAF. Subject: Air-Ground Operations, 11 August 1952.

Corbin, Thomas G., SAWC Commander. To Gen Gabriel P. Disosway, Tactical Air Command Commander. Subject: Quality of FAC Trainees, 20 January 1967.

Delia, E. J. Capt., Adjunct, Eighth Fighter Bomber Wing. To commanding general, FAF. Subject: Mission Summary, 17 January 1953.

Deputy Commander for Operations, Seventh Air Force. To Plans, Seventh Air Force. Subject: Misty FAC Operational Requirement, 15 March 1968.

Galligan, Walter T., Maj Gen. Director TACC, Seventh Air Force. To Deputy Director, TACC, Seventh Air Force. Subject: Vietnamization of SEA TACS, 7 July 1970.

Gleason, Robert L., Lt Col. To Col Ray Bowers, Office of Air Force History. Subject: Not given, 30 December 1971.

Greene, William G., Operations Analyst. To Maj George Partridge, Air-Ground Control Branch, Director of Operations. Subject: Comments on Working Copy of the Draft Report by the FAC and SCAR Working Group, 4 August 1969.

I DASC. To Chief, Air Force Advisory Team1. Subject: Phase-out of US FACs in ARVN System, 10 January 1971.

Partridge, George, Maj. To Lt Gen J. A. Van Fleet, CG EUSAK. Subject: Joint Air-Ground Operations Board, no date given.

Sheppard, Donald W., and James E. Risinger, Capts, Third TFW. To Director, Tiger Hound and Tally Ho Divisions, Seventh Air Force. Subject: In-flight Evaluation of PVS-3 Night Starlight Scope, 16 June 1968.

37th TFW. To Seventh Air Force. Subject: Not given, 14 December 1968.

———. To Seventh Air Force. Subject: Commando Sabre Night Operations, October 1968.

———. To Seventh Air Force. Subject: Special Operational Historical Report, 9 April 1969.
———. To Seventh Air Force. Subject: Report of FAC Training, 20 August 1968.
———. To Seventh Air Force. Subject: Report on FAC Training, 26 August 1968.
———. To Seventh Air Force. Subject: End of Training Comments/Recommendations of 366 TFW, 20 August 1968.
366th TFW. To Seventh Air Force. Subject: Not given, 20 August 1968.
432d TRW. To Seventh Air Force. Subject: Falcon FAC Report, 24 May 1969.

Memorandums

Bottomly, Col Heath. To Gen Norman O. Sweat, Deputy Director for Plans, Seventh Air Force. Subject: Not given, 5 January 1968.
Chief of Staff, GHQ, FEC. To Chief of Staff, USAF. Subject: Control of Tactical Air Support, 9 June 1950.
Commanding General, Far East Air Forces. To Chief of Staff, USAF. Subject: Requirements for Increased Combat Effectiveness, 10 June 1951.
Director of Plans, USAF. To Chief of Staff, USAF. Subject: CINCPAC Briefing on Jungle Jim. 16 October 1961.
———. To Chief of Staff, 1 March 1962.
White, Thomas D., Maj Gen. To Secretary of the Air Force. Subject: 4 May 1950. Not given.

Messages

Chief of Secretary of the Air Force. To JCS, 8 February 1963.
Chief of Staff, United States Air Force. To Joint Chiefs of Staff, 8 February 1963.
Chief of Staff, United States Air Force. To Pacific Air Force, 24 December 1964.
Commander in chief, Pacific Command. To Chief, Military Assistance Advisory Group, Vietnam, 16 November 1961.
———. To Defense Intelligence, 13 March 1963.

———. Commander in chief, Pacific Command. To Chief of Staff, United States Air Force, 15 March and 11 May 1963.

———. To Seventh Air Force, 13 August 1969.

2d Air Division. To Pacific Air Force, 10 January; 21 February; and 12 April 1964.

Detachment 2, Eighteenth Tactical Fighter Wing. To 2d Air Division, 18 January 1965. 2d Air Division. To Pacific Air Force, 22 March 1963; 29 September 1963; 5 October 1963.

Detachment 9, 2d Air Division. To Pacific Air Forces, 21 November 1961.

Joint Chiefs of Staff. To commander in chief, Pacific Command. 26 December 1961.

———. To commander in chief, Pacific Command. 1 November 1963. Pacific Air Force. To 2d Air Division, 30 October 1963.

———. To commander in chief, Pacific Command. 12 May 1964.

———. To commander in chief, Pacific Command 27 January and 4 February 1964.

Military Assistance Command, Vietnam. To commander in chief, Pacific Command, 3 October 1963.

———. To Joint Chief of Staff, 13 June 1964.

———. To 2d Air Division, 27 March 1964.

———. To 2d Air Division, 29 October 1964 and 20 November 1964.

———. To commander in chief, Pacific Command, 11 August 1964. 2d Air Division. To Pacific Air Force, 18 February 1963.

Pacific Air Force. To commander in chief, Pacific Command, 8 May 1962.

———. To Chief of Staff, Air Force, 1 January 1963.

———. To Chief of Staff, Air Force, 20 February 1963.

———. To Thirteenth Air Force, 8 May 1964.

Seventh Air Force. To CHJUSMAGTHAI, 10 March 1967.

———. To 432d TRW, 19 March 1969.

———. To 432d TRW, 19 March 1969.

———. To 432d TRW, 23 May 1969.

———. To 432d TRW, 24 April 1969. 2d advanced echelon. To Thirteenth Air Force, 21 April 1962.

Thirteenth Air Force. To Pacific Air Force, 27 January 1965.

2d Air Division. To Pacific Air Force, 10 January; 21 February; and 12 April 1964.

———. To Thirteenth Air Force, 23 January 1964.

———. To Thirteenth Air Force, 2 March 1964. To Chief of Staff, 15 April 1964. To Pacific Air Force, 20 April 1964.

———. To 23d air base group, 23 December 1964.

———. To 80th tactical fighter squadron, 25 December 1964.

———. To Pacific Air Force, 17 January 1965.

———. To Chief of Staff, United States Air Force, 15 March 1965.

———. To Pacific Air Force, 28 January 1965.

366th Tactical Fighter Wing. To Seventh Air Force, 10 November 1968.

388th Tactical Fighter Wing. To Seventh Air Force, 5 January 1969.

———. To Seventh Air Force and 432d TRW, 25 July 1969.

Manuals and Regulations

2d Air Division Regulation 55-5. 22 January 1963.

504th Tactical Air Support Group Manual 55-3. 1 March 1970.

Continental Air Command Regulation 26-1. *Organization-Tactical Air Command.* 11 August 1950.

Operations Order (OPORD) 439-67. *Combat Skyspot.* 10 March 1967.

Tactical Air Command Manual 2-4. *Tactical Air Control Party.* May 1965.

Tactical Air Command Pamphlet (TACP) 50-28. *J-Fire.* July 1989.

"Joint Task Force Operations" (Draft). HQ US Strike Command, MacDill AFB, Fla., 15 April 1964.

Studies

"Close Air Support Operations in Korea: Preliminary Evaluation," Operations Research Office, HQ FEC, February 1951.

"Cost Effectiveness of Close Support Aircraft," Langley AFB, Va., 1965.

Eckhardt, George S. "Command and Control, 1950–1969," Washington, D.C., Department of the Army, 1974.

"Evolution of Command and Control Doctrine for Close Air Support." Washington, D.C., Office of Air Force History, March 1973.

"Linebacker II: USAF Bombing Survey." Headquarters PACAF, April 1973.

"The Tactical Air Control System," in "Report on the Korean War," II. Maxwell AFB., Ala., Air University Library, Documents Section, M-U 35961-1, September 1954.

"The Vietcong," John F. Kennedy Center for Special Warfare. November 1965.

Whitson, W. L., et al. "Preliminary Evaluation of Close Support Operations in Korea," Operations Research Office, Far East Command. 1 February 1951.

Other Documents

AFXOPJ Book of Actions in SEA. 1961–64.

Far East Air Force Mission Summary. 16 November 1950.

Headquarters, Far East Air Force "Weekly Intelligence Roundups." April–May 1951.

Korean Evaluation Report. Volume III: "Operations and Tactics."

Weekly Activities Report, 27th Fighter-Escort Wing. 12–18 March 1951.

Weekly Activity Report, PACAF. June 26–3 July 1964.

Unpublished Materials

Air War College and Air Command and Staff School Studies. Air University, Maxwell AFB, Ala.

Brown, Donald R. "Guide for Case Study: Tactical Air in Limited War." Air University Library, Maxwell, AFB, Ala., undated.

Crawford, Thomas M. "The Airborne Forward Air Controller—Peacetime Casualty." Air University Study No. 3894, Air War College, Maxwell AFB, Ala., undated.

Crowe, Myron W. "The Development of Close Air Support." Air War College Thesis, June 1968.

Cunningham, D. D. "Close Air Support Aircraft." Special Study, Air Command and Staff School, Maxwell AFB, Ala., 16 May 1960.

"Effective SEAasia Tactics (TACS)," Headquarters USAF, draft, 1969.

Ella, Paul S.; Richard Joyce; Robert H. Williams, and William Woodworth. "US Army Special Forces and Similar Internal Defense Advisory Operations in Mainland Southeast Asia, 1962–67." Research Analysis Corporation, June 1969.

Lescher, Charles O., Jr., Maj, USAF. "Forward Air Controller Selection Criteria and Vietnam Tour Length." Maxwell AFB, Ala.: Air Command and Staff College Thesis, June 1968.

Momack, Stanley M. "Use of the Jet Fighter Aircraft as a Forward Air Control Vehicle in a Non-Permissive Environment." Research Study, Air War College, April 1976.

Operational Test and Evaluation Stabilized Night Observation Device (Eye_Glass)," Test Report, Special Air Warfare Center. Eglin AFB, Fla., undated.

Shackelford, William F. "Eleven Days in December: Linebacker II." Air War College Research Study, Air University, Maxwell AFB, Ala., 1977.

Staff Study, Assistant for Evaluation. DCS/Development USAF, subject: "What Can and Should the USAF Do to Increase the Effectiveness of Air-Ground Operations?," December 1950.

Summers, Charles, M., Maj, USAF. "Interdiction Concepts and Doctrine: 1954 through 1968." Air Command and Staff Thesis, Air University, Maxwell, AFB, Ala., May 1969.

"Tactics and Techniques of Close Air Support Operations, 1961–1973." Office of Air Force History, 1976.

"United States Air Force Operations in the Korean Conflict, 25 June–1 Nov 1950." USAF Historical Study No. 71, 1 July 1952.

"United States Air Force Operations in the Korean Conflict." USAF Historical Study No. 72, Maxwell AFB, Air University Library, Documents Section.

Wilkins, George I. "The FAC Factor in South Vietnam." Air War College Study, Air University, Maxwell AFB, Ala., November 1970.

End of Tour Reports

Doyle, M. M., Lt Col, and John P. Gilbert. February 1962–August 1963.

McDonald, A. K., Col, commander, Eighth TFWg. July 1969.

Mellish, David S., Lt Col. 15 January 1964.

Nash, Slade, Col, Deputy Commander for Operations and Vice Commander. Eighth TFW. January 1969.

O'Donnell, John F., Maj, 388th TFWg Tactics Officer. Subject: Tiger FAC Program, April 1969.

Pattillo, Charles C., Col, commander, Eighth TFW. June 1969.

Ruonavaara, Russell B., Lt Col, Operations Officer, 20th TASS. 10 May 1972.

Schmitt, John G., Maj. 2 September 1963.

Tompkins, Gary R., Capt. 18 October 1967.

Other Documents

Air-to-Ground Operations School, Introduction Pamphlet. 1994.

Freedman, Roswell and Ronald Brown. "The Evolution of Interdiction." USAF Course Outline, Air War College. USAFHRA, undated.

"Laos: April 1971." Staff Report, Subcommittee on US Security Agreements and Commitments Abroad, Committee on Foreign Relations, US Senate, 3 August 1971, GPO.

MACV Summary of Highlights. February 1962–February 1963.

"Summary of Misty Bronco Operations, April–June 1969."

TACLO Activity Report 17. 15 September 1968.
——— 18. 30 September 1968.
USAF Management Summary in SEA. 19 February 1971.
Yates, W. J., Col, chairman. Report. Subject: "Report on Joint Air-Ground Operations Conference held at Headquarters Fifth Air Force, Seoul, Korea, 8–22 August 1953.

Related Sources

Books

Cagle, Malcolm W., and Frank A. Manson. *The Sea War in Korea.* Annapolis: Md.: United States Naval Institute, 1957.

Craven, Wesley F., and James L. Cate, eds. *The Army Air Forces in World War II, Vol. 2; Europe: Torch to Pointblank.* Chicago: The University of Chicago Press, 1949.

"German Air Force Operations in Support of the Army." USAF Historical Study, Air University Library, Documents Section, M-U 27218, 1962.

Jones, H. A. *The War in the Air: Being the Story of the Part Played in the Great War by The Royal Air Force.* Volume 2 of 6. London, Clarendon Press, 1922–1937.

Knaack, Marcelle S., comp. *Encyclopedia of US Air Force Aircraft and Missile Systems.* vol I: *Post-World War II Fighters.* Washington D.C.: Government Printing Office, 1978.

Mirande, Henri, and Louis Olivier. *Sur la Bataille, Journal d'un Aviateur Francais a l'Armee Bulgare, Au Seige d'Air divisionrianople.* Paris, 1913.

Neumann, Georg P. *Die Deutschen Luftstreitkrafte im Weltkrieg.* Berlin, 1920.

Slessor, J. C. *Air Power and Armies.* London, Oxford University Press, reprinted by AMS Press, New York, 1936.

Smith, Peter C. *Dive Bomber! An Illustrated History.* Annapolis, Maryland, Naval Institute Press, 1982.

Standard Aircraft Characteristics: The T-6G Texan. Air Material Command. US Air Force, 12 April 1950.

———. *The F-51H Mustang.* Air Material Command, USAF. 3 July 1950.

———. *The F-80A Shooting Star.* Air Material Command, USAF. 25 January 1950.

Taylor, John W. R., ed. *Combat Aircraft of the World.* London: Ebury Press, 1969.

Taylor, Michael J. H., ed. *Jane's World Combat Aircraft.* London: Jane's Information Group, 1988.

Tedder, Arthur William. *Air Power in War.* London: Hodder and Stroughton, 1954.

———. *With Prejudice, the War Memoirs of Marshall of the Royal Air Force.* Boston: Little, Brown & Co., 1966.

The Accomplishments of Airpower in the Malayan Emergency (1948–1960), Concepts Division, Aerospace Studies Institute, Air University, May 1963.

Wise, S. F. *Canadian Airmen and the First World War (The Official History of the Royal Canadian Air Force).* Vol. I, Toronto: 1980.

Articles and Periodicals

Boggs, Charles W. "Marine Aviation: Origins and Growth," *Marine Corps Gazette 34* (November 1950).

Huston, James A. "Tactical Use of Air Power in World War II: The Army Experience," *Military Affairs, 14* (Winter 1950).

Laine, Serge. "l'Aeronautique Militaire Francaise au Maroc (1911–1939)," in Cooling.

Madelin, Ian. "The Emperor's Clothes Air Support," *Air University Review* (November–December 1979).

Official Documents

Air Forces and War. Text for Army War College Course, 1937–1938. Carlisle Barracks, Pa.: US Military History Institute, undated.

Attack Aviation 1935–1936. Air Corps Tactical School Text, United States Air Force Historical Research Agency (USAFHRA), undated.

Aviation in Support of Ground Forces. War Department Field Manual 31-35, Washington, D. C.: Government Printing Office, 9 April 1942.

Close Support of the Fifth Army. Headquarters, Mediterranean Allied Air Forces, 1945, Maxwell AFB., Ala., USAFHRA.

Dictionary of Military and Associated Terms—JCS Publication I. Washington D.C.: Government Printing Office, 3 January 1972.

Directive on Close Support Bombing, British War Office, WO 106/5162, 6 December 1940.

Heflin, Woodford Agee, ed., *The United States Air Force Dictionary.* Maxwell AFB, Ala.: Air University Press, 1956.

Mitchell, William. "United States Army, Provisional Manual of Operations," 23 December 1918.

Tactics and Techniques Developed by the United States Tactical Air Commands in the European Theater of Operations. Army Air Forces

Evaluation Board in the European Theater of Operations, March 1945.

The Employment of Combat Aviation. Tentative text, USAF, April 1939.

War Department Publication: *Field Manual 100-20.* "Command and Employment of Air Power." July 1943.

THIS PAGE INTENTIONALLY LEFT BLANK

Index

12th Tactical Fighter Wing: 127, 181
17th parallel: 109
187th Regimental Combat Team: 46
18th parallel: 161
199th Light Infantry Brigade: 113
19th parallel: 156, 161
19th Tactical Air Support Squadron: 110
19th TASS: 113, 117, 161
1Hs: 203
1st Air Cavalry Division: 113
1st Air Commando Squadron (Composite): 95
1st Brigade: 114
1st Commando Squadron: 128
1st Infantry Division: 113

20/40 formula: 131
20-channel VHF radio: 67
20th parallel: 213, 215, 217
20th Signal Company: 42
20th TASS: 113, 117, 152, 161
20th, 21st, and 22d TASSs: 114
21st TASS: 117
22d TASS: 117, 124, 161
23d TASS: 117, 147, 152, 161
24th Division L-17s: 34
24th Infantry Division: 30, 35
25th Infantry Division: 113
27th Wing: 36
2d Air Division: 111, 115

35th Fighter-Bomber Squadron: 25
366th Tactical Fighter Wing: 175, 182
366th TFW: 214
388th Tactical Fighter Wing: 187
38th parallel: 25–26, 29, 65
3d Brigade, 9th Infantry Division: 115
3d TFW: 176

416th TFS: 172
428th Tactical Fighter Squadron: 168
432d Tactical Reconnaissance Wing: 189
4400th Combat Crew Training Squadron: 84
44th and 67th Tactical Fighter Squadrons: 168
44th TFS: 168
45th Tactical Reconnaissance Squadron's (TRS) RF-51s: 67
460th tactical reconnaissance wing: 180
469th TFS: 187
49th tactical fighter wing: 214
4th Air Commando Squadron: 131

502d Tactical Control Group: 66
502d TCG: 42
504th tactical air support group: 116, 172
504th TASG: 118
507th Tactical Control Group: 82
51st Fighter Group: 36
56th Air Commando Wing: 160
56th Special Operations Wing: 152
5th Infantry Division: 114

6132d aircraft control and warning squadron (ACWS): 42
6132d tactical air control group (TACG): 38
6147th Squadron: 47, 76
6147th tactical control group: 42, 60
6147th tactical control squadron, airborne: 38
6147th TCG Deactivated: 74
6147th TCG: 67
6149th TCS: 73
68th Fighter All-Weather Squadron (FAWS): 25

80 Squadron: 4
80th tactical fighter squadron: 167
8th Fighter Group: 36
8th Tactical Fighter Wing: 191

A-10: 230
A-1: 128, 154, 168, 169, 203, 211
A-37: 167, 203, 206
A-4: 185
A-7: 167, 220

Abrams, Gen Creighton: 208, 210, 215
AC-119: 203, 205
AC-47: 127, 129, 131, 133, 154, 203, 205
Advance Headquarters, FAF: 37
advances in military technology: 233
AGOS: 61
Air America: 159, 168
Air Combat Command: 61
Air Commando: 84
air defense command: 16
Air Force doctrine: 241
Air Force Space Command: 236
Air Force/Army Agreement of March–April 1965: 125
air liaison officer (ALO): 40
Air mission priorities: 10
air operations center: 90
air superiority: 22, 77, 231
Air Support Control: 9
air warfare center: 61
airborne FAC: 45, 74
airborne tactical air coordinator (A-TAC): 32
air-ground controllers: 72
air-ground coordination: 232
Air-Ground Operations School (AGOS): 60
airpower's priorities in Korea: 19
Allied Forces Northwest Africa: 10
Almond, Maj Gen Edward: 33
ALO/FAC program: 77
America Division: 114
American I and IX Corps: 67
American policy: 65
Americans worked as assistant ALOs: 91
Anderson, Gen S. F.: 72
Anthis, Gen Bollen H.: 90
antiwar movement: 201, 209
Anyang-Inchon-Yongdungpo area: 68
Area Echo: 175
armed FACs flying OV-10s: 112
Armistice: 4, 73
Armstrong, Lt Frank H.: 48
Army 52d Aviation Battalion: 169
Army observers: 39, 58

Army of the Republic of Vietnam (ARVN): 94, 201
Army War College: 7
ARN-92: 190
Arnold, Brig Gen Henry H.: 7, 8
artillery-spotting airplane: 2
Ashau: 127, 134
Ashiya: 31
Aspin, Les: 235
ATC: 115
Atlanta/Falcon team: 190
Atlanta: 190

B-26: 66, 69, 72, 82, 84, 87, 95
B-29: 30, 66, 72
B-52: 133, 158, 163, 211, 216
B-57: 154
Bai Thuong: 162
Balkan Wars: 1
Ban Kari Pass: 153
Bangkok: 184
Barrel Roll Working Group: 187
Barrel Roll: 150, 157, 187–188
Barthelemy Pass: 162
Battle of Okinawa: 16
Battle of the Somme: 3
Battle, Maj Benjamin R.: 184
battles of An Loc and the highland regions: 215
Ben Karai: 175
Bien Hoa: 87, 176, 214
Blind Bat (C-130): 184
bomb damage assessment (BDA): 55
bomb tonnage: 201
Bosnia-Herzegovina: 237
Bottom-Up Review: 235
Bradley, Gen Omar: 11
Bright Star '94: 237
British, the: 2, 233
Brown, 1Lt Chester L.: 73
Brown, Dr. Harold: 110
Bryant, Lt James A.: 34
Bullpup: 168
Butz, J. S., Jr.: 122

C-119: 132
C-123 Candlesticks: 183
C-130 Blindbats: 183
C-130, C-123, and C-7: 211
C-130: 132, 133, 154, 211, 237
C-141: 237
C-47: 47, 52, 67, 68, 82, 84, 154, 158
Cairney, Capt Tom: 91
Cam Rahn Bay: 132
Cambodia: 126, 150, 163, 184, 201, 208
Camp Holloway: 169
Campbell, Maj John F.: 124
Carlton, Lt Col Merrill H.: 34 39, 45, 47
carrier-based pilots: 36
Carter Capt Tennis: 128
CAS: 18, 19, 31
   at night: 131
   coordinating requests for: 94
   effectiveness: 66, 76
   in Cambodia: 161
   sorties: 71
Casablanca Conference: 10
Characteristics of importance in any FAC aircraft: 229
China: 65
Chinese intervention in Korea: 65
Chinese, the: 26, 66
Chinhae: 31
Chinnampo: 46
Chochiwon: 35
choke point concept of operations: 152
Chonui: 34
Chosen Reservoir: 29
Chu Lai: 114
CINCPAC: 92, 167
CINCPACAF: 118
Clark, Gen Albert P.: 119
Clark, Gen Mark: 11
Clay, Gen Lucius Jr: 213
cluster bomb units: 129
Cole, Vic: 49
Combat Crew Training Center: 61
Combat Skyspot: 149

Combined VNAF-USAF staffs: 94
Commander of the Navy of the Far East (ComNavFE): 57
Commando Hunt: 156
Commando Sabre: 171, 178
Communist Losses in the First Year: 70
comparing Korea and Vietnam: 240
Constant Guard's aircraft: 214
continental air command: 16
Control of USAF air strikes: 120
control station Mellow: 38
controlling strike aircraft near friendly ground troops: 120
cooperation between FAF and Eighth Army: 67
cooperation with Vietnamese L-19 controllers: 93
Corbin, Maj Gen Thomas G.: 118
counterinsurgency activities: 81
Covey (O-1): 152, 184
Cox, Maj Jerry: 218
Cricket: 155

Da Nang: 113, 167–168, 174, 185, 214
DASC: 94, 116, 204, 211
Dean, Maj Gen William F.: 30
deep reconnaissance: 50, 57
Diem, Ngo Dinh: 82, 90, 92, 94
Dien Bien Phu: 133
Disosway, Gen Gabriel P.: 118
Dixie station: 22, 132
DMZ: 22, 126, 150, 163, 180, 185–186, 201, 213
Dong Hoi: 163, 169
dry monsoon: 149
Dwyer, Maj Gerald T.: 134

EC-121: 156
Edinburgh, Lt Aubrey C.: 69
Eglin AFB: 61, 84
Eighth Army: 21, 29, 31, 33, 36, 46, 60, 65, 69
Eighth Fighter-Bomber Wing: 72
Eighth Tactical Fighter Wing: 184
Eighth United States Army-Korea (EUSAK): 37
Eisenhower, Gen Dwight D.: 9
En-lai, Premier Chou: 26
EUSAK headquarters at Taegu: 37

Evans, Maj Douglas: 91
Eyeglass scope: 147

F-100: 127, 149, 154, 167, 169, 171, 176, 179, 185, 194, 230
F-105: 154, 167–169, 174, 176, 189
F-111: 167, 216
F-16 and A-10 pilots: 228
F-4 and A-7 strike aircraft: 216
F-4 FAC Section: 184
F-4 Phantom: 69, 127, 167–168, 180–181 183, 185–188, 230, 240
F-5: 167, 203, 206–207
F-51 Mustang: 26, 28, 33, 41
F-80: 230
F-80C: 26, 28, 31, 33, 36
F-82G: 25–26
F-84 and F-86 wings: 72
F-84: 33, 36, 69
F-86 Sabre: 30
FAC:
   aircraft, design of: 60
   concept: 45
   corps: 110
   effectiveness: 121
   in Korea: 45
   shortage: 114
   Survivability: 59
FAC/Reconnaissance Teams: 189
FAF: 32
Falcon AFB: 236
Falcon FAC unit: 190
Falcon/Laredo: 189
Far East Air Force Bomber Command: 65
Far East Air Forces: 20, 25–26, 32, 57, 66, 70
Far East Air Materiel Command: 38
Farm Gate: 87, 95, 109
Fast-FAC program: 195, 234
Felt, CINCPAC Adm Harry: 92, 94
Ferguson, Col James E.: 42
Field Manual 31-35, Air Ground Operations: 227
Fifth Air Force: 21, 25, 56, 65
Fifth Army: 11
fighter-bombers: 28

first American FACs in Southeast Asia: 91
First and Third Marine Divisions: 22
first comprehensive airborne forward air controller program: 45
first Farm Gate detachment: 109
First Marine Air Wing: 21, 32, 71
first USAF kill: 25
Fisher, Maj Bernard C.: 128
flak-suppression missions: 59
Flaming Dart: 169
Fleet Marine Force Pacific: 18
Fleeting targets: 193
Fort Benning tests: 9
Forward Air Controller Comparison: 194
forward air controller course: 61
French Army: 1
Fukuoka area: 28

G-3 air officer: 40
Geneva Accord: 81
Giap, Gen Vo Nguyen: 129
GPS information: 236, 238
Great Britain: 81
Groom, Col John F.: 154
ground commander: 57
ground controllers: 233
Guam: 16
Gulf of Tonkin: 22, 116, 132, 161, 176
Gulf War: 228
Gun Kill program: 193
Gunboat (later Gunship II): 132

Haiphong: 216
Haiti: 15
Hanoi: 82, 170, 215
Hargreaves, Capt John H.: 68
Harkins, Gen Paul D.: 89
Helio Aircraft Corporation: 82
history's longest truce talks: 73
Ho Chi Minh: 173
Ho Chi Minh trail: 128, 133, 147, 150, 154–155, 175, 201, 207, 210, 240
Hoengsong: 69

Hongchon: 69
Horner, Gen Charles A.: 236
Hubbard, Capt Wade: 218
Hudson, Lt William G.: 25
Hue Phu Bai: 186
hunter-killer teams: 179
Hurlburt Field, Florida: 61
Huston, James A.: 9

I and II Corps headquarters: 90
I Corps: 22
Ichon: 34
I Corps: 132
II Corps: 126
III and IV Corps: 22
III Corps Tactical Zone headquarters: 90
immediate CAS requests: 51
Inchon: 29
Inertial navigation systems: 238
infrared radar/optics: 125
interdiction campaign: : 65, 71, 148, 217, 234
International Control Commission (ICC): 81
interservice communication: 233
Iraqi Scud launchers: 237
Itazuke Air Base, Japan: 28, 31
IV Corps: 132
Iwo Jima: 15

jet FAC: 172, 192
J-Fire: 228
JOC: 19, 56
Johnson, Lyndon B.: 82, 133, 163, 169, 201
joint air-ground operations conference: 74
Joint Chiefs of Staff: 114, 169, 225
joint doctrine for close air support: 228
Joint General Staff: 127
joint operations center: 11
Jungle Jim: 84, 87, 89

KC-135: 116, 211, 237
Kennedy, John F.: 81–82, 87–89
Khe Sanh: 133–134

Khmer Republic: 208
Khrushchev, Nikita: 81
Killer Scout program: 228
King, Col Benjamin H.: 84, 88
Kirkpatrick, Maj Kenneth A.: 119
Kissinger, Henry A.: 216
Kochan, Lt Chester T.: 48
Kompong Thom: 209
Korat Air Base: 167, 185, 188
Korea: 228
Korean Military Advisory Group: 47
Korean People's Army: 31
Korean War: 15, 18
Kratie, Cambodia: 218
Kunsan: 41
Kyushu: 31

L-17: 34
L-19 (O-1): 42, 60, 67, 91, 93, 95, 110, 230
L-5: 34, 47, 60, 230
Laird, Melvin: 202, 208
Lam Son: 211
Lam, Lt Gen Hoang Xuan: 211
Langley AFB: 37
Laos: 118, 150, 155, 201, 207, 210, 240
Laredo FACs: 191
lasers: 125
Latiolas, Lt Col Stanley P.: 34
Lavelle, Gen John D.: 213
LaVigne, Capt Edwin Duffy: 68
LeMay, Gen Curtis E.: 82, 88–89, 95, 168
Lima Site 36: 187
Linebacker: 212
LORAN: 186, 190, 192
low-light-level television: 147
Luftwaffe: 8, 18
Luke AFB: 61

MAAG: 89
MacArthur, Gen Douglas: 25
MACV: 90, 148, 150, 161, 169, 211
Mang Yang: 126

Marine Corps aviation in Korea: 214, 227
Marines in I Corps: 130
marking rockets: 55
Marshall, Gen George C.: 8
Mayaguez incident: 233
Mayo, Capt Richard G.: 184
McNamara, Robert S.: 84, 90, 160
McPeak, Gen Merrill A.: 236
Medal of Honor: 128
Mekong River: 209
Mellow control: 37
Meyers, Col Gilbert L.: 42
MiG force: 28, 163, 170, 207
MIGCAP: 216
Military Advisory and Assistance Group (MAAG): 87
Military Assistance Command Vietnam (MACV): 23, 89, 202
Minh, Maj Gen Tran Van: 171
Misawa external fuel tanks: 36
Misty: 172, 174–175, 184, 191
Mitchell, Col William Billy: 7
Mitchell, Lt Frank G.: 34
mobile nuclear missiles: 236
Momyer, Gen William W.: 115, 160, 171, 195
Montgomery, British general Bernard L.: 11
Moore, Lt Gen Joseph H.: 115, 168–169
Morocco: 1
Morris, Lt Harold E.: 34
Moscow: 129
Mosquito: 38
   aircraft: 58
   Cavalry Division: 40
   commander: 45
   flexibility of: 46
   Mellow: 52, 67
   operation: 195
   planes: 67
   squadron: 36
   unit: 39
   Wildwest: 40
Mosquito-TACC communication: 52
Mu Gia and Ban Karai passes: 153, 155, 175, 186, 191
multisource tactical system: 237

Myers, Maj D. Wayne: 128

Nail (O-2): 152, 184
Nakhon Phanom: 147, 155
Nam Phong: 214
Nape: 153
Nash, Col Slade: 184
National Campaign Plan: 94
Naval fighter aircraft: 58, 132, 168
    A-1H: 168
    A-24 Dauntless: 8
    A-7: 153
    CAS: 15
    Corsairs: 68
    P-1: 155
Navy/Marines: 15
near-real-time intelligence: 237
Nelson, Lt George W.: 41
neutrality of Laos and Cambodia: 217
Neville, Lew: 49
Night air operations: 129, 145, 176, 191
Ninth Air Force: 11
Nixon, Richard M.: 158, 163, 201, 208, 214–215
NKPA and communist Chinese forces: 50
Nol, Lt Gen Lon: 208
North Korean Air Force (NKAF): 25–26
North Korean People's Army (NKPA): 26
North Vietnam: 201
North Vietnamese panhandle: 174
North Vietnamese: 170
northern Laos: 185
Northwest African Air Force: 10

O-1 Bird Dog: 110, 121, 147 154, 158, 169–170 230, 240
O-1 Raven controllers: 187
O-1, O-2, and OV-10: 117
O-2: 111, 147, 170, 174, 211
observers: 60
O'Donnell, Gen Emmett: 88
Okinawa: 16, 168
Operation:
  Daniel Boone: 160

    Harvest Moon: 114
    Linebacker II: 215
    Neutralize: 174
    Rain Dance: 187
    Ripper: 69
    Sea Dragon: 178
    Thor: 175
    Thunderbolt: 68
operations research office (ORO): 49
Ordnance Selection: 53
OV-10: 111, 113, 133, 147, 211, 230, 240

PACAF: 88, 90, 92, 115, 117, 169
Pacific campaign: 15
pacification program: 211
Panmunjam: 73
Pao, Maj Gen Vang: 157
Paris talks: 215
Partridge, General: 30, 38, 42, 76, 195
Pathet Lao: 162
Pave Spot: 147
Pave Wolf: 193
people sniffers: 125
People's Self-Defense Forces: 212
Persian Gulf War: 234
Phnom Penh: 201, 208
Photo reconnaissance: 180
photography: 125
Phouma, Souvanna: 150
Phoung Choy: 177
Phu Cat: 174, 179
Phuoc Long: 126
Pilatus Porters: 159
Plain of Jars: 162
Plei Me: 150
Pleiku: 114, 169
political and military objectives: 70
Pope AFB: 60
previously killed targets: 228
psychological warfare: 41
Pusan perimeter: 16, 29, 57

Quang Tri: 114, 211

Radar Bomb Scoring: 149
radar bombing: 206
radar-guided missions: 72
Ranch Hand: 89
Ratley, Capt Lonnie O.: 220
Raven: 152, 158–159, 187
RB-26: 95
reconnaissance wing: 72
Reed, Maj Lawrence L.: 118
regular South Vietnamese forces: 212
Republic of Korea (ROK): 25
Republic of South Korea: 65
RESCAP: 176
rescue combat air patrols: 176
RF-101: 154, 167–168
RF-4C: 133, 154, 180, 189, 211
Ridgway, Gen Matthew B.: 21, 67, 69, 75
Risinger, James E.: 176
ROK Air Force: 25
ROK Army: 35
Rolling Thunder: 152, 170, 212
Route Package:
    I: 161, 213
    II: 162
    III: 162
    IV: 162
    V: 162
    VI: 162, 216
    I and II: 213
    V and VI: 215
Rover Joe: 10
Royal Laotian Government: 150, 179
rules of engagement: 120
Rusk, Dean: 95

Sabres: 28
Saigon: 82, 92, 123, 201, 212
satellite targeting data: 236
SC-47: 84, 87, 92
search-and-rescue (SAR) missions: 178, 215

Seoul: 42, 69, 74
Seventh Air Force: 22, 112, 115, 124, 129, 172, 175, 179, 180–181, 183–184, 186
Seventh Fleet: 21, 37
  Task Force 77: 32
Seventh Infantry Division: 29
Sharp, Adm Ulysses S. G.: 167
Shaw AFB: 82
Shepherd, Lt Gen Lemuel C.: 18
Sheppard, Donald W.: 176
Sihanouk, Prince Norodom: 208
SLAR: 125
Snare Drum: 191
Snort (OV-10): 184
Song Ly: 114
Song Troc River: 177
South Vietnamese Air Force: 89
Soviet Union: 65
Soviets, the: 129, 170
Spaatz, Gen Carl A.: 10
space systems: 236
Space Warfare Center: 236
special air warfare center (SAWC): 118
SS Saint Paul: 179
starlight scope: 129, 147, 155, 178, 183
Steel Tiger: 152, 174, 181, 185
Stormy FACs: 183–184
Strategic Air Command: 127, 214
Strategic airpower: 225
strategic relocatable targets (SRT): 237
Stratemeyer, Lt Gen George: 66
strike control and reconnaissance (SCAR): 117
Struble, Vice Adm Arthur D.: 37
Sullivan, William: 159–160
Super Sabre: 167, 177
SUU-25 flare dispenser: 176
Suwon: 30, 68

T-28: 82, 84, 87, 92, 154, 158,
T-34 tank: 41
T-6: 31, 34, 38–39, 46–47, 55, 58, 60, 67, 76, 194, 230, 240
T-6 Airborne Controller course: 61

TAC: 50, 52, 90, 115
TACAN/ADF: 177
TACAN: 187
TACC: 204
TACP: 38, 50, 66, 93, 115, 205
Tactical Air Command: 16, 84
tactical air control center (TACC): 11, 28
Tactical Air Control Party team: 61
tactical air control system: 88
Tactical Air Coordinator-Airborne (TAC-A).: 46
tactical air direction centers: 42
tactical air navigation (TACAN): 48
tactical airpower: 20, 225
Tactical Operations Center; 94
   in Saigon: 127
tactical reconnaissance units: 12
TADC: 67
Taegu: 28, 36, 68
Taejon: 30, 34, 68
Takhli, Thailand: 214
Talon:
   Command: 237
   Lance: 237
   Night: 237
   Ready: 237
   Shooter: 237
   Touch: 237
   Vision: 237
Tan Son Nhut: 82, 87, 90, 92
Tarawa: 15
Target Discrimination: 54
Task Force 77: 37, 65, 161
Tchepone, Laos: 168, 180, 210
TENCAP: 236
Tet offensive: 116, 134
Thailand: 184, 207, 220
Thanh Hoa: 162
Third Marine Amphibious Force: 22
Third Marine Division: 29
Thirteenth Air Force: 90, 92
Tho, Le Duc: 216
Tiger Hound: 150, 154

Tiger: 185, 187
troop carrier wings: 72
troops-in-contact: 241
Truce Ceremony: 73
Truman, President Harry S.: 25
Tuy Hoa: 175
Twelfth Army Group: 11
two-ship FAC operation: 193

U-17: 158
Ubon: 185
UC-123 spray aircraft: 154
Udorn, Thailand: 157
Umsong: 34
UN air superiority: 26
UN Command: 21, 25, 65
UNC Army: 71
United Nations: 81
United States Far East Command (USFEC): 25
United States Strike Command (STRICOM): 75
US:
    25th Division: 68
    Army Air Corps: 5
    Army Air Service: 7
    Embassy in Vientiane: 151
    IX and X Corps: 69
    Marine Corps: 7
    military strategy: 81
    XXIV Corps: 211
USAF doctrine: 77
USAF units in Thailand: 116
USSR: 81

Van Fleet, Lt Gen James A.: 21
Vandenberg, Gen Hoyt: 11, 19, 65
Vang Pao, General: 187
Varvi, Col Charles: 240
Vesely, Brig Gen David L.: 236
VHF-Omnirange (VOR): 48
Vienna: 81
Vientiane: 201
Vietcong: 84, 92, 123, 169

infiltration: 123
infrastructure: 129
Ninth Division: 126
Vietnam: 225
Vietnamese:
   Air Force: 167, 171
   FACs: 91
   L-19: 92
   operations against the Vietcong: 88
   Skyraiders (AD-6): 92
Vietnamization: 201
VNAF FACs: 204
VNAF observer/FAC: 121
Vulcan cannon: 190

Walker, Lt Gen Walton H.: 33, 36
War at Night, The: 58
weather reconnaissance: 179
Westmoreland, Gen William C.: 121, 126, 128, 132, 169
wet monsoon: 149
Weyland, Gen Otto P.: 20–21, 41, 65
Wheeler, Gen Earle G.: 114
White, Maj Gen Thomas D.: 16
Wilkins, Lt Charles R.: 69
Wilkinson, Capt Dorrence E.: 69
Wolf: 184–186,
World War I: 1, 225
World War II: 2, 9, 225

X Corps: 33

Yaks: 34
Yalu: 20, 26, 29, 33
Yangpyong: 69
Yankee Station: 22, 132, 161
Yates, Col Dave: 185, 238

Mosquitoes to Wolves
The Evolution of the Airborne Forward Air Controller

Air University Press Team

Chief Editor
Preston Bryant

Copy Editor
Lula Barnes

Cover Art
Steven C. Garst

Illustrations
L. Susan Fair

*Composition and
Prepress Production*
Linda C. Colson

www.ingramcontent.com/pod-product-compliance
Lightning Source LLC
Chambersburg PA
CBHW082111230426
43671CB00015B/2667